Anthony Neilson

Plays: 2

Edward Gant's Amazing Feats of Loneliness!
The Lying Kind
The Wonderful World of Dissocia
Realism

Edward Gant's Amazing Feats of Loneliness!: '*Edward Gant* represents a plea for the imagination to be allowed to take what violent twists it will, without having to justify itself in terms of social commentary.' *Daily Telegraph*

The Lying Kind: 'Neilson turns to farce like an old hand. His play is littered with virtuoso twists which transform the simple scenario into a hilarious living nightmare. Besides Neilson's love of foul language, he also has Joe Orton's ear for exasperating word play and a similar feel for knockabout slapstick.' *Daily Mail*

The Wonderful World of Dissocia: 'Tackling the complex issue of mental illness and our society's approach to it, the drama exhibits real bravery in the boldness with which it explores the psychosis of Lisa . . . *Dissocia* is a sort of *Alice in Wonderland* for the twenty-first century, taking us into a looking-glass world in which the pleasingly surreal is quickly punctured by the frighteningly violent in this superb play.' *Sunday Herald*

Realism: 'An exquisite tragic-comedy for our times . . . it should strike a chord with anyone who's ever struggled to make sense of the modern world and their place in it. An absolute joy from start to finish.' *Herald*

Anthony Neilson was born in Scotland in 1967 and is a writer and director of theatre and film. Contrary to previous biographies, he has no children yet, nor any of the things that an adult should. He lives in London and considers it his home.

ANTHONY NEILSON

Plays: 2

Edward Gant's Amazing Feats of Loneliness!
The Lying Kind
The Wonderful World of Dissocia
Realism

with an introduction by the author

Methuen Drama

METHUEN DRAMA CONTEMPORARY DRAMATISTS

1 3 5 7 9 10 8 6 4 2

This collection first published in Great Britain in 2008
by Methuen Drama

Methuen Drama
A & C Black Publishers Limited
38 Soho Square
London W1D 3HB
www.acblack.com

Edward Gant's Amazing Feats of Loneliness!
first published by Methuen Drama in 2008
Copyright © 2008 Anthony Neilson
The Lying Kind first published by Methuen Publishing in 2002
Copyright © 2002 Anthony Neilson
The Wonderful World of Dissocia first published by Methuen Drama in 2007
Revised in this volume. Copyright © 2007, 2008 Anthony Neilson
Realism first published by Methuen Publishing in 2007
Revised in this volume. Copyright © 2007, 2008 Anthony Neilson
Introduction © 2008 Anthony Neilson

Anthony Neilson has asserted his rights
under the Copyright, Designs and Patents Act, 1988,
to be identified as the author of these works

ISBN: 978 1 408 10680 8

A CIP catalogue record for this book is available from the British Library

Typeset by Country Setting, Kingsdown, Kent CT14 8ES
Printed and bound in Great Britain by
CPI Cox & Wyman, Reading, RG1 8EX

Contents

Anthony Neilson
Chronology

1988	The Colours of the King's Rose (*radio play*)
1990	Welfare My Lovely
1990	A Fluttering of Wings (*radio play*)
1991	Normal
1992	Deeper Still (*short film*)
1993	Penetrator
1994	Year of the Family
1995	Heredity
1995	Jeffrey Dahmer Is Unwell (*co-written with Alan Francis and Mike Hayley*)
1995	The Night Before Christmas
1996	Meat and Two (*aka* Hooverbag)
1997	Twisted (*radio play*)
1997	The Censor
1999	The Debt Collector (*feature film*)
2002	Edward Gant's Amazing Feats of Loneliness!
2002	Stitching
2002	The Lying Kind
2004	The Wonderful World of Dissocia
2006	Realism
2007	God In Ruins

Introduction

The plays contained here are all comedies, of one sort or another. Two of them – *Dissocia* and *Realism* – use comedy as a 'delivery system' for more serious themes, whereas the other two – *Gant* and *The Lying Kind* – don't have much purpose other than to entertain. There are those who will think the latter two lesser plays for this – and they are perhaps less 'complete' as experiences – but I have become ever more aware of my (and my profession's) duty to entertain over the years and I have become quite addicted to the sound of an audience laughing.

Interestingly, reaction to these comedies has been even more polarised than the reaction to my more 'controversial' work. That is to be expected – one either finds something funny or one doesn't – but I suspect there is also a generational gap at work here. Matthew Pidgeon, the one actor who appeared in all these plays, recounted an illuminating story about meeting a particularly sour-looking woman after a performance of *Dissocia*. Tentatively enquiring whether she liked the play, the woman set him with a withering gaze and said, 'I don't do *zany*.' And yes, I will admit there is a lot of 'low' humour in the plays, and some *very* cheap gags. But it seems that, generally, my generation and subsequent ones seem to have less trouble with tonal variation. They seem to accept quite naturally that low humour can sit alongside seriousness and that darkness can move to light and back again within seconds.

It's hard not to seem pompous when writing an introduction to a collection of one's own plays, but I might humbly suggest (presuming your interest) that these four plays also represent an evolution in my personal style. While I have never been a particularly naturalistic writer, I have been pursuing an increasingly absurdist agenda. I currently believe that this form plays most fully to the strengths of the medium, allowing me to address serious themes in the most entertaining and accessible way possible, and also allowing for more fluidity between scenes and a deeper integration of set, lighting and sound design.

After a down period, in all senses of the phrase, *Gant* was really an attempt to let my imagination run loose. *The Lying Kind* was me trying to learn the mechanics of farce, and *Dissocia* was a breakthrough for me in bringing these elements of comedy, fairy-tale and even vaudeville together in the service of a more serious ambition. *Dissocia* was almost entirely subjective (in the first half at least) and *Realism* was a further exploration of this. I suppose – rather than adopting Absurdism with a capital A – I have been looking to find a way of writing that somehow moves in the way the mind moves. I do believe that the way we surf the internet (peculiarly similar to the movement of thought) and other elements of popular culture – the subjectivity of console gaming, the tangential nature of shows like *The Simpsons* – will have a huge influence on the very nature of narrative, and playwrights had best start addressing this if we want to stay relevant.

As a side note, I might add that the single biggest influence on me during this period was an evening of short plays written by children between the ages of ten and twelve, for a project called *Scene and Heard*. While they were all inevitably lacking in coherence, I was absolutely elated by the unpredictability of what these children produced; by their natural understanding of dramatic imperative, their genuine surreality and the pure little truths that occasionally exploded into the open. It's a cliché, but it graphically illustrated to me just how much I had to unlearn.

At the time of writing this, I am still unlearning. I suspect it will be a lifetime's work.

Anthony Neilson
2008

Edward Gant's
Amazing Feats of Loneliness!

As transcribed by Mr Anthony Neilson
For the illustrious Theatre Royal, Plymouth
This year of Our Lord, 1881

Edward Gant's Amazing Feats of Loneliness! was first performed at the Drum Theatre, Plymouth, on 13 May 2002. The cast was as follows:

Christine Entwisle   Madame Poulet
Stuart McQuarrie   Edward Gant
Matthew Pidgeon   Nicholas Ludd
Barney Power   Jack Dearlove

Director Anthony Neilson
Designer Bob Bailey
Lighting Designer Chahine Yavroyan
Sound Designer Matt Dando

The Players

Edward Gant	Himself
	Opium Den Client
	The Phantom of the Dry
Madame Poulet	Sanzonetta Tutti
	Louisa Von Kettelmein- Kurstein Frond
	Bear One
	Herself
Jack Dearlove	The Doctor
	A Pimple
	Salvatore Avaricci
	Edgar Thomas Dawn
	Bear Two
	Himself
Nicholas Ludd	Campanetti Tutti
	A Pimple
	Ranjeev the Uncomplicated
	Himself

Notes

The above castings, the transcript that follows and all stage directions therein are as accurate to the event witnessed as the transcriber's memory allows. In any further recreation of this extraordinary evening, all may be seen as moveable (where it is less than ludicrous to do so). These short histories may also be of use . . .

Madame Poulet was so known on account of her career previous to joining Mr Gant's troupe, wherein she took the aspect of a chicken and somehow simulated the actual laying of eggs. She took this act and, indeed, all her parts quite seriously and seemed, to the observer, to exist in a world of her own making. Gant seemed to have a peculiar fondness for her, though this is but conjecture on my part.

'Little' Nicky Ludd took to the stage as a child, most popularly impersonating a young Highland lassie.

Unfortunately, he carried on this act long beyond it was seemly to do so, wherein he fell upon hard and notorious times. Exploited by a radical political body, he was rescued by Mr Gant just as he was about to perpetrate a great and murderous treason upon the State. By the time of the evening transcribed, fuelled by rumours of a new theatrical realism in the East, he seemed to me disillusioned with Mr Gant and his methods. The animosity this engendered seemed most overtly directed towards Jack Dearlove, whose authoritarian nature appeared to inflame him.

Sgt Jack Dearlove, alongside Edward Gant, survived the infamous Charge of the Light Brigade. He believed that Gant had dragged him to safety that fateful day though − having been temporarily blind at the time − the veracity of this was never established beyond question. It hardly mattered, as Dearlove was devoted to the notion of service, and this perceived debt gave focus to his life. His immaculate devotion to Gant stretched from the earliest days of Gant's Midget Opera to the performance here transcribed. He was, as noted, at odds with Mr Ludd, whose notion of social enlightenment and insolent attitude towards Mr Gant embodied all he despised in the youth of the day.

I know not what became of the members of this troupe but dearly hope they are at peace, wherever they may be. I was but a lad when I witnessed the events herein, and set them down in the hope that their endeavours may echo beyond my own demise; I do so with thanks, for one of the two most astonishing evenings of my life so far . . .

Act One

Darkness . . .

Gant
    My good and pure ladies
    My brave and gentle men
    BEHOLD (if you will)
    The Oceanic Planet Earth!

Above us, the underside of a globe.

Behold the firmament's most precious jewel, around which
does revolve all the bodies of the Heavens

*One by one, the performers enter. Each carries a long stick, atop which
sway representations of the following. In procession, they circle the
suspended globe.*

    The Moon – la Luna.
    The Sun – le Soleil.
    The war planet Mars.
    The ringed planet Saturn.

Each performer, in turn, takes the light for his or her introduction.

The Moon held aloft by the heavenly Madame Poulet . . .

The Sun borne defiantly by our own Mr Nicholas Ludd . . .

And struggling bravely with both Mars and Saturn, my
steadfast Sergeant, Jack Dearlove . . .

The last of them exits. **Mr Gant** *is revealed.*

And holding the planets fast, to night's velvet train, the
silverpin points we call THE STARS!

*He throws up a handful of glitter, which catches the light and rains
back down to earth.*

Now let it come down, this watery world! *The globe shudders
but does not move.*

Now let it COME DOWN, this watery world!

The sound of a winch. Creakily, the globe winds downwards.

And let us (if we dare) take the aspect of God, gazing down (as does he) on this most various of his creations.

The descended globe is revealed as flat on top. Britain dominates the relief map: a naive, imperialist view of the world, bristling with Union Jacks.

Gant   A world of water, yes, but of many climates also: of sand and ice and trees and grass; of mountain, field and cloud. And on this Earth a billion creatures live, but most uniquely Man, who differs from all other beasts in one important way . . .

For while the beasts can be divided into those that form societies and those which bide alone 'tis only Man bestrides the two.

On the one hand, his great success has come about through partnership, and common effort –

Dearlove *and* **Ludd** *shake hands to illustrate this, while* **Madame Poulet** *acts out laying flowers on a grave to illustrate what follows.*

Gant   – yet, on the other, he has been gifted (or cursed) with the absolute knowledge of his mortality – and here his true uniqueness lies.

All three enact a hunting scene.

The beast senses danger at the *moment* it arises and forgets it the moment it has passed. But Man – Man lives in its shadow all the time. *He knows that he will die* –

Madame Poulet *falls.*

Gant   – and it is this terrifying fact –

Dearlove, *also, falls.*

Gant   – that imprisons each man within his own mind. And thus the most sociable of God's creations is far the most alone.

He taps his cane and the players exit.

Ladies and gentleman, as some of you may know, my name is Edward Gant: prodigy, soldier, traveller, poet – but always and ever a showman. As such, it has been my mission to bring you the most wonderous and bizarre that the world has to offer.

But what I bring you now is no mere freak show. You will gasp, yes, and you will marvel and you will see your share of grotesquerie. But the deformities on show this evening are not the deformities of the frame, but those of the heart and mind.

I have scoured every continent to find these most astonishing testaments. Alas, I cannot put before you the subjects themselves, but I will – with the help of my players – attempt to represent their tales to you as truly as time and talent will allow.

So without further ado, I present for your astonishment the Extraordinary! The Terrible! The AMAZING FEATS OF LONELINESS!

An explosion! And **Gant** *disappears.*

*

Ludd *and* **Dearlove** *enter, kicking the show off with a song.*

Ludd *sings and plays, hardly concealing his irritation at* **Dearlove**'s *banal accompanying illustrations . . .*

Ludd

    Ladies and gentlemen,
    Kindly let me address
    The first of our stories
    Of heartbreak and loneliness.
    Tragic, it may be,
    Sad and bizarre, but still
    We've added a dash of humour
    In the hope it will sweeten the pill.

    Our story takes place
    In the country we know as Italy,
    The Southernmost part at that
    In the region surrounding Sicily.
    Imagine the sunshine,
    Imagine the grapes on the vine,
    The smell of bread baking,
    The making and drinking of wine

At this point, **Ludd** *surreptitiously remonstrates with* **Dearlove**,
attempting to halt his actions. This only partially succeeds: **Dearlove**
continues his actions behind **Ludd**'s *back.*

Ludd

    But first let us travel
    To Italy's capital Rome,
    Where Mr Edward Gant
    Had the fortune to own a small home.
    He can never return there,
    If he does it's the end of his world,
    His one souvenir
    Is the tale you'll now hear –
    Sanzonetta, the Pimple-Faced Girl!

The two exit, and we can see that they will be having words backstage.

Madame Poulet, *in character, is now on stage, crying softly.*
Gant *enters.*

Gant   Just as a mother cannot ignore her baby's cry, no gentleman can happily pass a weeping woman. And so I found myself by the La Trevi fountain one winter, offering solace to a girl with a pockmarked face . . .

*

Girl   You are kind, Sir, to sit with me in the cold.

Gant   Not at all, my dear. It is no burden to sit with a beautiful girl.

Girl   You needn't humour me. I know I am not that.

Gant   Perhaps I see deeper than your tortured skin.

Girl   Then you are kinder still and I must reward you.

She hands him a pearl necklace.

It is all I have to give.

Gant   My dear girl – I cannot accept this –

Girl   You must. There is little enough kindness in the world. It should be rewarded when it occurs.

Gant   But this is a valuable thing. Is it not precious to you? Besides, I hardly think the Italians are ready for a man in jewellery.

Girl   Is there no special lady in your life? Give it her, with my blessing.

Gant   There are many ladies in my life.

Girl   Then give them one each!

She unloads a heap of them into his hands.

Gant   Are they imitations?

Girl   No, Sir, they are not.

Pause.

Gant   Do you mean they are stolen? Tell me you are not a thief.

Girl   They are real, Sir, and I am very far from a thief. But I have been much stolen from.

Gant   Intrigued, I pressed her further and she revealed to me then the extraordinary events of her life . . .

Her name was Sanzonetta Tutti and she was one of two sisters born to modest society. A normal girl in childhood, from the age of fourteen she was afflicted by severe attacks of pimples.

She was subject to ridicule, of course; but, to make matters worse, her sister, Campanetti had blossomed into the most gorgeous womanhood . . .

*

Campanetti *flounces in with a bouquet of flowers.*

Campanetti   My, but I am tired of these suitors!

Sanzonetta   Which one was that?

Campanetti   Guffini, the librarian's son.

Sanzonetta   I thought you said he was nice.

Campanetti   The backwards are often nice; they haven't the wit to be nasty.

Sanzonetta   The flowers are well chosen.

Campanetti   Which proves my point: were he as wise as he is ugly, he'd have brought a pig's arse and perhaps gained in the comparison!

Pause.

There is so much stress involved in choosing a husband! Especially now you have become ugly: all Papa's expectations are shouldered by me alone. Sometimes I envy you, Sanzonetta. It must be curiously restful, knowing no one would touch you with a gondolier-pole.

Pause.

My goodness; the shadows thrown by your pimple-heads
show it has gone six o'clock! Mashetti, the horse-butcher's
son is due to call at seven; I must prepare.

Oh, and Sanzonetta, I do not wish to be cruel but – should
you answer the door to him – would you mind putting a
bucket over your head, lest he spill his guts on the marbling?

Pause. **Sanzonetta** *nods.*

Campanetti   You are a darling!

*

Gant   Campanetti could not have known the agony her
careless remarks caused her sister.

Sanzonetta had tried everything to cure her affliction; taken
every remedy, seen every doctor, adopted any habit that
might lessen the attacks. There was every chance the condition
would pass in time; the danger was that it would leave her –

*

The **Doctor** *enters.*

Doctor   – irreversibly scarred!

Sanzonetta   Scarred? You mean – for ever?

Doctor   It stands to reason, Signora; your skin bubbles
hot like a cauldron. If this should persist for long enough
then, yes, of course – it will scar you.

Sanzonetta   Is there no way I can avoid this fate?

Doctor   Fate cannot be avoided, Sanzonetta. That's why
they call it fate.

Pause.

However, you can take care not to exacerbate the condition.

Take for instance, the boy who compared your face to a pizza. Cruel words, yes, but not wholly inaccurate. Each one of your tomato-red pimples contains a substance not unlike melted mozzarella. It is this that gives them their eye-catching white points. Now – if you apply sufficient pressure to these pimples, they will rupture, expelling their cheese in an often quite dramatic fashion.

Sanzonetta   No – how disgusting!

Doctor   Disgusting, yes, but you may also find the sensation of – ejaculation – strangely satisfying. Do not underestimate its allure; you rupture one, then another and soon the pimples will be singing to you, luring you as if hypnotised. 'Squeeze us,' they will sing. 'Expel our sweet cheese! Squeeze us!'

You must deny them, Sanzonetta! Their song serves only to lure you to the rocks! No matter how tempted you are, you must close your ears, strap down your hands, resist, resist!

Sanzonetta   Yes, I will!

Doctor   And come back in a month.

*

Gant   Sanzonetta was as good as her word – at first. But the doctor also spoke the truth. The song of the pimples sounded louder every day . . .

Sanzonetta *tosses and turns in her bed.*

Pimples (*sing*)
   Squeeze us, Sanzonetta –
   Expel our cheese – squeeze us . . .

Sanzonetta   No, I won't – I won't – !

The song grows louder and louder.

No – please – I don't want to be scarred – !

The song reaches a pitch and she jumps out of bed.

Yes! All right! I will do what you ask! But cease your endless song!

She runs to the mirror.

Gant   Wretched and broken, Sanzonetta chose the most taut and swollen pimple on her once lovely face. She pressed her knuckles to it, either side, and applied all her strength to its stubborn core.

The **Pimples** *moan, ever more frenzied: 'Yes, yes, yes!'*

She felt the pressure build and build – felt the tiny hairline cracks split across her tightening skin, her knuckles whitening with the strain and then – AND THEN – AND THEN – !

The **Pimples** *reach a pitch.* **Sanzonetta** *cries out and then –*

A tiny pearl rolls across the floor.

Pause. She picks it up, studies it, smells it.

Campanetti *enters.*

Campanetti   What is all this commotion, Sanzonetta?! You know I need my beauty sleep!

Pause.

What is that you have there?

Sanzonetta   Nothing . . .

Campanetti   Let me see. Sanzonetta – Sanzonetta!

Sanzonetta *gives her the pearl.*

Campanetti   Where did you get this? Did you steal this from my box?

Sanzonetta   No, I swear!

Campanetti   Don't lie to me, sister. Where else would you come upon a pearl such as this? It is certain no gentleman gave it you.

Sanzonetta   It is no pearl, Campanetti.

Campanetti   What do you take me for? You think I do not know a pearl when I see it? And a quite exquisite one at that . . . Come now, confess. Where did this come from, if not from my box?

Sanzonetta   It came from – my face.

Campanetti   From your face? Have you gone mad, Sanzonetta?

Sanzonetta   No, truly, I –

Campanetti   For either you believe it yourself or you believe that I will believe; and each of these is clearly madness.

Sanzonetta   I am as disbelieving as you, my sister, but I swear it; I attempted to squeeze one of my pimples and that is what came forth.

Pause.

Campanetti   Show me, then.

Sanzonetta   I will try.

She tries again, groaning with the effort.

Campanetti   This had best be no trick, sister; for it is quite the most revolting thing to witness!

With a final squeal, another pearl pops out and rolls across the floor. **Campanetti** *picks it up and studies it. She looks at her sister, amazed.*

Campanetti   It's a pearl!

Sanzonetta   I know.

Campanetti   It came from your face!

Sanzonetta   I know!

Pause.

Campanetti   Do you realise what this means?! If each of your pimples harbours a pearl of this perfection?!

Sanzonetta *shakes her head.*

Campanetti   It means that we are rich, my sister! It means that we are rich!

*

Gant   The sun was dawning by the time Sanzonetta had forced the last pearl from her ravaged, bloody face. This crop alone would have been sufficient to raise them into the lower ranks of privilege, but – to Campanetti's delight – a day later, her sister's face was once more in bloom.

Within months, Campanetti had established a thriving business, trading in pearls of such quality that the Tutti name was soon famous the length and breadth of Europe. Their newfound wealth allowed the two sisters to acquire a substantial country home in Sicily.

But – while Campanetti lived the high-life – Sanzonetta's circumstances had hardly improved . . .

*

Campanetti *enters, dripping with pearl jewellery.*

Campanetti   Sanzonetta – what are you doing in the sunlight? You know production slows in the sunlight!

Sanzonetta   But it is damp in the cellar.

Campanetti   I know, my dear. But we must satisfy this Parisian order; they have paid us handsomely for a prompt delivery.

Sanzonetta   You mean they have paid you handsomely.

Campanetti   I mean what I said, my sister. Your share of the proceeds lies in your account.

Sanzonetta   Exactly; and it will continue to lie there, as I am never allowed the time to spend it!

Campanetti   I sympathise, my dear, I do. But only God knows how long your bounteous condition will continue. We must take advantage while we can. Your day will come, my sister.

Sanzonetta   Easy for you to say; it would seem your day is upon you and has been for many a month.

Campanetti   Sanzonetta – I have just this moment returned from Spain. In the morning, I set sail for England. What more can I do than play my part?

Sanzonetta   You could begin by changing the name of our company.

Campanetti (*sighs*)   Sanzonetta –

Sanzonetta   I know you will say you are protecting me, but I do not see how it protects me to name it The Campanetti Pearl Company.

Campanetti   It is a matter of convenience, nothing more.

Sanzonetta   So you say. But, sister – I never see the wonder on the client's faces, never see my pearls adorn their necks. Why should I also be so disavowed? Why can it not be known that I am the source of these wonderful pearls?

Campanetti   Don't be a fool, Sanzonetta; you think the great and good would be so keen to wear our pearls if they knew they came from a teenager's face? No – the truth would ruin our business and do you no credit, either. At the moment, people merely think you ugly; would you prefer that they deride you as a freak?

Reluctantly, **Sanzonetta** *shakes her head.*

Campanetti   Then you have your answer.

Pause. **Sanzonetta** *starts to trudge back to the cellar.*

Campanetti   Oh, Sanzonetta, I nearly forgot: I have news that may interest you.

Sanzonetta *stops.*

Campanetti Do you remember – before your . . . condition set in – the weekend we spent in Milan?

Sanzonetta Yes?

Campanetti Do you remember the young man you strolled with in the garden?

Sanzonetta Salvatore?

Campanetti Salvatore Avaricci. You took a shine to him, if I recall?

Sanzonetta *looks down, embarrassed.*

Campanetti Come now, admit it. You talked about him all the journey home.

Sanzonetta I admit he was a dashing young man.

Campanetti But he'd have nothing to do with the likes of you; isn't that what you said?

Sanzonetta He's the heir to the Avaricci fortune . . .

Campanetti Indeed. Well – I forgot to tell you, but I chanced to run into him recently.

Pause.

He remembered you, my sister.

Sanzonetta He did?

Campanetti In great detail.

Sanzonetta Well – but – what did he say? About me?

Campanetti He said a great deal. But to cut a long story short . . . we are to be married next spring!

Pause.

So you see: you should never judge a book by its cover. Are you happy for me?

Sanzonetta   Of course . . .

Campanetti   Sanzonetta – look at me?

She holds her sister's face and stares at her.

Goodness, is that the time? You'd best get off to the cellar.

Campanetti *exits.* **Sanzonetta** *trudges off to the cellar.*

*

Gant   At that moment, for all her potential riches, Sanzonetta felt quite the poorest girl in the world.

The next day Campanetti set off on her trip across the water, leaving Sanzonetta alone once more. This was her sister's great error; for that week, their home received an unexpected visitor . . .

Sanzonetta *is in the cellar, dispensing pearls. A knocking from above.*

Avaricci   Hello?!

Sanzonetta *sits up, panicked.*

Sanzonetta   My goodness; who is that?!

Avaricci   Hello?!

Sanzonetta   Hello?!

Avaricci   Hello?! Where are you?!

Sanzonetta   Where is that lazy maid of ours? Drunk again, I suppose!

Avaricci   Where are you?!

Sanzonetta   I'm down here!

Avaricci   Down where?!

Sanzonetta   I shall come to you!

Avaricci   And I shall come to you!

Sanzonetta *puts on her veil and leaves the cellar.* **Avaricci**
descends the staircase. They call to each other as they draw nearer:
'Hello?!', 'Hello?!'

Avaricci *enters at the same time as* **Sanzonetta**.

Avaricci   Campanetti!

Sanzonetta   Signor Avaricci!

Avaricci   Campanetti?

Sanzonetta   No I – I'm afraid Campanetti is in England.
She is not due back until tomorrow.

Pause.

Avaricci   You do not fool me, my love. Take down that
veil and let me see your beautiful face.

Sanzonetta   I am not Campanetti.

Avaricci   This is Campanetti's home, is it not?

Sanzonetta   Yes, Signor.

Avaricci   And you are no maid; for she is vomiting by the
ponds. So who else lives here?

Sanzonetta   I am her sister. Sanzonetta.

Pause.

Avaricci   Campanetti – God will punish you for such
wickedness!

Sanzonetta   I am who I say, Signor.

Avaricci   My dearest – you should not confuse my longings
with my humour. There is a place for perversity and this is
not it.

Sanzonetta   Is it so hard to believe that I am Sanzonetta?

Pause.

Avaricci   Show me your face.

Sanzonetta I would rather not, Signor.

Avaricci *unsheaths his sword.*

Avaricci I'm afraid I must insist.

Sanzonetta Do not ask this of me, please.

Avaricci This is the home of my betrothed. The door stands open. I trust you see my point.

Sanzonetta But I am – ugly, Signor.

Avaricci You will be more so if you do not comply this instant.

Pause.

Sanzonetta Promise me that you will say nothing hurtful.

Avaricci You have my word.

Sanzonetta *lowers her cowl.*

Avaricci Dear Christ in Heaven! Your face! Your hideous, appalling face!

Sanzonetta You promised me!

Avaricci Why do you walk the Earth, foul fiend?! What terrible purpose have you here?! Be merciful, Sanzonetta; return to whence you came!

Sanzonetta Your compassion overwhelms me, Signor Avaricci.

Avaricci You have my every compassion, Sanzonetta, but you do not belong here. I would not have had you die, but die you did. Why is your spirit not at rest?!

Pause.

Sanzonetta I am not dead, Signor.

Avaricci No, Sanzonetta, you are – you must accept it, if you are ever to find peace!

Sanzonetta   Signor Avaricci, I assure you – I have a bad complexion, but I am not dead. Here, touch me –

Avaricci   No, get back!

Sanzonetta   Why do you think that I am dead?

Pause. She extends her hand

Touch me.

Slowly, timidly, he reaches out and touches her.

There. Am I not flesh and blood?

Pause.

Avaricci   Sanzonetta?

Pause.

But – Campanetti told me you were dead!

Sanzonetta   Campanetti?

Avaricci   Yes – I met her at a drinking contest in Bavaria. She told me you had died in Brittany, from a surfeit of eels. You mean this was a lie?

Pause. He stands.

I fear I have made a fool of myself, Signora. How can you ever forgive me?

Sanzonetta   It is not you I will need to forgive, Signor Avaricci. I suppose she also told you about the Campanetti Pearl Company?

Avaricci   Yes, in that it's a company she grew *herself* from *nothing* with *no help from anyone* and that she *personally* scours the planet for the finest pearls available, which is the reason she charges *an extra twenty per cent* over and above the asking price and that once we are married she intends to *sell* the company and use the profits to *leave this dump* and live the rest of her life in *luxury* with me in my palace in *Monaco*.

Pause.

Why?

Pause.

Sanzonetta   I think we should talk.

*

Gant   And talk, ladies and gentlemen, they did . . .

Signor Avaricci discovered the truth about his bride-to-be, and Sanzonetta showed him the true source of the so-called Campanetti pearls.

In silhouette, **Avaricci** *vomits.*

Gant   Avaricci knew then that his marriage to Campanetti was not to be. But, just as one Tutti sister was taking leave of his heart, another was stealing in . . .

*

Avaricci *and* **Sanzonetta** *return from their talk.*

Avaricci   No, he said that there was no place in the Catholic Church for the sexual molestation of children.

Sanzonetta   Did he?

Avaricci   Yes, so they're building one.

Pause.

Sanzonetta   My goodness, it has fallen dark . . .

Avaricci   Goodness, yes; so it has . . .

Sanzonetta   When did that happen?

Avaricci   I have no idea.

Pause.

Sanzonetta   Well . . .

Pause.

Avaricci   Of course you know what this means?

Sanzonetta   What?

Avaricci   The sun has crept away so as not to disturb us.
It knows it has outstayed its welcome.

Sanzonetta   It is well-mannered.

Avaricci   And perceptive too.

Pause.

Avaricci   Sanzonetta – take down your veil.

Sanzonetta   Please, Signor, we have had such a pleasant
afternoon. Let us not spoil it now.

Avaricci   Sanzonetta, if I have responded violently, it was
to your face, not your soul.

Sanzonetta   Call me vain, but that is little comfort.

Avaricci   You must understand; despite my inordinate
wealth, I am in many ways a shallow man. I have struggled
for little in my life. Your sister is just the latest in a long line
of impossibly beautiful women I have courted but, in truth,
I have felt little for anyone.

Pause.

Until now, that is. Until meeting you.

Sanzonetta   You could not love one as ugly as I, Signor.

Avaricci   No; but that is the point. I think fate has
brought me here today. I think God has sent you to me.

Sanzonetta   To what end?

Avaricci   To make me a better man.

Pause.

Sanzonetta, I will admit – my fascination with pearls is well known. That they were Campanetti's trade played some part in her appeal. 'But here,' God is saying, 'Look: a woman so ugly you would not have shat in her mouth if she were hungry. But look closer – these deformities conceal the very thing you find most beautiful.' You see?

He gets down on one knee, holding her hand.

Loving you will be my struggle. And with God's grace I will overcome my shallowness and find happiness at last.

Sanzonetta　Stop, Salvatore – your words pour forth like wine and I am giddy with it!

Avaricci　As am I. But this is good; I want us to get giddy with it!

Sanzonetta　But you are promised to my sister.

Avaricci　She has shown you no such consideration.

Pause.

Come, Sanzonetta, let your veil fall away, and with it your chains! Let me kiss the pearls from out your skin! Let me reap your tender harvest!

Sanzonetta　Salvatore! You have your wish, for good or ill. Here!

She lets the cowl fall.

I give myself to you, Salvatore; Farm me! Farm me!

They embrace.

*

Gant　The very next day, Sanzonetta gathered up her belongings and fled with Avaricci to his residence in Monaco, where they lived out the summer in something close to bliss.

Their combined wealth was such that Sanzonetta had no more need to sell the fruits of her skin. She grew her pearls slowly, in the full light of day and only for her true love, Salvatore.

Avaricci *enters, dressed for all the world like a pearly king.*

Gant   Avaricci was no less content. He had been with many beautiful women in his time but – for a man obsessed with acquisition – it had never been enough. One can never truly possess a woman whose beauty is available to all men's eyes; but Sanzonetta's beauty was known only to him. She was his and his alone.

He farmed her gently, once a week, and used the pearls to build a small church on the grounds, in which they would be married as soon as work was done.

*

Sanzonetta *lies on the bed, reading a letter.*

Avaricci   What are you reading, my love?

Sanzonetta   It is from that society journal, *Buongiorno*. They wish to report on our wedding. How should we reply?

Avaricci   I tell you how we shall reply: I shall use the letter for my ablutions and we shall post it by return.

Sanzonetta   Their intentions seem quite honourable. Can we not allow their request?

Pause.

Avaricci   If it will please you, my sweet –

She embraces him. He kisses her and accidentally gets a pearl.

Another for the pulpit.

They nuzzle lovingly.

Campanetti *suddenly appears, looking wretched and poor and wearing a cowl.*

Campanetti   Ah how sweet! The Eunuch and the Jezebel!

Sanzonetta   Campanetti!

Avaricci   What brings you here?!

Campanetti   Why, Signor Avaricci – I have come to receive my invitation to your wedding, for the mail has clearly failed me! I notice you have found a use for my sister's pearls. Congratulations – a church you smell before you see. But why stop there? Perhaps you can use her other waste products for a bridal suite!

Sanzonetta   Do not blame him, my sister. I felt it would be wrong to invite you and that you would not have come, in any case.

Campanetti   Oh, but you are wrong, my sister! You may have cheated me of my business and my standing and my self-respect but make no mistake, I will be at that wedding – but not as a guest. As the Bride!

She pulls away the cowl to reveal a huge and bulbous pimple on her forehead.

You see, my love? You see what I have grown for you?

Avaricci   It's revolting, Campanetti!

Campanetti   Yes, and how I have longed to hear those words ! All those months in the dark, caked in the fat of oxen, all to hear you say those words!

Sanzonetta   What have you done to yourself?

Campanetti   Oh, do I detect fear in your voice, my traitorous sister? Then it is well placed. For now I am all a man could desire; beautiful in face and bulbous of pimple. Can you imagine the size of the fucker in this?! Why, it will put your puny petits-pois to shame!

She approaches **Avaricci**.

Campanetti   It is all for you, my love. And though my skin has grown taut as the breeches of a priest at choir practice, I have resisted all temptation to set it free. I offer it to you now, as a symbol of my devotion. Will you receive my pearl, Salvatore?

Avaricci (*tempted*)   Campanetti, I – cannot.

Campanetti   You must. You must or I shall let it grow till it impinges on my brain!

Sanzonetta   No, my sister, it will kill you!

Campanetti   If I am denied this moment, I will welcome death!

Pause.

Sanzonetta   Receive her pearl, my love.

Avaricci   Sanzonetta – are you sure?

Sanzonetta   I trust you, my darling.

Campanetti   Touching, is it not? How little she knows of the ways of men!

Sanzonetta   Perhaps. But I know the ways of mine.

Campanetti   We shall see. Once he has my pearl in his hands, we shall see how much he differs.

Pause.

Sanzonetta   Receive her pearl, Salvatore.

Pause. **Avaricci** *goes to* **Campanetti**.

Avaricci   I do this for you, my love.

Campanetti   I almost feel sorry for her.

Avaricci   Silence, woman. Deliver up your pearl.

Campanetti *uses her fists to squeeze and squeeze the huge pimple on her forehead, groaning with the effort as her sister did before her.*

Suddenly, it explodes, showering **Avaricci** *with pus. He staggers back in disgust.*

Avaricci   Achh!

Campanetti   No! No! Where is my pearl?! Where is my beautiful pearl?!

Avaricci   Get out of my palace! Get out and never return!

Campanetti   No, but it must be here! It's in here somewhere, my love, I promise you!

She searches frantically in her forehead.

Sanzonetta   There is no pearl, Campanetti, only cheese!

Avaricci   Take her from my sight, my love, take her!

Campanetti   No, please, my sweet, it is here, I tell you!

Sanzonetta   No, Campanetti – we are sisters, but this trait we do not share. Come –

Campanetti   No, wait, here – here!

She holds up a handful of jelly.

It is here, within this jelly, see – see, my love!

She searches within the jelly: nothing.

Where can it umbrella?

They look at her, puzzled.

It flog me spaghetti . . . Bubble ark abalone!

Sanzonetta   Why does she speak so strangely?

Campanetti   I cannot teat the pump garden!

Avaricci   Wait – look: this is no mere jelly; this is your brain!

Pause.

Sanzonetta   Oh no – Campanetti!

She looks at them confused.

Campanetti   The kissy summer sunshore!

Then drops down dead.

Sanzonetta *and* **Avaricci** *stare down at her corpse.*

*

Gant   That is a sad tale indeed, Signora; but I hope you did not blame yourself –

Sanzonetta   No, Signor Gant, I did not.

Gant   Then that is good; nor should you have. I take it, then, that the marriage did not occur?

Sanzonetta   Oh no, Signor Gant, it occurred. The marriage went ahead as planned.

Pause.

Gant   I'm not sure I understand, Signora. You said you had been much stolen from . . .

Sanzonetta   Wait, Signor Gant – my story is not ended yet.

I did marry Signor Avaricci and all was well at first. We continued our lives as happily as ever; I can recall no great disagreements, no noticeable dimming of our passion. And yet, one spring morning, I woke alone . . .

A letter lay on Salvatore's pillow . . .

She hands the letter to **Gant***.*

Gant (*reads*)   'My darling Sanzonetta . . .
    'I told you once that I was a shallow man. It seems, to my shame, that this is no less true today. I can do you no more good than to state this very plainly: I have left you for an oyster named Martine.'

Pause.

'Believe me when I say you have played no part in my discontent. The restless heart is mine and mine alone.
                    'Forever yours, Salvatore Avaricci.'

Pause.

Sanzonetta   I sense, Signor Gant, that you understand what it is to lose in love, so I will not bore you with the details of my grief. But I made it then my mission to confront him and his oyster mistress.

It was a long and tiresome search, spanning much of Europe. I finally tracked them down to a diplomatic function in Vienna. I hired the most lavish dress I could and bribed the doorman fifteen pearls to let me in.

I moved through the waltzing couples as one moves through a dream. They parted before me with an almost magical precision. Finally, at the heart of the throng, I saw them . . .

Avaricci *is dancing with* **Martine** *the oyster.*

Sanzonetta   He danced with her as he once did with me. Looked at her as he once looked at me. I had played this moment in my mind so many times – how I would rage at him, show him my raw sorrow, shame him into wanting me once more.

Yet now the moment had arrived, I could but stand there. And strangely, I felt something close to tenderness. I remember thinking, here is another way in which I differ from my sister.

I let the dancers swallow me up once more, and drifted to the sidelines till the waltz came to an end.

Pause.

Gant   You did not even speak to him?

Sanzonetta   I spied him alone on the balcony later and we exchanged niceties, as if nothing so unusual had occurred.

Gant   You did not touch on his betrayal at all?

Sanzonetta   I simply asked him why– why he had left me and the bliss we had had in our grasp? What this Oyster had that I did not?

Pause.

Gant   And how did he reply?

Pause.

Sanzonetta   Mystery.

Pause.

He said she had . . . mystery.

And, with this, **Sanzonetta** *takes her leave . . .*

*

Gant   Mystery, yes . . . of course; who among us can deny its allure? We devour it second only to food and drink.

Yet there are those who would seek to deny it. These are the dull fellows who come to me and say, 'But Gant – you cannot expect us to believe such a preposterous story! Surely,' they say, 'you should devote yourself to the truth of life?'

I answer in two ways. Firstly, that I simply recount the tale as 'twere told to me. Secondly, that – whilst I have no way of knowing what is false in Sanzonetta's story – this much I do know; that life is not merely the space between sleeping – and that the truth of life lies least of all in the facts.

Ladies and gentleman, you have now completed the first course in this evening's menu. Accordingly, I shall allow you a brief moment to digest it. I pray you will return refreshed, your palates clean and ready for my next feat of loneliness which I can guarantee you – in the least financial sense of the word – will be yet more amazing still . . .

Exit.

Act Two

Gant *enters.*

Gant I am forbidden to tell you in what way I was
connected to Mr Edgar Thomas Dawn, but connected
we were; and he was thus within his rights to approach
me as I relaxed at the Gentleman's Club in the Rangoon
Grand . . .

*

Edgar *approaches* **Gant** *at his table.*

Edgar Sir, will you excuse me, but I must ask your
assistance: and if you will shake my hand, you will understand
why you must lend it, if you can.

Gant *shakes his hand. Obviously something happens.*

Gant Gant, Edward Gant. Of the 93rd Highlanders, the
Seven Oaks Order and Midget Opera T.C., at your service.

Edgar Thank you, Brother Gant. My name is Edgar . . .
Edgar Thomas . . . Dawn . . .

He sways woozily.

Gant You seem unsteady, Brother Edgar. Here – sit
down.

Edgar *nods his thanks as* **Gant** *helps him into the chair.*

Gant Will you take your chances with the water?

Edgar If you will grant my wish, I'll have no need of it,
Brother. Nor of bread, nor sunshine, nor any of the hateful
staples of existence.

Pause.

Gant What is it you would have of me, Brother Edgar,
that would render you so . . . independent?

Edgar I would have you kill me.

Pause.

Gant   Come now, Brother. I cannot think your life is so bad.

Edgar   Can you not?

Gant   The gift you ask is grave indeed. I cannot grant it on a whim.

Edgar   No.

Pause.

No, of course not, Brother. And you must excuse my insolence. Think it only the actions of a desperate man, and remember me kindly.

He is about to go when **Gant** *stands.*

Gant   Brother Edgar.

Edgar *stops.*

Gant   I have seen death, Sir, and it is no friend of mine. But nor is it a foe. It is a tool, borrowed from God, that we use to engineer the world. Its use can be for good or ill. Perhaps if you tell me the source of your woes, I can better judge its application.

Pause.

Edgar   The source of my woes? Yes, I can tell you that and better; I can give it a name.

Louisa von Kettelmein-Kurstein Frond.

Louisa *appears, laying down a picnic blanket.*

Edgar   It hardly matters how I met her; only that I did. At first I thought her but a medley of my past loves – the smile of one, the locks of another, the careless shrug of another still . . . But it soon came clear my Louisa was no pale reminder of them; but rather they who had served to point the way to her.

Pause.

She was my fate, Brother Gant, come down in female form.
I had no choice but to love her . . .

*

A field. **Louisa** *is eating as* **Edgar** *returns.*

Louisa   Jammy ring?

Edgar   No, no, I used a dockleaf.

Louisa   No, I mean would you care for a jammy ring?
Papa made them this morning.

Edgar   Really? Well; what a peculiar name.

He watches her lovingly.

How funny you are.

Louisa   In what respect?

Edgar   Oh, I don't know. With your little nose and
your . . . jammy, jammy ring.

Louisa   Am I your great, great love?

Edgar   It would appear that you are.

Pause.

Louisa   I am bereft of undergarments.

Pause.

Edgar   How funny you are.

Pause.

No, but I think you are . . . I think you are my great love –
I know you are – which brings me quite neatly to what I was
going to say and why I brought you here today, to where we
first ever kissed; it seemed the right place for me to ask you
this – thing I'm going to ask you –

Louisa *lifts out another cake.*

Edgar   No, don't have another jammy ring –

Louisa   They're delicious!

Edgar   No, but – because I'm going to ask you something.

Louisa   So?

Edgar   Well, just – please, my dearest – you can have one, just – wait a moment . . .

She sits with the jammy ring hovering at her mouth.

No, can you –

Louisa   What?

Edgar   Can you actually just – Louisa, my dearest –

Louisa   It's attracting flies!

Edgar   Just one moment –

Louisa   I wish you would just say what it is then, and be done with it!

Edgar   No, but it requires –

Louisa   These damnable flies !

Edgar   I'm asking for your hand –

Pause.

Louisa   In marriage?

Edgar   In marriage, yes; my sweetheart, my darling, my sunshine and showers.

Pause.

Louisa   I have no words.

Edgar   You need only one.

Louisa   And you don't mind about my . . . ?

She looks down at herself.

Edgar   I wouldn't have them any other way.

She suddenly embraces him.

Louisa   Edgar, my love! I do, I will. Yes! My love.

Edgar   I think I have never been happier than now. And it seems all nature does agree!

Louisa   Ow!

She touches her neck.

I think I have been bitten . . .

Edgar   I see the culprit – a foul and vicious wasp. How dare you sting my sweet Louisa?!

He beats it to death.

There. He has paid full penalty for his crime.

But **Louisa** *is going into shock . . .*

Edgar   'Tis only a wasp's sting, my sweet . . .

Louisa   I feel strange . . .

Edgar   Have you not been stung before?

Pause.

Louisa?

Louisa   Something is happening to me . . .

Edgar   What?

She begins to shake uncontrollably.

Louisa! What is wrong with you?!

Louisa   I don't know – the world is turning black –

Edgar   What do you mean?

Louisa   I fear I am . . . slipping away – Edgar . . .

Edgar   No, don't be absurd – !

Louisa   I'm losing you, my love –

Edgar   But it's only a wasp sting – Louisa . . . !

Louisa   Hush now, hush – There is no better day to die.

Edgar   No, Louisa, listen; this cannot be! It was only a wasp, you cannot die – I forbid you to die, Louisa, I FORBID IT!

He looks around for help, distraught.

Louisa   Know that I would have married you, Edgar. That there is another world where I did, and where we still wake up together – only now the birdsong is joined with the laughter of our children. It is there I go to be with you now . . .

Edgar   Then I will follow!

She grabs him, urgently.

Louisa   No! No, you must promise me – you must live your life in joy, you must do that for me!

Edgar   No – Louisa –

Louisa   It is a sin, Edgar – you must not sin for me. If you join me it must be God's will alone. Promise me, Edgar, if you love me. Promise me.

Pause.

Edgar   I promise.

Louisa   You can – have those – jammy rings . . .

And with this, she dies.

*

Edgar   Need I tell you, Brother Gant, that God made an enemy that day?

It seemed I was no longer flesh and bone and sinew but a creature carved of pain alone.

For years I raged from place to place, fighting, drinking and trying to womanise. I became hopelessly addicted to opium and even sank so low as to canvas for Gladstone. I knew things had to change.

Despite the Liberal Government, I made the decision to go on with life. I destroyed every letter sent me by Louisa, every rendering of her. Anything I could find that in any way conjured her, I loaded on a pyre and burned from out my sight.

But still I could not free myself from the quicksands of my grief. One image of her remained to haunt me, outwit my grasp, unburnable.

He taps his forehead.

Here, my Brother, here it was stored; within my mind's imagining. Playing like a diorama in my skull.

I thought myself beyond hope; until that chance encounter in an opium den in Hastings . . .

*

A **Man** *lies on a mattress, out of his head on opium.*

Man   That is a sad tale, my friend, and I can offer no solution –

Edgar   You misunderstand me, Sir, I was not –

Man   Hold on, you didn't let me finish. I can offer no solution but one. Tell me: are you a wealthy man?

Edgar   Once I was of reasonable means, but no longer.

Man   A pity.

Edgar   Why a pity? There are no riches on this earth enough to buy peace for my soul.

Man   Wrong, Sir. The rich can buy anything; a round trip to Nepal, for example.

Edgar   I do not need a holiday, Sir.

Man   It would be far from that. This would require a treacherous journey into the mountain ranges, the most inhospitable terrain known to man.

Edgar   And why would I choose to holiday there?

Man   You would not. Instead, you would seek out Ranjeev the Uncomplicated, an ancient fakir who has made his home there.

Edgar   And why would I holiday with him?

Pause. The **Man** *is still.* **Edgar** *shakes him.*

Man   Eh?

Edgar   Why would I holiday with Ranjeev the Uncomplicated?

Man   You would not. But rumour has it he can lift the torment from men's minds as cleanly as you would lift a bullet from out a leg.

Edgar   You mean – he could rid me of this last image of Louisa?

Man   It is only rumour, my friend. But I don't see why not.

Pause.

Edgar   He is a fakir, you say?

Man   An old fakir, yes.

Edgar   An old Indian fakir.

They begin to laugh.

Man   A wizened old fakir!

The laughter grows uncontrollable.

Edgar   Here – I hope the 'fakir' is not a 'faker' –

They lose themselves in hysterics.

Man   I wish you well, my friend!

The laughter subsides. Pause.

Have you got anything to eat?

*

Gant   Decency prohibits me from telling you how this
tortured soul went about raising the money for his expedition
to Nepal. Let us just say that, after two years in Plymouth,
he was of sufficient means to set sail for the East.

By the time Edgar neared the summit of the range, he was
alone; his sherpas having either died, fled or simply gone in
the huff with him. A terrible snowstorm blew up and Edgar
found himself exhausted and consumed. He lay there, near
the roof of the world, and drifted into unconsciousness . . .

*

Edgar *wakes in a cave.*

Edgar   Where am I? What is this place? Hello?!

Backstage, the other players provide the echo to his words.

No reply but my own . . . Perhaps I have died. Yes: perhaps
I have died and gone to Heaven!

But if this is Heaven, where is my sweet Louisa's welcome?
Where be the cherubs and their tender ministrations? And
why is my mouth as dry as a suffragette's chuff?

Perhaps this is not Heaven, but the other place. Have I been
so wretched in my grief? Has God turned his back on one
so taken with his own misfortune? Forgive me, gentle one,
I implore you! Be merciful in death to one so robbed in life!
I beseech you, Lord! I beseech you!

He collapses in tears. **Ranjeev** *enters.*

Ranjeev   Excuse me, Sir, but I was wondering if you
would mind beseeching your God a little quieter, as the
sound does tend to travel.

Edgar   Who are you?

Ranjeev   I am the one you seek.

Edgar   You are Ranjeev the Uncomplicated?

Ranjeev   In a word: yes.

Edgar   Then this is not the Promised Land?

Ranjeev   No, it's a cave.

Edgar   But nor is it Hell itself.

Pause.

Ranjeev   It's a cave.

Edgar   Your name is well earned.

Ranjeev *nods his thanks.*

Edgar *looks back out of the cave entrance.*

Ranjeev   It is true to say you came close to death. Moments more and the mountain would have claimed you.

Edgar   Yes, I remember feeling wretchedly cold . . . and sitting down for a rest and then . . . I must've fainted, like a woman. How dreadfully embarrassing.

Ranjeev   No, no, Sahib – This mountain is known for its treacherous cold. This is why the natives know it as Sangavi-al-jaheer.

Edgar   Which means?

Ranjeev   Mountain of treacherous cold.

Edgar   Treacherous indeed: even thick tweed offers no protection.

Ranjeev   That is what I most admire about the English; at their most stylish when style is least required.

Edgar   Thank you, my friend. But – English or not – it would seem I owe you my thanks.

Ranjeev   Sir, please – I need no thanks for what I did.

Edgar   Allow me their expression at least.

Ranjeev   I neither need nor deserve them.

Edgar   On the contrary, you deserve a great deal more. You ventured outside, at no little risk to yourself, and dragged me to safety, did you not?

Ranjeev   Yes . . .

Edgar   Then why would you not deserve my gratitude?

Ranjeev   Because your ear broke off.

He shows **Edgar** *the ear.*

*

Gant   Later – when the screaming had ceased – Edgar told the mystic of his plight. Ranjeev the Uncomplicated sat silent and serene throughout the recounting and pondered his answer long and hard . . .

*

A long, hard pause. Finally, **Ranjeev** *speaks.*

Ranjeev   It is true what they say. I can do this thing you ask.

Pause.

Edgar   Pardon?

Ranjeev   IT IS TRUE WHAT THEY SAY. I CAN DO THIS THING YOU ASK.

Edgar   Oh, right, good.

Ranjeev   And so do all respond at first. But there are –

Edgar *cups his non-existent ear.*

Ranjeev   BUT THERE ARE DANGERS HERE.

Edgar *still can't hear. He turns so that his existing ear is towards* **Ranjeev**.

Ranjeev   THERE ARE – there are dangers here.

Edgar   I am content with that. All that matters is I am freed of this torment; the means are unimportant.

Ranjeev   With respect, Sahib: there is worse in life than death.

Edgar   Than my death, yes. Than hers – than my beloved Louisa's death – no, my friend: there was no worse, not in my life. Nor will there ever be.

Pause.

Ranjeev   Very well.

He rises.

It will require me exposing the very essence of your being. Touching the very core of the tortured soul within you.

Edgar   And how will this come about? Through meditation, song and deep massage?

Ranjeev *opens a box full of horrendous trepanation items.*

Ranjeev   No. By drilling a hole in your head.

Pause. **Edgar** *stares at the gruesome instruments.*

Edgar   I see. So it is to be done with trepanation.

Ranjeev   Oh yes; with *extreme* trepanation.

Edgar   *Extreme* trepanation?

Ranjeev   It cannot be done lightly.

Edgar   No, I suppose not.

Pause.

Purely as a matter of interest – could you refresh me as to what exactly this procedure involves?

Ranjeev   The spike takes purchase of the skull, anchoring the cutting tool as it shears a perfect circle from its hard, bony plate. The disc is removed, laying bare the throbbing brain. Then I will introduce a device that will apply pressure to the brain whilst also acting to close the wound.

Pause.

Edgar   Righty-ho . . .

Ranjeev   You will no longer be plagued by the image of your loss –

Edgar   Well, that's the main thing . . .

Ranjeev   Listen carefully, Sahib. The image of your beloved will be gone, but not the memory of what occurred. You will know that you loved and that you lost. But your memories will be like empty rooms.

Edgar   The emptier the better.

Ranjeev   There is one thing further: once this device is in place, it can never be removed. The moment it is removed, the image of your beloved will return and blood will flood your head, bringing instant death. Do you understand, Sahib? You cannot remove it, even for a moment.

Edgar   I understand.

Ranjeev   Not even if it gets itchy.

Edgar   Not even if it gets itchy.

Ranjeev   It does get very itchy.

Edgar   Listen – I was in the Camel Corps. There's nothing you can tell me about itching.

Pause.

Your well-meaning words are noted, my friend, and well taken 'n all. I came here to find peace, by hook or by crook. You have my blessing to proceed.

Ranjeev   As you wish.

Standing behind **Edgar**, **Ranjeev** *assembles the diabolical trepanatory tool.*

Ranjeev   Will you be going on holiday this year?

Edgar   I shouldn't think so. Spent all my money coming here.

Ranjeev   I know; it's so expensive, is it not?

Edgar   It's not so much the travelling as paying the guides not to kill you.

Ranjeev   It's terrible. Now, I'm just going to take a little off the top, nothing off the back.

Edgar   Proceed.

Alarmingly, **Ranjeev** *is consulting an instruction manual.*

He gently taps the spike, trying to penetrate **Edgar**'s *skull.* **Edgar** *does his best to cope.*

Edgar   Goodness. What a very strange sensation.

Pause.

So at the moment you're attempting to penetrate my skull, are you?

Ranjeev   That is correct, Sir.

Edgar   Right.

Ranjeev   Try not to nod, Sahib.

Edgar   Right, of course.

Pause. **Ranjeev** *looks perplexed. It isn't working and the manual makes no sense.*

Edgar   It's typical, isn't it? All these years of torment I've suffered and yet, now, sitting here, it doesn't seem so very bad. I think it might be the mountain air.

Pause.

Not that I'm saying we shouldn't proceed or anything. Just, it would be funny, wouldn't it, if I was sitting here having my skull opened when all I really needed was a holiday! It'd be just like the thing.

Ranjeev *stops. The manual requires another piece of kit to be used. He sees the instrument in the trepanation box.*

Ranjeev   There we are . . .

Edgar *stands.*

Edgar   Oh, well – that wasn't so bad, was it? Bit of sweat on the old palms but apart from that . . . Almost relaxing in its way.

Ranjeev   I have done nothing, Sahib.

Edgar   You're too modest, my friend. I can tell you are greatly skilled.

Ranjeev   No, I really have done nothing, Sir. The spike is not yet in.

Pause.

Edgar   Not even a bit?

Ranjeev *sits him back down.*

Edgar   But it was bloody agony!

Ranjeev   It will be easier now. Hold your nerve, Sahib.

Edgar   Look – I'm holding my nerve but – it is clean, isn't it? This spike thing?

Ranjeev   Perfectly. Hold still.

He screws down the cutting tool.

Edgar   Oh dear! That was – a tad painful.

Pause.

You're sure that it's clean, are you?

Ranjeev   Are you suggesting that we Indians are dirty, Sahib?

Edgar   No, not at all, I just –

Another grind on the implement.

Oh, Ma*ma*!

Ranjeev   I know that is what you English think. That we are no cleaner than the dogs you accuse us of eating.

Edgar   No, you misunderstand me –

Ranjeev   You think that we do our business in the street, like animals.

Edgar   I can assure you, Ranjeev, I meant no –

And one more for luck.

Ranjeev   We are in, Sahib!

Edgar   Oh – ! Good show.

Ranjeev   Now – this is where it gets messy . . .

*

Gant   Ladies and gentlemen – we shall spare both you and the laundryman the gory spectacle that followed.

Suffice it to say that it was all over within twelve hours . . .

*

Ranjeev *is soaked with blood.*

Edgar *sits, harrowed, with his hand on his head.*

Ranjeev *holds a long cork.*

Ranjeev   Now, Sahib, the hole has been cut and the brain is exposed. Can you still recall the face of your beloved?

Edgar   The what?

Ranjeev   The face of the woman that you loved.

Edgar   Oh, Louisa. Yes. Yes, I can.

Ranjeev   Then savour it, Sahib. It is for the last time.

Edgar   Goodbye, my love, until God brings us together once more.

Ranjeev   Now – when I tell you – remove your hand and I will push in the cork, thereby ridding you of your pain.

Pause.

Now, Sahib – remove your hand!

He does so, and – with some effort – **Ranjeev** *pushes the cork into* **Edgar***'s head.*

Ranjeev   It is in, Sahib. The cork is in!

Edgar   Thank the Lord!

Ranjeev   Give me your hand –

He places **Edgar***'s hand on top of the cork.*

Ranjeev   Now you must maintain this pressure on the cork. The blood in your skull will solidify around it, locking it to your brain.

Edgar   How long will it take?

Ranjeev   A month, to be safe.

Edgar   A month?! I can't walk around like this for a month!

Ranjeev   You must, Sir. If the cork comes loose, you will die instantaneously!

Edgar   Then I must endure the indignity. For I swore to my Louisa that I would never –

Pause.

Wait! What is this?! I still see her face!

Pause.

Ranjeev! I still see my Louisa's face! Only now – 'tis more vivid than ever!

Pause.

No! I see her as she died – her face as she died! My poor Louisa, no! I can think of nothing else! Something has gone wrong, Ranjeev! The surgery has failed!

Ranjeev   Oh.

Pause.

Well – I tried.

Edgar   What do you mean, you tried?! No – Louisa! She haunts me worse than ever! What have you done to me, you swine?!

Ranjeev   Look – I tried, it didn't work out; what do you want me to say?

Edgar   But – I thought you had done this before!?

Ranjeev   Yes, but not on a man!

Edgar   Not on a man?

Ranjeev   No, on one of those, what do you call them – a goat.

Edgar   A goat?!

Ranjeev   Goats have feeling too, you know.

Pause.

Well, not this one; not any more.

Edgar   You have not performed it on yourself?

Ranjeev   You think I am insane?!

Edgar   But what am I to do?! The image of her dying is fixed behind my eyes as if I lost her only yesterday!

Ranjeev   You are so impatient, you English. You think you take what you want, exactly when you want it. In your impatience to escape the pain of loss, you have made it more so. You have brought this on yourself.

Edgar   How dare you blame me for your incompetence?! Why, I ought to strangle you where you stand!

Ranjeev   You would need both hands for that, Sahib.

Edgar   You fiend!

Ranjeev   I am a mild man, Sahib, but I will not be insulted in my own cave.

He bustles **Edgar** *out.*

Edgar   You can't send me out in this condition!

Ranjeev   Watch me.

He bundles him out.

Edgar   God will punish you for this, Ranjeev.

Ranjeev   My God can take your God any day!

Edgar   No, he can't!

Ranjeev   There are two ways down the mountain, Sahib. A quick way and a slow way. I would advise you take the slow way.

Pause.

And don't come back!

*

Back in Rangoon . . .

Edgar   So now you understand why I ask you for a favour so grave, Brother Gant.

I have lived this last year in the most debilitating torment. I sleep only minutes at a time. Even opium offers only momentary relief.

I would have removed this infernal cork long ago were it not for my promise to Louisa. This is why it must be the work of another to deliver me unto God.

What say you, Brother? Will you do what I ask?

A long pause, then **Gant** *rises.*

Gant   Ladies and gentlemen – I have decided to curtail this story for reasons that will later be revealed.

Gant *walks off, leaving* **Edgar** (**Jack Dearlove**) *bewildered on stage. Pause.*

Jack *is about to leave the stage, when* **Gant** *returns.*

Gant   I have decided also to forego our usual interval. We shall continue with the show momentarily.

He leaves again, taking **Jack** *with him.*

There is a long moment of silence, while the stage stands empty . . .

Eventually, the player, **Nicholas Ludd**, *enters.*

Ludd   Ladies and gentlemen – while my fellow-actors prepare the stage for our next story, I should like to meanwhile occupy you with some poems of my own devising. The first is entitled 'The Night Watchman'.

Pause.

> All night,
> He watches
> The night.
> The night
> Watchman
>
> The day
> He does not watch,
> He's not
> The day
> Watchman

One day
He might watch
The day
But not
Tonight.

Tonight
He watches
The night,
The night
Watchman.

Pause.

Thank you.

He looks behind to see if they are ready yet. They are not.

My next poem is entitled, 'What Need Have I of Whimsy?'

Pause.

What need have I of whimsy?
Give me potatoes instead
My child can live without whimsy
Without 'taters, she will be dead.

What need have I of your whimsy?
Repeal the Corn Laws instead
My family can live without whimsy
The Corn Laws will see us all dead

Pause.

Give me not your whimsy
Give me 'taters and Corn Laws –

No –

Pause.

Give me not your whimsy
Give me 'taters and – have the Corn Laws, um –

He stops, obviously having dried.

Um –

Long pause. And then, the sound of thunder: smoke billows onto the stage.

A figure in a cloak drifts on. It is **Gant**.

Gant   Nicholas Ludd!

Ludd   Who are you?

Gant   I am the Phantom of the Dry! I appear to thespians whose lines have escaped them; I live a whole lifetime in those yawning seconds of helplesness and pass, like a butterfly, when they end!

Ludd   Have you come to me with my lines, Phantom?

Gant   I have not. I bring instead a lesson.

Ludd   What good is a lesson to me now, when the audience is hanging on my words?

Gant   The only thing this audience will be hanging is you, my friend, for your crimes against poetry!

Pause.

Ludd   I think they would rather my poems than your whimsy. Wouldn't you, ladies and gentlemen?

He addresses this to the audience, who will more than likely ignore him.

Gant   An overwhelming response. Nonetheless, let me return to the lesson –

Pause.

I hear your thoughts, thespian! You stand here at a loss and think yourself the loneliest soul in the world, am I correct?

Ludd   No.

Pause.

Gant   I think so!

Ludd   No, actually.

Gant   Yes, and you should be ashamed! Take my hand and I shall put your selfish thoughts to rest!

Ludd *takes his hand. There is a flash, and they are transported.*

Ludd   My goodness! Where have you taken me, terrible Phantom of the Dry?!

Gant   To the land of the small hours, where the lonely wander endlessly!

Ludd   Wait – where are you going?

Gant   I told you – I live only the few yawning seconds of your helplessness; I have no intention of spending them with you.

Pause.

I will return when you have learnt the error of your ways; or remembered the next line of your poem – whichever comes first.

He exits, dramatically.

Ludd   What a fat and *whimsical* fool! His strategy is doomed to failure; for if I were not the loneliest creature on earth when he plucked me up, I most surely am now!

Pause.

  Give me not your whimsy . . .
  Give me corn and –

No, that's not it . . .

A full-size **Bear** *appears in the background.*

Bear One   Excuse me, Sir?

Ludd *turns.*

Ludd   Good Lord! A full-grown bear!

Bear One   Please, kind Sir, I mean you no harm. I am merely a child's plaything, abandoned and astray.

Ludd   What do you want of me?

Bear One   Only a few pennies, Sir – a few pennies for an imaginary cup of tea. Can you spare it?

Ludd   Imaginary, did you say?

Bear One   Yes, Sir, an imaginary cup of tea, just to keep me warm on such a night. Can you spare it, Sir?

Ludd   I'm afraid I have no money.

Bear One   None, Sir?

Ludd   None. In fact, I am not even here.

Bear One   Where are you, Sir?

Ludd   I'm on stage in Plymouth. I've just dried.

Bear One   Dried, Sir ?

Ludd   Forgotten my lines.

Bear One   Oh, I see. That must be lonely, right enough. That must be the loneliest thing in the world.

Ludd   Exactly my point.

Bear One   So you're an actor, then?

Ludd   I try.

Bear One   And what are you currently drying in?

Ludd   An unintelligible travelling vanity project by an opium-addicted buffoon who thinks himself a visionary!

Bear One (*nods*)   Cos I'm in showbusiness myself. Nothing so grand as that, of course. I've just got a song that I sing so's to make a few pennies. I'll sing it for you, if you like. It's very nice, and all for the price of an imaginary cup of tea.

Ludd   Look, I've told you –

Bear One   Yes, Sir, you have. It's just often people say they ain't got none, when they have.

Ludd   Yes, well, this time I'm telling the truth.

Pause.

You have your answer, bear; be off with you. I am trying to recall my lines.

Bear One   Perhaps I can help you, Sir.

Pause.

And all for the price of an imaginary cup of tea.

Ludd   If you ask me that again, Bear – !

Bear One   I'm sorry, Sir – please don't beat me. It's just that I am so very, very thirsty.

Pause.

Ludd
Give me not your whimsy,
Bring me Corn Laws and –

The **Bear** *is hanging around.*

Ludd   Be off with you then.

Bear One   Yes, Sir. Sorry, Sir.

The **Bear** *trudges away slowly. Pause.*

Ludd   Look – if all you want is an imaginary cup of tea, why not simply make it yourself?

Bear One   Oh no, Sir, that's not how it works. I can't make myself one, no. There'd be no point in that at all.

Ludd   Why not?

Bear One   Because it's not the tea, Sir, it's the whole thing – having it made for you, having someone hold it to your mouth, pour it in . . . Oh, it's grand, Sir.

Ludd   I'm sure there must be someone in this lonely land who will do this for you.

Bear One   There is a filthy old tramp, Sir, who will do imaginary things for money. All the abandoned playthings go to him.

Ludd   Would he not consider waiving his fee?

Bear One   He sometimes forgoes the money, Sir. But there is always a fee.

The **Bear** *hides its face in shame.*

Ludd   Good God! What kind of a hell have you brought me to, cruel Phantom of the Dry?!

Pause.

But where is your owner, Bear? I take it you had one once?

Bear One   Oh, yes, Sir. Indeed. And he was good to me, Sir, good as gold. What happened – it wasn't his fault, not really. He fell in with a bad lot, is all, and that's easily done, let me tell you.

Ludd   What is it that happened?

Pause.

Bear One   I'd rather not go into it, Sir, if it's all the same to you.

Ludd   Why not?

Bear One   It just upsets me, is all. I'd really rather not.

Pause.

Ludd   I tell you what: if you recount what happened . . . I'll make you some imaginary tea.

Pause.

Bear One   You would do that for me? What about cake?

Ludd   Imaginary cake?

The **Bear** *nods.*

Ludd   Go on then, yes. If you will tell me what happened.

Pause.

Bear One I was with him since he was a baby. Gorgeous, he was: golden hair in loose, silky curls. He used to worry about me dying, you know. 'What will I do when you die?' he would say. Sometimes he would say it over and over, till he brought himself to tears. To tears, Sir. And then he would hug me tight to his chest.

Pause.

But he changed, Sir. He'd always been a bright and happy soul but all of a sudden he was filled with self-loathing.

Ludd Self-loathing?

Bear One Oh, yes, Sir. He would hit himself, Sir.

Ludd Hit himself?

Bear One Yes, Sir. He would turn my face to the pillow but I could hear him, Sir, beating himself mercilessly, sometimes two or three times a day. Harrowing, it was, Sir – I mean, why would a young boy beat himself so?

Ludd I daresay he had his reasons.

Bear One Oh, but not only that, Sir –

Ludd No?

Bear One He was constantly wanking as well, Sir.

Ludd I am growing impatient with this story, Bear!

Bear One He fell in with some boys, Sir. Not bad boys in themselves but cruel, as boys can be. One day, they saw me on the bed and they mocked my friend; said he was a weakling, Sir, and a mummy's boy. He denied it, of course. He said I was just there by accident, but they didn't believe him. They picked me up and threw me back and forth. I could see my friend was upset and so could they, which only fired them with further mischief. 'Don't cry, Sir,' I was thinking. 'Don't let them see you care,' and he managed, Sir – he kept the tears at bay. They were almost convinced. But there was one more test to pass . . .

Pause.

'If you truly don't care about this stupid toy,' they said, 'Let us see you torture it.'

Ludd   How beastly!

Bear One   They bashed my head off the bureau and twisted my arms and punched my nose. Then they threw me to my friend. 'Punch him,' they said, and soon they were taunting and chanting and it wasn't his fault, Sir, he couldn't resist.

Pause.

He punched me. Just gently at first; but the boys all cheered, so he did it again, harder this time, and then again and then, like a fire, the laughter spread to my friend and I knew then. I knew I had lost him.

Pause.

Later on, he hugged me and wept and said he was sorry but I was never allowed back on the bed. I sat on the chair for months and then the lady put me in the cupboard.

Pause.

Ludd   That is a strangely depressing story.

Pause.

Bear One   May I have my tea and cake now?

Pause.

Ludd   Yes. Of course.

Fuming with embarrassment, **Ludd** *sets about making the imaginary tea in painstaking detail, while the* **Bear** *looks eagerly on.*

He cuts a slice of cake and puts it alongside the tea on an imaginary tray.

He carries it to the **Bear** *and lifts the cup to its lips. It starts to drink.*

Another **Bear** *appears at the back, watches for a moment, then approaches.*

Bear Two   Is that imaginary tea you're having?

Ludd   No, sod this – I'm not having this! This is ludicrous! GANT?!

He turns to the audience.

I'm sorry, ladies and gentlemen, but I can't go on with this. I'M NOT GOING ON WITH THIS, GANT, DO YOU HEAR ME?!

Bear Two (*whispers*)   What are you doing, Ludd?!

Ludd   I'm stopping the show, Jasper – that's all right, isn't it? To just stop the show when you feel like it?!

Bear Two (*whispers*)   Of course it's not all right!

Ludd   Well it's all right for Gant – it's all right for him, isn't it? So why's it not all right for me?! COME ON, GANT! SHOW YOURSELF!

Bear Two *then attempts to manhandle him off the stage.*

Ludd   Get your hands off me, Jasper! I won't be silenced!

Bear One (**Madame Poulet**) *takes her head off and approaches the audience. She has a tiny body strapped to her chin.*

Poulet   Ladies and gentlemen – I know it doesn't look like it, but this is actually meant to happen –

Ludd   Don't tell them that! Ladies and gentlemen –

Bear Two *tackles him again, bringing him to the floor. They grapple on the stage.*

Poulet   Um – the bear and the man did then wrestle most um – wrestlingly – upon the floor –

Ludd *breaks free. (Note: in these sequences, the lines are of secondary importance to the realistic creation of chaos.* **Poulet** *may improvise this mock-narration at her discretion.)*

Ludd   Come on, Poulet, what's the matter?! This is what he wants, isn't it?! Give the people a show! Well, here you go, ladies and gentlemen! Nicholas Ludd's amazing feat of sanity!

Bear Two   Shut up, Ludd!

Ludd   I've had enough of it, Jasper; he's made a monkey out of me, out of all of us, for far too long!

Bear Two   He hasn't made a monkey out of me.

Ludd   Oh don't be ridiculous; look at yourself, man! Look at her! Look at this –

He flaps the little body strapped to **Madame Poulet***'s chin.*

Ludd (*to the audience*)   Do you know what this is, ladies and gentlemen? A backstreet abortion! She comes on later as a Backstreet Abortion! Now how pointless – and tasteless – and sick is that?!

Bear Two *attacks him again.* **Madame Poulet** *tries to drag them apart.*

Gant *appears on the balcony.*

Gant   Jack!

They stop and look up at him.

Let him be.

Ludd *struggles to his feet.*

Ludd   Ah, there he is! There he is, ladies and gentlemen, the great Edward Gant: prodigy, soldier, traveller, poet, but always and ever an absolute bulb! Well, I've had it, Gant, do you hear me?! I've had it with your lies and your pretentiousness! I'm leaving this flea-bitten show once and for all!

Bear Two *takes his head off: it is, of course,* **Jack Dearlove***.*

Jack   I'll not have that, Ludd. I'll not have you call Mr Gant a liar!

Ludd   Oh, wake up, you old fool! He's lied to us all along! You think he's ever going to put in your stupid war story?

Jack   Next season, actually, yes.

Ludd   It's dung, Jasper, and you know it! We won't be doing your war story, any more than anything with any kind of reality at all!

Pause.

Never mind that there's writers out there trying to deal with real people and real issues! 'Yes, Nicky, but we have to Trojan Horse it,' he says. Three years later and the only horse we've had is the one with the magic cock! He's betrayed us! You've betrayed us, Gant! And those are *my* poems, and they're *good* poems, they have *meaning* – which is more than this piece of nonsense has – and you used them for a cheap joke! Well not any more! And I *know* the next lines, ladies and gentlemen:

>   Give me none of your whimsy,
>   Give me potatoes and corn,
>   For whimsy is made for the dying
>   Not for the ones being born!

He bows.

I thank you! I thank you!

Gant *claps.*

Gant   Bravo, Nicky; very good. I always knew you had it in you.

Jack   Mr Gant, should I . . . ?

He nods towards the audience.

Gant   No, no, Nicky is right. We have no secrets from them. And he's right about something else. I have betrayed you. All of you.

He sets off down to them. Pause as they consider his pronouncement.

Poulet Does that mean I can take off my abortion?

Jack I don't know what any of it means!

Ludd It means I'm right, Jasper.

Jack My name is Jack, do you understand?! Jack Jack Jack! And you've got no right to talk to Mr Gant like that, to call him a liar! Why he's the bravest, most honest man I ever met!

Ludd And he saved your life, I know – !

Jack He did save my life! He did, ladies and gentlemen. The Charge of the Light Brigade, it was, and I had come off my horse, and I was lying there in the mud and the blood – the blood and the mud – the mud and the blood!

He passes out.

Ludd And that's as far as he ever gets with *that* story, ladies and gentlemen.

Madame Poulet *starts to strut and cluck like a chicken.*

Ludd Dear God . . . !

Poulet
    Ladies and gentlemen, do not go!
    Guess what I've got down below?
    Watch, as from, between my legs,
    I drop half-a-dozen eggs!

Pause.

Does anyone happen to have a hard-boiled egg at all? In its shell, preferably.

Gant *enters.*

Gant It's all right, Madame Poulet.

Jack *stands to attention, salutes.*

Jack Dearlove, Sergeant, Jack, Sir!

Gant At ease, Sergeant.

Pause.

Ladies and gentlemen; as you can see, our performance has taken an unexpected turn. You are free to leave if such candour embarrasses you.

Jack *starts to leave.*

Gant   Not you, Jack.

Jack   Sir, I must register my disapproval of this business.

Gant   Noted, Sergeant.

Jack   Thank you, Sir.

Ludd   'Thank you, Sir.' Listen to him!

Jack   You need a lesson in loyalty, Ludd, and I'm just the man to give it you!

Ludd   Ah, Jack – the thing with people like you is that you need to be led, and it doesn't matter why or by who! You're a company man, Jack!

Jack   I don't take that as an insult.

Ludd   I didn't think you would.

Poulet   You are being unfair, Mr Ludd. We all owe Mr Gant a great deal. You, for one, would be in prison for treason.

Ludd   That's a damnable lie and you will retract it!

Poulet   I will not. You attended a Royal Gala with explosives strapped to your chest; what is that if it is not treason?

Ludd   I told you – it was a corset sold me by an Irishman! But even so, what of it? Does it mean I am in his debt for ever? What is the point of saving someone only to enslave them?!

Gant   You have always been free to leave, Mr Ludd.

Ludd   You said you had a vision!

Gant   I did. And this is it.

Ludd   Exactly. This is it. This is your examination of
loneliness. Nothing about the poor or the needy, the sick or
the dispossessed. Just a mish-mash of preposterous stories
and cheap innuendoes.

Poulet   To be fair, Mr Ludd, most of the cheap innuendoes
are yours.

Ludd   That's not the point! What does it have to do with
the real loneliness of real people?!

Gant   Nicholas, Nicholas – this has always been your
problem; you can never see the woods for the trees.

Ludd   No, Gant – it's you that cannot see what is
happening all around you. These people want to see real life
as it is lived, not the opium-fuelled fantasies of an egotist!
And if we do not give what they seek, they will turn away
from the theatre and who will remain to play to? The rich
and the idle, and that is all!

Gant (*amused*)   Don't forget the critics. Whose ranks it
seems you have joined.

Ludd   How dare you!

Gant   No, you show great aptitude. You have that rare
ability to misinterpret a man's aims and then hound him for
not achieving them.

Jack   Genius, Sir. (*To* **Ludd**.) That's genius, that is.

Ludd   Oh, shut up, Jasper!

Jack   Don't you call me that, Ludd!

Ludd   Gant is no genius!

Jack   Tell him not to call me that, Sir!

Ludd   I'm just saying that we had a chance here; but
you're still running a freak show! And we are the freaks!

Pause.

Gant   Are we done now?

Ludd   Yes, I am done. Well and truly done.

Pause.

Gant   Mr Ludd is correct. I am no genius and have never claimed to be. In fact, I doubt the word itself; it is merely the term used by the talented to account for those more talented than themselves.

Jack   Genius!

Pause.

I mean . . .

Gant   Oh, my friends, my friends. What a long road has brought us here.

Pause.

Mr Ludd makes a fair point. There is real loneliness out there and an appetite to see it reflected. But that is not what this show is about. It is not about survival, but all that is superfluous to survival: love and dreams and imagination and . . . love.

Pause. He ventures into the audience.

In a world where death is at our shoulder every hour, even the smallest act of creativity is a marvellous, courageous thing. The fact that this audience has come here tonight, to dream along with us – that is an act of courage, of hope; an amazing feat of loneliness. Do you see?

Pause.

Poulet   But why did you say you had betrayed us?

Gant   I have betrayed you because I have been dishonest. I have compromised the truth for the sake of entertainment. (*To* **Ludd**.) Not reality; the truth.

Pause.

But you are right, Mr Ludd. We cannot go on with this. There will be no more. This will be the last show.

Poulet   The last?!

Jack   With respect, Sir, have you taken leave of your senses? You cannot be swayed by this guttersnipe!

Ludd   How dare you call me guttersnipe?!

Gant   Please, gentlemen. The decision is mine alone.

Poulet   But why, Edward, why?

Pause.

Gant   Edgar Thomas Dawn: a man who felt the pain of loss so strongly that he undergoes cruel and brutal surgery.

Pause.

In our story, the operation goes wrong and he is condemned to live with the image of his loss for ever. Now what is this saying?

Jack   Never trust an Indian, Sir.

Gant   Not exactly. What it says is that there is no worse punishment than to live out your life in pain.

Jack   How very true, Sir.

Gant   No, Jack, it is a lie. There is far worse than living your life in pain.

Poulet   But what could be worse than that?

Gant   Simple, my dear – living your life without it.

Pause.

Jack   I'm sure you must be right, Sir, but it sounds very wrong.

Ludd   It's drivel, that's why! Another woolly bourgeois fantasy!

Gant   I bow to your great experience, of course. But
indulge me for a moment.

Pause.

Let us say that the surgery worked. That the image of his love
is gone from his mind. He knows that he loved, and that he
lost, but he has no face to embody that loss. The pain is but
a notion; it has no effect on his heart.

Jack   I like it, Sir! It is altogether cheerier.

Gant   Wait a moment, Jack. The pain of losing her has
gone. But so has the joy of loving her. He remembers his
time with her as if it were but a tale, told him by a stranger.

Pause.

Time passes, but he never finds such a love again. He is
content, but only that; never angry nor inspired – simply
content.

Pause.

Jack   I'm confused. I thought being content was good.

Poulet   But he feels no passion, Jack!

Jack   Oh, right.

Pause.

And that's bad, is it?

Gant   Yes, Jack. Edgar's love for this woman was the
defining moment of his life, yet he cannot savour it. He is
like a man with no taste buds at the perfect meal.

Jack   Ah. Well, now you put it that way, yes, that would
be annoying, to be sure.

Poulet   Is there nothing he can do to reverse the situation?

Gant   Of course.

Pause.

He can remove the cork.

Jack   But that would kill him!

Gant   Indeed. But before he dies, he will see his Louisa's face once more.

Ludd   Sentimental dung!

Poulet   But he cannot do this, Edward. He will have broken his vow to her.

Gant   Exactly. 'If we are to meet again,' she said, 'it must be by God's will alone.'

Poulet   So what will he do?

Gant   What indeed?

Pause.

Jack   I don't see what's wrong with the story as it stands. Let us leave it as it is.

Gant   No, my friend. I meant what I said. There will be no more shows.

Poulet   But why? What will we do with ourselves?

Gant   My sweet Madame Poulet, I have always been fond of you. You are a warm breeze across my heart. I have no doubt that a woman of your beauty and talent will go on to greater things.

Ludd   If not, there's always the egg-laying.

Gant   Exactly. And Jack – my timepiece, my constant – while ever men need decency and valour, there will be a place for you.

Ludd   If not your boring war stories.

Gant   And Nicholas – you have your passion for reality. I suspect you will come to find it misplaced, but then it is the journey, not the arriving.

Pause.

Ludd   Look – I know I've come on a bit strong –

Gant   Hush now. Do not disappoint me.

He turns to the audience.

My good and pure ladies. My brave and gentle men. I hope you will find it in your hearts to excuse our indulgence; and that it is some consolation to have at least been present at an event. Namely, the last ever performance of *The Amazing Feats of Loneliness*.

My name – is Edward Gant!

For the first time, he removes his top hat.

Prodigy! Soldier!

And now we can see –

Traveller! Poet!

– like **Edgar Thomas Dawn***, he has a cork in his head!*

Gant   But always – and ever – a showman!

And, with this, he removes the cork from his head.

Blood spills down across his face . . .

Sanzonetta – !

He smiles sadly –

Forgive me . . .

– and then collapses to the ground.

Madame Poulet *is the first to go to him, followed by* **Jack***, who feels for his pulse.*

Ludd   Is he . . . ?

Pause. **Jack** *nods.*

Pause.

Poulet   Take him off! Ludd!

Quickly, **Ludd** *and* **Madame Poulet** *drag* **Gant***'s corpse off the stage, leaving* **Jack** *alone.*

Jack   Um – ladies and gentlemen –

Pause. The skyhooks lower. On the verge of tears, **Jack** *crosses to the planet Earth and reattaches it to the hooks. He shouts up into the rafters.*

Take up the world!

The world creaks back up into the rafters.

He stares at the audience, searching for the words. He can find only these:

Edward Gant is dead.

And he exits, not quite sure which way to go.

(Note: it is up to you how the curtain call is taken, in character or not. But you might ask yourself whether what we have seen should be taken as truth, or whether it has all been just an artifice created by Gant, ever the showman. The decision is yours.)

The Lying Kind

The Long Kind

The Lying Kind was first performed at the Royal Court Theatre, London, on 23 November 2002. The cast was as follows:

Gobbel	Thomas Fisher
Blunt	Darrell D'Silva
Gronya	Alison Newman
Garson	Sheila Burrell
Balthasar	Patrick Godfrey
Reverend Shandy	Matthew Pidgeon
Carol	Kellie Shirley

Director Anthony Neilson
Designer Bob Bailey
Lighting Designer Chahine Yavroyan
Sound Designer Neil Alexander

Characters

Gobbel
Blunt
Gronya
Garson
Balthasar
Reverend Shandy
Carol

Act One

A residential street. Iced with snow.

A main door − number 58. A sprig of plastic holly pinned to it. To one side of the door, a window − in which a small artificial tree glows with Christmas lights. Behind it, the room is dark.

In the distance, we can hear a group of people chanting something indistinct. It sounds aggressive.

The chanting passes away.

*Enter **Blunt** and **Gobbel**, two police constables.*

Gobbel   Did you hear that?

Blunt *is holding a piece of paper, checking for the door number.*

Blunt   This is it − number 58.

He tries to see into the house.

Gobbel   People shouting something. Did you hear it?

Blunt   Never mind that. Let's get this over with.

Pause.

He nods at the door.

Pause.

Gobbel   What?

Blunt   Ring the bell.

Gobbel   Me?

Blunt   Of course you.

Gobbel   Why me?

Blunt   Because you lost the toss.

Gobbel   To *tell* them − Not to ring the *bell*. Nothing about ringing the *bell* − !

Blunt　It's part and parcel.

Gobbel　Eh?

Blunt　If you don't ring the bell, they won't know we're here. And if they don't know we're here, you can't tell them, now, can you? Part And Parcel.

Pause.

Gobbel　Can't you ring it?

Blunt　I could. But it would set a dangerous precedent.

Gobbel　Would it?

Blunt　Certainly it would. If you say you're going to do something, I have to know you'll honour that to the letter. Remember what the sarge said – Can't trust your wife, you end up divorced. Can't trust your partner – you may well end up dead.

Gobbel　What, from ringing a doorbell?

Blunt　Today it's a doorbell. Tomorrow it's a madman with an axe and a sawn-off shotgun.

Pause.

Gobbel　We're not working tomorrow.

Blunt　I don't mean it literally.

Gobbel　Tomorrow's Christmas Day.

Blunt　I know that. (*Pause.*) Just go ahead and ring the bell.

Gobbel *nervously approaches the bell. He hesitates.*

Gobbel　How old are they?

Blunt　Who?

Pause. **Gobbel** *nods at the house.*

Blunt　The parents?

Gobbel *nods.*

Blunt   How should I know?

Gobbel   Well, how old's the . . . ?

He nods at the house again.

Blunt   Deceased.

Gobbel   How old is she?

Sighing, **Blunt** *gets the scrap of paper out of his pocket.*

Blunt   Thirty-four.

Gobbel   Thirty-*four*?!

Blunt   What *about* it?

Gobbel   Well – if she's thirty-four – that means they must be . . .

Blunt   What?

Gobbel   *Old*!

A momentary flicker betrays **Blunt**'*s concern. Pause.*

Blunt   Not necessarily.

Gobbel   Thirty-four?!

Blunt   Maybe they had her at sixteen.

Gobbel   Sixteen?!

Blunt   People have children at sixteen.

Gobbel   Not these days . . .

Blunt   But we're not talking about these days though, are we? We're talking about thirty-four years ago.

Pause.

Gobbel   Thirty-four plus sixteen . . .

Blunt   Fifty.

Gobbel   That's old!

Blunt   No it's not!

Gobbel   Fifty's old –

Blunt   Not these days it's not.

Gobbel   I thought we weren't *talking* about these days!

Blunt   Well, we are *now* . . .

Gobbel   Eh?

Blunt   We're talking about these days *now* –

Gobbel *wrestles with this.*

Blunt   Look – All I'm *saying* is that fifty isn't what it was.
Fifty's just middle-aged now. Fifty – is what forty was, ten
years ago.

Gobbel (*pause*)   What, thirty?

Blunt   What's the matter with you?! Their daughter's
been killed on the motorway – !

Gobbel   *Sssshhh!!*

Blunt   Well, it's not an easy thing to hear at *any* age, is it?!

Gobbel   No, but – I mean – at least if they were young . . .

Pause.

Blunt   What?

Gobbel   Eh?

Blunt   At-least-if-they-were-young *what*?

Gobbel   Well – they'd still . . . have their whole lives . . .
ahead of them.

Pause.

Blunt   You just open your mouth, don't you? You open
your mouth and meaningless words just tumble out, like
brain-damaged skydivers.
Now go ahead and ring the bell!

Again, **Gobbel** *contemplates. Again, he hesitates.*

Gobbel   The bell.

Blunt *nods.*

Gobbel   Not the knocker?

Blunt   No, the *bell.*

Gobbel (*nods*)   Right.

Pause.

Why not the knocker?

Blunt   Why not the *bell?*

Gobbel   It might give them a fright.

Blunt (*pause*)   Well, then use the *knocker* then!

Gobbel   D'you reckon?

Blunt   Whatever you *like*!

Gobbel   Right.

He rubs his cold hands together and approaches the bell.

You ready?

Blunt *nods, tensing himself.*

The holly takes **Gobbel***'s interest.*

Blunt *watches as he inspects it.*

Gobbel   This holly's a bit loose . . .

Pause.

I'll just use the bell.

Blunt *sighs heavily.*

Gobbel   Ready?

Blunt   Stop asking me if I'm ready! Just ring the bloody thing!

Again, **Gobbel** *rubs his hands and approaches the door. Again,* **Blunt** *tenses.*

Yet again, **Gobbel** *hesitates.*

Blunt   What is it *now*?!

Gobbel   I'm scared!

Blunt   Oh, don't be ridiculous!

Gobbel   You're not scared?

Blunt   What's there to be scared of?

Gobbel   Because they might be old and frail and hearing this – it could *kill* them. Blunt! The shock could kill them stone *dead*!

Blunt   Don't talk rubbish!

Gobbel   You do it then! If I'm talking rubbish, you do it!

Blunt   I did the last one!

Gobbel   So you're more experienced!

Blunt   I don't *want* to be more experienced! I want to be *less* experienced!

Gobbel   You can't be *less* experienced!

Blunt   I can be less experienced than I'll be if I have to experience it *again*!

Gobbel   Yes, but not yet!

Blunt (*pause*)   *You* – are going to ring that bell – if I have to use your severed hand to do it!

Gobbel *is a little shocked by* **Blunt**'s *ferocity.*

Gobbel   There's no reason to be like that.

Blunt   There's a hundred reasons and they're all you!

Pause.

Gobbel   There's no need to be nasty about it.

Blunt   I'm not *being* – ! (*Pause.*) Look – I'm no happier about this than you. But being a policeman can't be just moving on buskers or exchanging friendly banter with the Countryside Alliance. There's bound to be some bad bits too. We knew that when we joined.

Pause.

Think of it this way: it's Christmas Eve. We just have to do this one thing and then that's us, for two whole days. Think about that. Two whole days of getting up whenever the fancy takes us. No trudging around all day in stiff new shoes. We'll get the fire going –

Gobbel   Both bars?

Blunt   Both bars, why not? And we'll sit there with our feet up, sipping warm brandy from the fancy glasses; paper hats, Eric and Ernie and the friendly smell of slowly roasting turkey . . .

Pause. **Blunt** *gets lost in his own reverie.*

Gobbel   Blunt?

Blunt   Mmm?

Gobbel   I couldn't get a turkey.

Blunt   Why not?

Gobbel   They didn't have any left.

Blunt   So what did you get?

Pause.

Gobbel   Dutch sausage.

Pause.

Blunt   Dutch sausage.

Gobbel   You know, the ones like that – (*He makes a horseshoe shape.*) Like a magnet. In a bag and you / boil them.

Blunt   I know what it is.

Gobbel   They're not as Christmassy as turkey but they're a lot quicker to cook.

Pause.

They're nice with beans.

Blunt   Well, we can discuss that *later*. What I'm saying is that we have to look beyond the task at hand; not at the stormy seas around us but at the calm horizon ahead. You see?

Gobbel   The calm horizon ahead.

Blunt   Exactly.

Gobbel (*nods*)   Not the stormy seas around us . . .

Blunt   The calm horizon ahead.

Gobbel (*nods*)   Right.

Blunt   Got it?

Gobbel   Yes.

Suddenly, **Gobbel** *reaches out to press the bell – this time, it's* **Blunt** *that stops him.*

Blunt   What are you doing?!

Gobbel   I'm ringing the bell!?

Blunt   You didn't ask if I was ready!

Gobbel   I thought you told me not to!?

Blunt   I didn't expect you to listen!

Pause. **Gobbel** *points at him.*

Gobbel   You *are* scared!

Blunt   Nonsense!

Gobbel   You are! You're just as scared as I am, and you're right because it's terrible! Because it's Christmas Eve and they're in there all warm and nice with the holly and the tree and no idea that any minute now it's all going to be ruined! Their lives are going to be ruined and it's us that's going to ruin them!

Blunt   Stop saying that!

Gobbel   I thought we were going to help people, not ruin their lives!

Blunt   It's not our fault what's happened!

Gobbel   It'll be our fault they know about it!

Blunt   Well, someone's got to tell them!

Gobbel   Do they? Why? Maybe they don't want to know! Who are we to go telling people things?!

Blunt   You're talking rubbish!

Gobbel   Am I? Everybody doesn't have to know everything, you know! Haven't you ever been happy not knowing something?

Blunt   What are you talking about?

Gobbel   It's true though, isn't it?

Blunt   It's nonsense! How would I know if I was happy not knowing something unless I knew what it was I didn't know?!

Gobbel   No, because you said – you *told* me – when Racquel went off with that man on your honeymoon –

Blunt   That was completely different –

Gobbel   You told me; you wished you hadn't found out!

Blunt   Found *them*! I wished I hadn't found *them*!

Gobbel   Because you were happy not knowing!

Blunt   I wasn't happy, I just didn't know! And now all I feel is twice the idiot. Once because my wife was betraying me with a hot-dog seller, and twice cos all the time it was happening I was wandering round town in a massive sombrero!

Pause.

Gobbel   A sombrero.

Blunt *nods, ruefully.*

Gobbel   I didn't know.

Blunt   Fine if you never find out. But you do. And so will they. All you're doing is delaying the inevitable.

Gobbel   Good! It's always rotten anyway!

Blunt *notices someone standing offstage.*

Gobbel   Why can't good things be inevitable? Why can't being happy or rich be inevitable? But they're not. It's just rotten things like dying and getting ill –

Blunt *pats him quiet.* **Gobbel** *turns to see what he is seeing.*

Pause.

Blunt   May we be of any assistance at all?

Pause. And then a huge person enters – a brick shithouse, complete with blue-ink graffiti and the face you only get from a hard, hard life. This is **Gronya**.

As she approaches, **Gobbel** *edges behind* **Blunt**. *She takes a while to look them up and down, dragging on her cigar.*

Gronya   Seen any people?

Pause.

Blunt   People?

Gobbel   People . . .

Blunt   Could you perhaps be a little more . . . specific?

Gronya   A *bunch* of people.

Pause.

Blunt   A bunch of people.

Gobbel   A bunch of people . . .

Gronya   A bunch of people with signs. Chanting stuff.

Gobbel   That's what I heard, remember? People chanting something –

Blunt   We heard them, but we didn't actually see them.

Gobbel   It was coming from over there.

Gronya   Over there?

Blunt   Yes – over that way, somewhere.

She doesn't move. Pause. **Blunt** *and* **Gobbel** *shift nervously.*

Gobbel   Why's she staring at us like that?

Blunt   I don't know.
Is there a problem at all?

Gronya   You tell me.

Pause.

Blunt   I don't *think* so . . .

Gronya   So why're you here?

Blunt   We're here on a police matter.

Gronya   Is that right? And what would that be then?

Blunt   I'm afraid we're not at liberty to divulge that.

Gronya   Not at liberty.

Gobbel   That means we can't tell you.

Gronya   Are you trying to be funny?

Gobbel   No, sir.

Blunt *elbows* **Gobbel**.

Blunt   Excuse my colleague. He also has difficulty with left and right. But – in answer to your question – no: we are not attempting to be humorous.

Gronya   Just it's a funny thing to say; 'At Liberty'. Makes me think it must be in your mind. Makes me think maybe someone *is* at liberty. Now who would that be?

Pause.

Gobbel   What's she on about?

Blunt   I don't know.

Gronya   You don't know. Well, maybe *this* – will refresh your memory.

Facing them, she opens her jacket, flasher-style. They stare at her chest.

Gobbel   PAPS?

Gronya   You what?

Gobbel   That's what it says!

She's wearing a T-shirt that does indeed say 'PAPS'.

Gronya   That's PARENTS AGAINST PAEDOPHILE SCUM. Ring any bells?

Blunt   Weren't you the ones that set fire to the shoeshop?

Gronya   That's never been proved, but yes – that's us. We're a small but highly organised group of local parents that has come together to combat the threat of paedophile scum being in the area and potentially buggering or otherwise touching up our kids.

Blunt   Well, that's all very well, miss, but –

Gronya   That's *Mrs*.

Blunt (*pause*)   Mrs. (*Pause.*) But – with respect – I'm afraid I fail to see the immediate relevance.

Gronya   Oh, you 'fail to see the immediate relevance', do you? Well – it just so happens that today we got a tip from a very reliable source that there happens to be such a dirty child-molesting bastard living in this actual vicinity. And that furthermore, this fact is known by you – the Dibble – and has been for quite some time. So what do you say to that?

Blunt   We don't know anything about it.

Gobbel *shakes his head.*

Blunt   But then we wouldn't; there's a special unit deals with all that.

Gronya (*nods*)   Is that so?
Cos then we got *another* tip. Said the coppers know that we know, and that they're going to smuggle the dirty nonce bastard out of town before we can get to him and administer the punishment he so richly deserves. (*Pause.*) I suppose you wouldn't know anything about that either?

Gobbel   Well, you suppose *wrong.*

Blunt   Right.

Gobbel   Right?

Blunt   She supposes *right.* We don't.

Gronya   Well, that's lucky for you. Cos if there's anything I hate *worse* – than a dirty, stinking paedophile – it's the dirty, stinking *traitors* that protect them. Wouldn't you agree?

They are non-committal. **Gronya** *approaches them, menacingly.*

After all, a paedo's sick, like a rabid dog. He can't help himself. All you can do with a paedo is just –

She makes a sudden gesture and sound, like snapping at a twig. They flinch.

– Put Him Down, like the animal he is.

Pause.

Whereas the SCUM – that apologise for them – and protect them – and hide them in places where good, decent people live – they've got no excuse. Cos they should know better.

And if I was to ever get my hands on a pair of dirty traitors like that – I wouldn't just –

She makes the snapping gesture again. Again they flinch.

– put them down – no: that would be too quick. I'd want to make them *suffer* – like little abused kids *suffer*. And speaking as someone who grew up having her twat spanked by nuns on a daily basis, I'd say I was just the person to do it, wouldn't you?

Blunt   I suppose so.
Gobbel Yes.

Gronya *moves in closer, circling behind them. They're terrified.*

Gronya   Good. So we're all in agreement. Isn't that nice?

Gobbel   It's lovely.

Gronya   It's lovely. Good. So you would tell me if such a pair of traitors happened to be in the area, wouldn't you?

Blunt   (*nods*) Yes, absolutely.
Gobbel (*nods*) Definitely, we would!

Gronya   Of course you would. And you'd tell me if there was a plan to smuggle out the pervert, wouldn't you?

Blunt   We would, if there was, of course – !
Gobbel We'd sing like canaries, wouldn't we?'

Gronya   Good. So it shouldn't be any trouble to tell me why exactly you should so *coincidentally* happen to be *here* of all places on a quiet Christmas Eve, now should it?

Pause.

Blunt   We'd like to, honestly, but we simply just can't!

Gronya   Right. But *you* can know, can't you, and the
Prime Minister can know and the bloody social workers can
know, but *us* – the people that have to *live* here – we're not
allowed to know, are we? Cos we can't be *trusted* with that
information, can we?

Blunt   Look – with respect – I understand your concerns
but I promise you, you've got the wrong end of the stick.
Hasn't she?

Gobbel   She has, she really has –

Blunt   I mean, if you knew how wrong you were –

Gobbel   She can't see the wood for the trees.

Blunt   It's actually almost funny, isn't it?

Gobbel   It *is* funny!

Blunt   Forgive me but it is –

Gobbel   It's hilarious!

Blunt   If only we could tell you how –

Gronya *knocks their helmets together, cutting off their laugher.*

Gronya   Now you listen to me, you pair of nellies – my
kid's got a spacesuit; it don't make him a fucking astronaut!
So don't be thinking I'm squeamish. I've done for more pigs
than Melton Mowbray and there's a bunk down Holloway
the shape of my arse to prove it! So you tell me what you're
doing here or I'll stuff your todgers so far up your bum'oles
that every time you go pee-pee, you'll blow up like a pair of
puffer fish!

Blunt   Now, just hold on a minute; you can't talk to us like
that. We're Officers of the Law, and we've been trained to
deal with tougher customers than you – haven't we?

Gobbel   When was that?

Blunt   What do you mean, 'when was that'?

Gobbel   Was that the week I was off with shingles?

Blunt　The point is that you don't scare us, Miss . . . Mrs. We can't tell you why we're here and even if we could, we wouldn't. So go ahead and do your worst, but I'll tell you this; our lips will remain absolutely *sealed*!

Gronya (*nods to* **Gobbel**)　And does that go for you too?

Gobbel　It goes *double* for –

Gronya *suddenly grabs their crotches in her vice-like fist, and* **Gobbel** *instantly screams:*

Gobbel　SHE'S DEAD!

Gronya　What?!

Gobbel　THE GIRL!

Blunt　Gobbel – shut up – !

Gronya　What girl?! Did the filthy nonce kill a girl?!

They shake their heads and manage a strangulated 'No'.

What then?! Tell me, or I swear to Christ, I'll go clockwise on you!

They are in terrible pain.

Gobbel　Blunt – I think – we should – tell her!

Blunt　We can't, it's – personal!

Gobbel　So – is *this*!

Gronya　What happened to the *girl*?!

She grips tighter. They scream.

Blunt　An accident – on the road – !

Gronya　On the road?!

Blunt　Coming home!

Gronya　On the road coming home?!

Blunt　That's why we're here –

Gobbel   To tell them –

Blunt   That their daughter died – !

Gobbel   On the way home – !

Blunt/Gobbel   For Christmas!

Pause. She lets them go and they fall to their knees.

Gronya   For Christmas?

They nod, kneading at their groins, dealing with the pain.

Gronya   That better not be a cover story. I know how you lot operate; you make up a cover story so you can smuggle them out!

Blunt   It's true, I swear.

Pause.

Gronya   You better not be lying. Not about a thing like that.

Pause.

You've heard nothing 'bout this paedo?

Blunt *shakes his head.*

Gronya   You don't know who he is? Or where he lives, or anything about him?

Blunt   Don't you?

In the background, the distant sound of the crowd chanting. **Gronya** *almost sniffs the air.*

Gronya   We will. Don't you worry. We've got friends in high places and they're on it right now. So tell your mates not to bother – this one's not slipping the net. Lynching him'll be our Christmas present to kids everywhere; the gift that keeps on giving.

Pause.

Have a nice Christmas.

Gobbel (*still recovering*)   And you!

Gronya *leaves.* **Blunt** *stares at* **Gobbel.** *Pause.*

Gobbel   What?

Blunt   'And you'!

Pause.

Gobbel   Just being polite . . .

Blunt   I can't feel my legs, can you?

Gobbel *crawls over and feels* **Blunt**'s *legs.*

Blunt   Not mine – yours!

Gobbel *feels his own legs.*

Blunt   Not with your hands!

Gobbel   What else am I going to feel them with?!

Blunt *rises, painfully, to his feet.*

Blunt   If you'd rung that bell when I told you, none of that would've happened.

Gobbel   It was you that stopped me!

Blunt   Well, I'm not stopping you now. Let's get it done and get out of harm's way.

Pause.

Gobbel   What do I say again?

Blunt   Don't you remember *anything*?

Pause.

Blunt   First, confirm identity.

Gobbel   Yes, that's right. 'Could you confirm that you know a person by the name of . . .'

Blunt *looks at the piece of paper.*

Blunt   Caroline Conner.

Gobbel   Caroline Conner –

Blunt (*nods*)   And they say 'Yes . . . ?'

Gobbel   Oh uh – (*Remembering.*) Please state your exact relationship to the deceased.

Blunt   Not 'the deceased'!

Gobbel (*pause*)   Who then?

Blunt   Say her name! Not 'the deceased'; they don't know she's deceased yet, do they?!

Gobbel   Please state your exact relationship to Miss Conner.

Blunt   And they say 'Parents' – And you say . . . ?

Gobbel   May we come in for a moment?

Blunt (*nods*)   'What's all this about, Officer?'

Gobbel   I'm afraid we have some . . . bad news. For you.

Pause.

Blunt   Prepare yourself . . .

Gobbel   I'm afraid you'll have to prepare yourself for . . . a shock.

Pause. They stare at each other, the horror of it dawning.

Gobbel   I'm sorry to inform you . . .

Blunt   . . . that your . . .

Gobbel   That your . . . daughter . . .

Blunt   That she's been . . .

Gobbel   That your daughter's been . . .

Pause. **Gobbel** *gasps like a fish.* **Blunt** *is also stricken with fear.*

Gobbel   Blunt! This is terrible!

Blunt   I know; but we have to do it. We can't go back not having done it. Our careers would be over before they've even begun!

Gobbel   Can't we just say they weren't in?

Blunt   Are you joking? The sarge'd peel our skulls like two satsumas. No – we have to tell them. Just remember; not the stormy seas around us . . .

Gobbel (*nods*)   The camel racing ahead.

Blunt   Exactly.

Blunt *gently ushers him towards the door.*

Gobbel   The camel racing ahead, the camel racing ahead, the camel racing ahead . . .

Pause. He nods grimly.

Right.

He straightens himself. Pause.

Are you ready?

Pause. **Blunt** *nods solemnly.*

Agonisingly slow, **Gobbel**'s *finger stretches out, just touching the skin of the bell. His arm trembles.*

Blunt   Press it –

Gobbel   I'm trying – !

Blunt   What do you mean, trying?!

Gobbel   I'm trying but I can't – !

Blunt   Why not? What's wrong?

Gobbel   My finger's too short!

Blunt   Why, you – !

Blunt *grabs* **Gobbel**'s *arm and presses it into the bell.*

The bell explodes in a puff of smoke and rings continuously; it's hideously shrill.

Blunt *and* **Gobbel** *run around like panicked sheep in a tiny pen, trying to get the thing to stop.*

Gobbel *takes his shoe off and starts hammering at it. Finally, it stops. The mechanism falls off the door frame.*

Pause. All composure gone, they quake in front of the door.

Blunt   Oh, my nerves – !

Gobbel   I've forgotten what I'm suppose to say!

Blunt   Put your shoe back on!

Gobbel   The camel racing ahead, the camel racing ahead, the camel racing ahead –

Blunt   Wait – shh! (*Pause.*) Can you hear anything?

Gobbel *shakes his head. Pause.*

Gobbel   Maybe there's no one in!

They put their heads to the door, listening. Pause.

There's no one in!

Joyous, he grabs **Blunt** *by the shoulders.*

Blunt, we're saved! There's no one in! We're – !

Above the door, a light comes on.

Pause. Their shoulders slump in resignation. They look at each other.

Blunt   We'll get through it.

Gobbel   Together?

Pause.

Blunt   Yes. Together.

Their arms creep around each other's backs.

A shape behind the glass.

The sound of locks opening. One, two, three . . .

And then the door swings open.

A small woman stands before them, older and more fragile than they could ever have imagined. Her hair is already shock-white. She stares at them with bulging eyes.

A frozen moment until **Blunt** *nudges* **Gobbel**.

Gobbel   Mrs Conner – ?

Pause.

Garson   She's dead, isn't she?!

They're stunned.

My little girl is dead, isn't she?!

Pause. She grabs **Gobbel** *by the lapels.*

TELL ME!

Gobbel   Yes! Yes! She's dead!

Pause. **Garson** *pushes* **Gobbel** *away and wanders out into the street.*

Garson   I knew it – I felt it in my heart – in here – I felt her leave this world – !

She sways slightly.

Blunt   We're very, very sorry, Mrs Conner.

A man's voice from inside.

Balthasar (*off*)   What is it, dear?! What's wrong?!

Bathasar, *her husband, appears. He is astoundingly old too.*

What's happened?

Garson   She's dead! Our little girl is dead!

Balthasar   Dead?!

He looks at **Blunt** *and* **Gobbel**.

Blunt   I'm afraid so.

Balthasar   Oh no –

He supports his sobbing wife.

Balthasar   How?

Blunt (*pause*)   An accident. On the road.

Garson *lets out a terrible moan and sags in his arms.*

Balthasar   Oh no, Garson – !

Gobbel   She's dead, Blunt! We've killed her!

Garson   My baby girl!

Blunt   Should we call an ambulance?

Balthasar   No, no, I just need to sit her down –

Blunt   Of course, yes.

Balthasar *escorts his weeping wife back down the hall.*

Blunt *goes to help but* **Gobbel** *stops him.*

Gobbel   Blunt –

Blunt   What?

Gobbel   She knew.

Blunt   We need to go and help him –

Gobbel   But how did she know?

Blunt (*pause*)   I suppose there's just things a mother knows. No explaining them, is there?

Pause. **Gobbel** *shrugs.*

Blunt   Come on then.

They go in, closing the door behind them.

Act Two

The living room.

It's very much an old person's home in ornament and design, though with well-travelled Bohemian overtones.

A large sash sags from the roof saying: 'Welcome Home Dearest Daughter'.

A Christmas tree with presents under it.

Balthasar *has sat* **Garson** *down on the sofa and is feeding her whisky in an attempt to calm her.*

Blunt *and* **Gobbel** *enter, awkwardly, at a loss*

Garson   I told you, didn't I? I said –

Balthasar   Ssshh now – drink this –

Garson   I saw it – something terrible, I said, something terrible, and you didn't believe me!

Balthasar   It's all right, dear, it'll be all right –

Garson *pushes the whisky away.*

Garson   No it won't! Nothing'll ever be all right again!

Balthasar   Shush now – I'm here –

Garson   I don't want *you*! What good are you?! I just want my baby back! My sweet little baby girl!

As she sobs, **Blunt** *and* **Gobbel** *can only look at the floor. She begins to shudder.*

Balthasar   We all want her back, dear. We all do.

Garson   Don't you lie to me! You never gave a damn about her or me or anyone!

She breaks away from **Balthasar** *and approaches* **Blunt** *and* **Gobbel**.

She was so beautiful, so – beautiful! If you'd seen her – her beautiful eyes – I saw them, those beautiful eyes but blind and lifeless – lifeless!

She grabs their hands.

And I felt her – felt her leave this world – like they lift a baby from your arms – felt her die, in here!

She presses their hands to her belly.

Balthasar   I'm sure they understand, dear – come on now –

He gently takes her shoulders, but she resists.

Garson   Don't believe him – he never loved her – never loved me – he'll smile and smile but don't believe him, he's a liar, he's –

And she faints in his arms. **Blunt** *helps* **Balthasar** *support her.*

Gobbel   That's it, she's dead!

I told you, Blunt – we've killed her stone dead!

Blunt   Stop saying that! She's not *dead*!

She's not, is she?!

Garson *groans.*

Balthasar   No, no, I think it's just the shock. I think she just needs a lie-down.

Blunt   Why don't we call an ambulance?

Garson   No!

Balthasar   No, officer, really. She doesn't like doctors at the best of times. I just need to get her to the bedroom, lie her down for a while.

Blunt *helps them stand.*

Balthasar   That's it, I've got her.

Blunt   I'll help you.

Balthasar   No, it's fine – she can manage – you can manage can't you, dear?

Blunt   It's no trouble.

Blunt *opens the door for them.*

Balthasar   No, thank you, but she doesn't like strangers in the bedroom. I can manage, really. You have a seat, I'll be back in a moment. Come on, dear . . .

Blunt   Don't you worry about us.

Balthasar *escorts his wife away. The door closes, leaving* **Blunt** *and* **Gobbel**.

Blunt   A lot of help *you* were!

Gobbel   I think we should call for an ambulance.

Blunt   You heard what he said; she doesn't like doctors.

Gobbel   She didn't look too good.

Blunt   Well, you wouldn't, would you? (*Pause.*) Wait till he gets back; see what he says.

Pause. They exchange a grim look.

Awful.

Gobbel   Terrible.

They sit down, **Blunt** *in the armchair,* **Gobbel** *on the sofa. Pause.*

They look old for fifty.

Blunt *scowls at him. Pause.*

Gobbel *stares up at the sash.*

Gobbel   Look at that.

Blunt (*nods*)   Awful.

Gobbel   D'you reckon?

Pause. **Blunt** *sees* **Gobbel** *still staring upwards.*

Blunt   Not the *sash*. The *situation*.

Gobbel   Oh – yes; awful.

Pause.

I can't imagine anything worse.

Blunt   No.

Pause.

Apart from murder. When a child's murdered, that's worse.

Gobbel (*nods*)   Apart from that, you're right. Nothing worse than a child being murdered.

Pause.

Blunt   Suicide, maybe.

Gobbel   D'you reckon?

Blunt (*nods*)   On a par.

Gobbel (*nods*)   On the mother too.

Pause.

Blunt   I mean the *same*. On a *par*.

Gobbel (*nods*)   Both of them.

Blunt *sighs, shaking his head.*

Gobbel   Gav said he was on a suicide the other week, did he tell you?

Blunt (*nods*)   Awful.

Gobbel   What was the story with that?

Blunt   Oh, some kid playing on a Ouija board. Thought the devil had possessed him. Ended up hanging himself. Only thirteen he was. Awful.

Gobbel (*shakes head*)   Terrible.

Pause.

Wonder what Rolf Harris thinks of that.

Blunt   Rolf Harris?

Gobbel   Well, he must've got it off him, mustn't he? Never seen anyone else play one.

Pause.

Blunt   'Wobbleboard'.

Gobbel   Eh?

Blunt   Rolf Harris plays a 'wobbleboard'.

Pause.

Gobbel   What did *you* say?

Blunt (*sighs*)   Never mind.

Pause.

Gobbel   He seems a nice old fellow, doesn't he?

Blunt *shrugs in agreement.*

Gobbel   Doesn't seem fair, does it?

Blunt   It's always the way. The cruel and the ruthless shoot to the top. It's the kind ones get it in the neck. I'm living proof of that.

Gobbel   You mean like Racquel leaving you for the hot-dog man?

Blunt   Do you have to keep bringing that up?

Gobbel *shrugs an apology. Pause.*

Blunt   Of course, you know what he was before he was a hot-dog seller?

Gobbel (*pause*)   Single?

Blunt *stares at him. Pause.*

Blunt   Apart from that. (*Pause.*) A bullfighter. Which
proves what I said about the cruel. Mind you, I suppose it'd
come in handy, given her temper.

Gobbel   If you ask me, you're better off without her.

Blunt   Not really; a year later she made half a million
pounds on the stock market.
(*Pause.*) Still − I'd rather be kind and get nowhere than
successful and cruel.

Gobbel   Me too.

Blunt *snorts.*

Gobbel   What?

Again, **Blunt** *snorts.*

Gobbel   I'm not going to get anywhere!
Where do you think I'm going to get to?

Blunt   Nowhere . . .

Gobbel (*pause*)   You're just saying that.

Blunt   Not at all. In fact, in your case, even getting
nowhere might be setting the sights too high.

Gobbel   D'you reckon?

Blunt   Absolutely.

Pause. **Gobbel** *hugs* **Blunt**.

Blunt   What are you doing?!

Gobbel   That's the nicest thing anyone ever said to me!

Blunt *pats him uncomfortably, trying to shift him.*

Blunt   Yes, well, that's − good −

Gobbel   Happy Christmas, Blunt − !

Blunt   Yes, and you − now −

Gobbel   I wouldn't rather go nowhere with anyone else but you!

Balthasar *comes in, catching them in the hug.*

Balthasar   Oh – excuse me –

Blunt *casts* **Gobbel** *off and stands.*

Blunt   Oh, Mr Conner, no, he's just – a bit upset about – your situation. We both are.

Balthasar   Well, that's very . . . very *kind* of you . . . yes.

Gobbel   How's his wife?

Blunt   How's Mrs Conner?

Balthasar   Oh, well, she's having a little sleep just now –

Gobbel   Are you sure?

Balthasar   Am I – ?

Gobbel   Are you sure she's asleep?

Balthasar   Am I sure – ? Oh, yes, no; I'm sure she's asleep, yes . . .

Blunt   Excuse our concern; it's just that shock can sometimes be dangerous. Especially when the person in shock is, well . . .

Gobbel   Old!

Blunt   Where are your manners?

Balthasar   Oh no, really, officer, no need. You don't get to this age without being old.

Blunt   No, quite. But you're sure we shouldn't call a doctor? Maybe some sedatives would help.

Balthasar   No, that's very kind, but really; she's not much truck with that sort of thing. If it can't be scraped off bark, she won't take it, bless her. But she's a tough old bird, that's for sure. Got that way in the Blitz. Ten years old and

shifting rubble she was; still the same skin on her hands.
Tough old bird for sure.
Anyway, I must thank you, Constable . . . ?

Blunt   Blunt.

They shake hands.

Balthasar   How do you do?

Blunt   And this is my colleague, Constable Gobbel.

Balthasar   How do you do?

They shake hands.

Gobbel   No, how do *you*?

Balthasar   Balthasar.

Gobbel   No, *Gobbel.*

Balthasar   Gobb – ? (*Pause.*) Oh – no, that's me; *I'm*
Balthasar –

Gobbel   Oh – !

Balthasar   Sorry, I didn't make myself clear –

Blunt   It's not you; his helmet's a little tight.

Balthasar   His – ? Oh well, anyway, as I was saying – I
must thank you for all your kindness. It can't be pleasant
having to deliver such news, and tonight of all nights.

Blunt   No, well, you're right; it's a grim task but –
ultimately it's a matter of duty. We just want you to know
how very sorry we are for your sad and tragic loss.

Balthasar   Well, thank you, Officer, I appreciate that; for
my wife, more so than for me.

Pause. **Blunt** *and* **Gobbel** *look a bit puzzled.*

Balthasar   That must sound terrible, mustn't it? It's not
that I'm not sad, I am, it's just that, well – she wasn't
actually *mine*, you see . . .

Blunt/Gobbel   'Ohhh' . . . !

Balthasar   It probably shouldn't make a difference, should it? It's just that I never had much contact with her, to be honest. Or rather, she never had much contact with me, I don't know why. Never really accepted me. Bit jealous, I think, though goodness knows why. It's not as if I got between them. No one ever did.

Pause.

Forgive me; I'm sure you've got better things to do than listen to some old fool get maudlin . . .

Blunt   Not at all –

Gobbel   It's a pleasure.

Balthasar   You're very kind. (*Pause.*) It's time, you see? You'd think at this age you'd treat every minute like gold. But you don't; you still think you've time for everything.

Pause as they respectfully absorb this.

Blunt   Speaking of which, there are a few minor details I'm afraid we have to –

Gobbel   Blunt!

The living-room door swings open to reveal **Garson** *standing there, wide-eyed and mad-looking, staring right at* **Blunt** *and* **Gobbel**.

Blunt   Mrs Conner!

Balthasar *turns and sees her. She doesn't like the look of him.*

Balthasar   Oh now – what are you doing up?

Pause.

Blunt   How are you feeling?

Pause. Her face softens into a charming smile.

Garson   Why, thank you for asking, Captain, but I'm fine now. I always get a little sick approaching Gibraltar, I don't know why.

She pushes an imaginary trolley towards them.

Balthasar   Oh no, dear – come on now –

Garson   Would you and the Viceroy care for some tea?

Balthasar   No, dear; the Captain's had some tea –
I'm terribly sorry; she goes a little funny sometimes,
especially under stress. Come back to your cabin for now,
dear –

He puts his arms at her shoulders and she turns on him.

Garson   Get your hands off of me, you *prick*!

*He recoils. Again, she smiles and turns to **Blunt** and **Gobbel**.*

Will Darjeeling do?

She holds up an imaginary teapot.

Garson   Cups, gentlemen?

*They look to **Balthasar**.*

Balthasar   I'm terribly sorry but it's probably best to
just . . .

*Pause. They raise imaginary cups – **Blunt**, awkwardly; **Gobbel**,
naturally – and she pretend-pours them each a cup of tea.*

Garson   Cream and sugar?

Blunt   Um – no, that's fine for me, thank you.

Gobbel   Just sugar for me.

*She scoops out an imaginary spoonful of sugar and is about to put it in
the imaginary cup when **Blunt** blocks her.*

Blunt   That'll be fine as it is, thank you. We don't want
the Viceroy losing all his *teeth*, now do we?

Garson (*to **Gobbel***)   Ooh, he's a harsh one, that Captain,
isn't he? But he's not all rules and regulations below deck,
are you, sir?

Gobbel   Isn't he?

Blunt   Amn't I?

Garson   Put it this way; every time we girls go into his cabin he just 'happens' to be in the altogether, don't you, sir?

Balthasar   Oh no, dear, please . . .

Gobbel *looks suspiciously at* **Blunt**.

Garson   I'm sure it's coincidence but there's some of the girls not so sure. One of them's taken to walking in backwards, so I heard. Naughty Captain!

She prods his stomach. **Gobbel** *still staring at him.*

Under the eyes of suspicion, **Blunt** *pretends to drink his tea. He meets* **Gobbel**'s *gaze.*

Blunt (*pause*)   What?

Balthasar   All right now, dear; they've got their tea – let's be getting you back to your cabin –

She pulls away from his gently guiding hand.

Garson   Who are you?!

Balthasar   You know who I am, dear; now let's not make a scene –

Garson   You're not a passenger on this ship! You're not crew! Captain – this man is a stowaway!

Blunt   No –

Garson   He is! He shouldn't be here –

Blunt   He's not a stowaway, he's your husband –

Garson   What do you mean, my husband? I'm not married?! (*Pause.*) What's going on here?

Blunt   He's only here to look after you. I give you my word as Captain.

Garson   Do you?

Gobbel   And mine as Viceroy.

Balthasar *puts his hand on her shoulder. Unsure, she begins to acquiesce.*

Balthasar   Come on, dear, please . . .

Garson   Will the gentlemen require anything further?

Blunt   No – thank you. That'll be all.

Garson   Then if you don't mind, sir, I will retire to my cabin for a spell. I've lost my beautiful baby, you see, and I'm a little out of sorts.

Gobbel   Carry on.

Garson   Thank you, sir. I'm sure I'll be my old self again by evening.

Balthasar   That's right, dear; come along . . .

He starts to lead her out.

Gobbel   Don't forget your trolley!

Garson   Oh!

She returns to collect her trolley.

Silly me.

She wheels it out.

Balthasar   I'm terribly sorry about all this – You're not in a rush, are you?

Blunt (*pause*)   Um – no, not at all. You go ahead.

Balthasar *exits.*

Blunt *stares very deliberately at* **Gobbel**.

Blunt   'Don't forget your trolley'?!

Pause. **Gobbel** *shrugs, ashamed.* **Blunt** *shakes his head, at a loss. He sits down.*

Gobbel   Poor old Mrs Conner.

Blunt   It's not good that. Once they start going like that
. . . beginning of the end.

Gobbel   D'you reckon?

Blunt   This'll only speed it up. Awful.

Gobbel   Terrible. Poor old Balthasar.

Pause.

It's sad he didn't get on with his daughter.

Blunt   But she wasn't his daughter, was she? That's why
they didn't get on.

Gobbel   My parents weren't my parents either, I still got
on with them.

Blunt   I thought you didn't?

Gobbel   I don't get on with them *now*. But I used to.

Blunt   So when did you stop getting on with them?

Gobbel   When they told me they weren't my parents.

Blunt *looks puzzled. Puzzlement turns to anger.*

Blunt   Right – that's it! When he comes back, you're
going to fix a time for him to come and identify the body
and then we're leaving, before I lose what's left of my mind!

Gobbel (*pause*)   Wait a minute – *I* have to fix a time?

Blunt   Yes, you.

Gobbel   No, no – I had to ring the bell and I had to tell
them but that's not part of telling them –

Blunt   I don't remember you telling anyone anything!

Gobbel   I did so!

Blunt   She guessed it!

Gobbel   But then I confirmed it.

Blunt   Only because she shook it out of you. And then you stood there gasping like a fish while I did everything else!

Gobbel   That's a rotten lie! I rang the bell and I told them and now it's as much your turn as mine! And that's the living end of it!

Pause. **Blunt** *nods, disappointed.*

Blunt   I see.

This always works – **Gobbel** *visibly crumbles.*

Gobbel   What?

Blunt   Look at that tree.

He points commandingly at the Christmas tree. **Gobbel** *doesn't look.*

Gobbel   Why?

Blunt   Look at it!

Pause. **Gobbel** *looks at the tree.*

Blunt   Look at those presents.
Look how lovingly they've been wrapped.
You think those presents will ever be opened?

Pause.

Gobbel   We can't open them . . . ?

Blunt   Of course we can't! That's my point; *No One Ever Will.* Those presents will stay wrapped. Weeks will turn to months, months will turn to years. And still they'll sit there, waiting, as the colours fade, waiting, as the dust gathers, for ever waiting . . . for the Child That Will Never Come.

Pause.

Gobbel   Poor presents . . .

Blunt   Never mind the presents – what about that old lady through there, demented with grief?! Old Balthasar that you say you feel so sorry for! But here you are arguing about whose *turn* it is! And you've the cheek to call yourself kind! Why the word's like dust in your mouth!

Gobbel   I am kind! You're the one that's not kind and I'm just as kind as you, if not kinder!

Blunt   Well, we'll see about that, shall we?

Gobbel   Yes, we shall!

Blunt   Right – well, I'm going to the toilet. And when I come back I'll expect you to have concluded our business here!

Gobbel   Fine!

Blunt   Fine!

He goes to the door. He peers cautiously out. Pause.

Gobbel   Blunt?

Blunt *stops, looks at him.*

Gobbel   Is a viceroy better than a captain?

Blunt   *NO!*

Blunt *exits.*

Gobbel *is left to mutter and sulk.*

Gobbel   Think you're so kind, but you're not . . . not kind to me . . . I'll show you . . . We'll see who's kind . . . Yes, sir – we need you to come and identify your daughter's body . . . yes, as soon as possible . . . Tomorrow? Yes, that would be ideal . . . *Thank you, you've been very kind* . . . Not at all, sir . . . *No, but much kinder than the other one . . . glad it was you that told me, not him . . . probably my wife would be dead now if it hadn't been you, probably would have dropped dead right there on the spot* – Oh really, sir, please . . . *No, no I insist, I'll be telling the sarge all about it – I wouldn't be surprised if you get promoted there and then – and have a present too – have the biggest present there with love from me and my wife because actually we're your parents –* You're my? – *Yes, we're your actual parents and all this has just* *been a big thing to get you here so we can tell you –* No! – *Yes, and all these presents are actually for you but we just had to find out if you were the kindest one –*

Balthasar *returns.*

Balthasar   I'm terribly sorry (to have kept you) –

Gobbel *jumps, spilling presents.*

Gobbel   Dad! Oh – sorry – I was just –

Pause.

Balthasar   Has the other constable gone?

Gobbel   Oh – um – just – to the toilet.

Balthasar   Oh. I hope he's found it. Bit of a funny layout, this house. Mind you, I suppose if a policeman can't find the toilet I don't know who can!

He laughs. **Gobbel** *jollies along.*

Balthasar *pours himself a drink.*

Balthasar   You must excuse my wife. She gets a little confused now and then –

Gobbel *sees* **Blunt** *appear outside the window, looking a bit confused. He holds up his hands in bemusement, then wanders away.*

Balthasar   I keep telling her she should go and see a doctor about it but of course she won't hear of it. It can all be a little embarrassing at times.

Gobbel *nods sympathetically, looking for a chance to say what he has to say.*

Balthasar   She worked on a cruise liner, you see, and this is, oh – some forty years gone – but sometimes she gets the idea she's back on it. I don't know why. It was only a few months of her life, so I don't know why it's so significant to her. I mean, we hadn't even met by then. Still, time like this, maybe it's good not to know what's going on.

Pause.

Gobbel   I'm awfully sorry about what's happened.

Balthasar   Yes, thank you . . .

Gobbel   And I'm sorry we had to tell you.

Balthasar   Oh no, really, you mustn't. It's not your fault.

Gobbel   It isn't, is it?

Balthasar   Of course not, not at all. These things happen. She'll get over it in time.

Gobbel   D'you reckon?

Balthasar   Oh yes, like I said, she's a tough old bird. She's had her share of tragedy across the years. Lost her brother, Theo, in the war . . . Her younger sister, Fenella, she died of malaria. Martha, she went over a cliff in that caravan . . .

Pause.

Her nephew, Harold – he was electrocuted. Her best friend died of a jellyfish sting. And then her parents – both of them to cancer, so yes . . . She's had her share.

Pause.

Gordon, her other brother, he died of pneumonia and his wife caught it off him and she died too and her Uncle Callum, they never even found him. But she survived all that and if you can survive all that then she'll survive this. I mean, as harsh as it sounds and as much as she loved her, at the end of the day, it's only a dog, isn't it?

Pause. **Gobbel***'s face freezes over.*

Blunt *enters.*

Balthasar   Ah there you are – did you find it all right?

Blunt   Yes, thank you – Has my colleague discussed the matters I mentioned with you?

Gobbel *is staring at* **Blunt**, *frozen in horror.*

Balthasar   Matters?

Blunt   I can see from his expression that he has not. So it would seem that it is, once again, down to me!

Gobbel   No, wait – !

Blunt   I don't want to hear your excuses, Constable. I've had my fill of them this evening –

Gobbel   No, but Blunt – !

Blunt   We – will discuss it – LATER.

Pause. **Gobbel** *sits down, face in hands.*

Blunt   Now, as I was saying; I'm afraid that before we can conclude our business, there are a few routine, though unhappy, procedural matter we must attend to. The most pressing of which, I'm afraid, is the matter of identification.

Balthasar   Oh . . .

Blunt   I'm afraid so.

Balthasar   Will a pension book do?

Pause.

Blunt   Oh, no, no – not you – We know who you are. No, I mean identification of – the *deceased*.

Balthasar   The – ? Oh, right – well – is there any need for that?

Pause.

I mean, you say it's her and I'm quite happy to take your word for it . . .

Pause.

Blunt   Well, I appreciate your confidence, but that's not exactly –

Gobbel *tugs at his sleeve.*

Gobbel   Blunt – !

Blunt   *I* – AM NOT *SPEAKING* – TO *YOU!*

Gobbel *retreats.*

Blunt   I'm afraid it's standard procedure; someone always has to identify the body.

Balthasar   Oh, I see – It's just I'd rather not put her through that, you understand – not in her present condition –

Blunt   Oh, but it needn't be your wife . . .

Balthasar   No?

Blunt   No, no; just someone who knew the deceased. You'd do as well –

Balthasar   Me . . . ? (*Pause.*) I don't want to be difficult, Officer, really I don't, but is this absolutely necessary?

Blunt   I'm afraid so. As strange as it may seem, mistakes have been made. It's highly unusual, but it has been known, so . . .

Balthasar   Yes, I see. It just seems – (*Pause.*) I mean, is she going grey?

Pause.

Blunt   Well, that does tend to happen –

Balthasar   Bad teeth – one broken at the front?

Pause.

Long, very prominent teats.

Pause. **Blunt** *clears throat.*

Blunt   I'm afraid I wouldn't have any of that information, sir . . .

Balthasar   Oh dear – I'm sure it's her. Long-haired but patchy – you know; down below –

Blunt   Down below?!

Balthasar   Yes, you know . . . smells a bit mangy –

Blunt   Mr Conner, please! (*Pause.*) Now I know you weren't close but there's such a thing as respect for the dead. I doubt Mrs Conner would appreciate you talking in such a fashion, now, would she?

Balthasar   Well, no – she wouldn't. But then I was the only one who smelt it –

Blunt   I beg your pardon?!

Balthasar   Well, me and the postman. I think he smelt it, though he never actually said –

Blunt   Do you realise what you're saying?

Balthasar   I don't see what the fuss is –

Blunt (*to* **Gobbel**)   He doesn't see what the fuss is!

Gobbel   But Blunt –

Blunt   Be quiet! You don't see what the fuss is?

Balthasar   Well, not really, no, I mean – she's dead, isn't she?

Blunt   And so?

Balthasar   Well, we're not going to have her stuffed or anything –

Blunt   There's no need for sarcasm.

Balthasar   Well, can't you just burn her and be done with it?

Blunt   Burn her and be – ?!

Pause.

Well, well, well! And to think my colleague and I were only just saying how cruel fate was to the kind. But once again our compassionate natures have been deceived!

Come, Constable. We've done our duty here. Please give our condolences to your good lady wife.

Balthasar   But she's a dog!?

Blunt   Nonetheless – please convey them.

As they approach the door, **Gobbel** *gets his attention.*

Blunt   For God's sake, what is it?!

Gobbel *whispers in his ear.*

The penny drops. **Blunt** *seizes* **Gobbel**'s *shoulder. They stand frozen for some time.*

Balthasar   Look, I'm terribly sorry, Officer, I seem to have offended you somehow – I like dogs, really I do, I just –

Pause. **Blunt** *turns to him.*

Blunt   Dogs.

Balthasar (*pause*)   Well, what do *you* call them?

Pause. He is at a loss.

I tell you what; our daughter Carol's due any minute and it was her that gave us the dog, so she knows what it looks like. She might be a bit tired because she's driving here from Bristol, but I'm sure she could do whatever has to be done. How about that?

Pause.

Blunt   Dog.

Pause.

Yes, you see – Mr Conner – Balthasar – It would seem that there's been a small . . .

Pause.

Actually, quite a *large* . . . misunderstanding.

Balthasar (*pause*)   Misunderstanding?

Blunt Yes, you see – you're talking about . . . a dog.

Balthasar *nods.*

Blunt Which went . . . missing, did it?

Balthasar Yes, about a week ago.

Pause.

Why? What's wrong?

Pause.

Blunt Well, you see . . . the thing is . . . what we're talking about . . .

Balthasar *looks a little pained, as you might with indigestion.*

Balthasar Yes . . . ?

Blunt Well, you see – you're talking about . . . a dog . . .

Balthasar *nods through another twinge. He rubs his chest.*

Blunt Whereas what we're actually talking about . . .

Balthasar *groans a little.*

Gobbel What's wrong with him?

Blunt What's wrong with you?

Balthasar (*pained*) I'm fine; go on –

Blunt He's fine.

Gobbel Why's he rubbing his chest like that?

Blunt Why are you rubbing your chest like that?

Balthasar It's nothing, just a twinge; what you're talking about is what?

Blunt What we're talking about is . . .

Another twinge, worse, and **Balthasar** *has to sit down.*

Balthasar Oh dear –

They help him.

Blunt   Are you all right?

Balthasar   Yes, yes, really; I just . . . just need a little . . . sit-down . . .

Gobbel   He's gone all white!

Balthasar   I wonder if you'd be so kind as to pass me . . . that pill bottle . . . on the sideboard . . .

Gobbel   Pill bottle!?

Blunt   Pill bottle on the sideboard!

Gobbel *gets the bottle.*

Gobbel   They're tiny, Blunt! Tiny pills!

He gives it to **Blunt***, who gives it to* **Balthasar***.*

Gobbel   That's bad, Blunt – tiny pills are bad! Why does he need tiny pills?!

Balthasar *shakes his head, trying to unscrew the top.*

Balthasar   Do you think you could . . . ?

He passes the bottle to **Blunt** *to open.*

Gobbel   What's wrong with him?!

Balthasar   I'm fine, I just –

Blunt   He's fine!

Blunt *passes* **Balthasar** *a pill.*

Gobbel   He doesn't look fine – !

Blunt   Do you need some water?

Balthasar *shakes his head, puts the pill in his mouth, swallows it.*

Pause.

Gobbel   His skin's all grey and baggy!

Blunt   Of course it is! (*Pause.*) I mean – Will you be *quiet*?!
Let the man recover!

Balthasar *exhales.*

Blunt   That's it. Just relax. Deep breath in. Deep breath
out. Deep breath in. Deep breath out.

Gobbel *breathes along but exhales on the in and inhales on the out.*

Blunt   Deep breath in. Deep breath out. Deep breath in.
Deep breath out.

Balthasar *starts to breathe heavier, put off by* **Gobbel**.

Blunt   Deep breath in. Deep breath – will you stop that?!

Gobbel   Stop what?

Blunt   Stop breathing!

Gobbel   Stop breathing?!

Blunt   Stop breathing out of time! It's messing *me* up,
never mind him!

Gobbel   I got off to a bad start.

Balthasar   I'll be fine now, really. I'll be fine . . .

Blunt   Are you sure?

Balthasar   Oh yes, really. Just a little twinge, that's all. I
get them if I don't take my pill on time. But I'll be fine now,
thank you . . . (*Pause.*) Thank you.

Gobbel   What's wrong with you?

Blunt   I don't think that's our business, do you?

Balthasar   No, no, I don't mind. Just a little trouble with
the old ticker, Constable; another pleasure of old age.

Blunt   But nothing too serious?

Balthasar   Well . . . Three heart attacks in the last two
years.

Blunt   Three?!

Gobbel   That's nearly one a year!

Balthasar (*nods*)   They offered me a pacemaker but I didn't fancy it. Be like you'd swallowed a clock, don't you think? Of course, the doctor thinks I'm mad. Says I should treat every day like my last.

Gobbel   Your last what?

Balthasar   Well-day, I suppose. But how you do that? I said, if it's all the same to you, I'd as soon treat my last day like all the rest. Seems more achievable, don't you think?

Pause.

Goodness – you look more worried than me! But he exaggerates, that doctor; I mean, according to him, my heart's so weak you could kill me just by creeping up behind me and bursting a paper bag!

Gobbel   A paper bag!
Blunt   A paper bag?!

Balthasar   A paper bag, can you imagine? I said, whatever you do, don't tell Garson, she'll be getting ideas. Be the perfect crime, wouldn't it?

Anyway – what was it you were saying?

Blunt   Saying . . .

Balthasar   You said I was talking about a dog but you were talking about . . . ?

Pause.

Gobbel   A victim!

Balthasar (*pause*)   A victim?

Pause.

Blunt   Yes, you see – you were talking about a dog . . . whereas to us, it's . . . a victim.

Gobbel   Of crime.

Balthasar   Oh . . .

Blunt   Yes; be it a dog or, or be it – um . . .

Gobbel (*pause*)   A non-dog –

Blunt   A non-dog, yes –

Balthasar   A non-dog?

Blunt   Yes – dog or non-dog, to us it makes no difference; they're all victims to us and we treat every case exactly the same.

Balthasar (*nods*)   Oh, I see. You'll have to excuse me, Officer. I'm a little behind on all this animal rights business. Growing up during the war, we were mainly worried about people. Still, I suppose it's the fashion these days.
So will that do? If Carol identifies the body?

Pause.

Blunt   Well – in *principle*, yes, it's just . . . You see, the thing is . . .

Balthasar   I'm expecting her any moment. She should have been here by now but I suppose the roads are busy; everyone coming home for Christmas. But I'd say it won't be more than fifteen minutes or so, so you're quite welcome to wait. What do you think?

Blunt (*pause*)   What do I think . . . ?

Blunt *looks at* **Gobbel**, *who shrugs*.

Gobbel   If it's just fifteen minutes . . .

Balthasar   Then that's what we'll do. Would you like a drink at all? There's orange juice or tea if you fancy – I'd offer you something stronger but I suppose you're not allowed, are you?

Gobbel *looks hopefully at* **Blunt**.

Balthasar   I won't tell if you won't.

Blunt   I suppose if it's just one . . .

Balthasar   That's the ticket – !

Gobbel   D'you reckon?

Blunt   How much worse can things get?

The doorbell rings. **Blunt** *and* **Gobbel** *stare at each other.*

Balthasar   Talk of the devil, there's Carol now! With all
sorts of nonsense that'll need carrying in, if I know her. Just
you help yourself to whatever you want. Now –
Goodness, I'm a little nervous actually. She's been in Africa
for three years with that what-d'you-call-them – ? the
clothes shop – Oxfam, you know, so we haven't seen her . . .
D'you think I should get Garson up? No – it'll be a surprise
– How do I look?

They stare at him. Pause.

Old, I suppose.

Pause.

Blunt   Not at all.

The bell rings again.

Balthasar   Righty-ho . . . COMING, DEAR!

Balthasar *exits.*

Gobbel   Who do you think it is?

Blunt   I know who it's not.

Gobbel   But maybe it is, though! Maybe there's been a
mistake! Maybe we've got the wrong house or something!

Blunt (*pause*)   No, I checked the number.

Gobbel (*pause*)   But maybe they got it wrong at the
station – ! They might've, mightn't they?

Blunt   They might've . . .

Gobbel   So maybe it's her! Blunt – maybe she's alive!

Garson   Maybe who's alive?

Startled, they turn to see **Garson** *in the doorway again.*

Blunt   Mrs Conner – !

Garson   What's going on here?

Gobbel (*pause*)   There's someone at the door –

Garson   At the door?

Gobbel (*pause*)   At the front –

Blunt *stops him with a gesture that says 'Leave it to me'.*

Blunt   *Someone* – is *boarding* – the *ship*.

Pause.

Garson   What are you talking about, you stupid man? Where's that damn fool husband of mine?

Gobbel   He's gone ashore.

Garson   He's gone ashore?!

Blunt   He's gone *to the door*.

Garson   Why?

Gobbel   Because there's someone at it.

Garson   I can see that. What are you doing here?

Pause.

Blunt   We came to tell you – you know – the bad news we told you . . .

She looks puzzled.

Don't you remember?

Pause.

Garson   My baby?

Blunt   Well . . . sort of.

Garson   My beautiful baby . . . (*Pause.*) She was so
beautiful. So happy to see me. So scared when I was gone.

Pause. She looks at them.

Would you like to see my bum, mister?

Gobbel *leaps with surprise.*

Garson   I'll show you if you want, I don't mind.

She turns and starts to lift her skirt. **Blunt** *stops her, in a panic.*

Blunt   No, really, thank you but we're fine – !

Garson   I don't mind, really I don't –

Blunt   I'm sure, but really – don't you think you'd be best
off having a little rest?!

He starts ushering her out the door.

Garson   Why?

Blunt   Well – your husband says it's –

Garson   My *husband*! Who cares what he says, the gutless
freak!

Blunt   I'm sure you don't mean that –

Garson   Oh no, of course not. After all, why would
someone say something they meant? And how could they
mean it about nice old Balthasar, right?

Gobbel   He's always been nice to us.

Garson   'Nice'! God protect us from 'nice'! And I suppose
you're 'nice' too, are you?

Blunt   We try our best . . .

Garson   Yes, I can smell it on you. Like cheap soap.

Blunt   Well – you know what they say; it's nice to be nice.

Gobbel   To see you –

Blunt/Gobbel   Nice!

She turns her back to them and lifts her skirt.

Garson   Wheee!

They scream.

Blunt   Mrs Conner, please!

She hobbles away from them, trying to pull her tights down.

(*To* **Gobbel**.) Help me get a hold of her!

They manage to grab her and try to pull her tights back up.

And just then, the vicar – **Reverend Shandy** *– enters.*

Shandy   What on earth?!

Blunt *and* **Gobbel** *stare at him in horror. Pause.*

Blunt   This isn't how it looks – !

Garson   How *does* it look?!

Balthasar *pushes past the vicar.*

Balthasar   Oh dear, I'm so sorry about this – ! Garson, dear, *please* try to control yourself!

Garson   Oh yes, cos we don't want a fuss, do we? No – nothing worse than a messy awful *fuss*!

Balthasar   No, but look, dear; the vicar's here –

This gets her attention.

Garson   Ah, the new vicar –

Shandy   Well, it's been a month or two, but yes –

He extends his hand.

Reverend Shandy. But you can call me Hans.

She doesn't take it.

Garson   I hear the last one left with his halo round his ankles. After all that nasty business at the raffle. But that's the liar's punishment, isn't it?

Balthasar   You're being a little rude, dear –

Garson   D'you know what that is, Reverend? The liar's punishment?

Shandy   According to Aesop, that he won't be believed, even when he speaks the truth.

Garson   No. That he can never believe anyone else, even when they speak the truth.

Shandy   That's very good. I'll remember that for a sermon.

Garson   Yes; a little sweetcorn in the turd.

Balthasar   Oh no, dear, please –

Shandy   It's all right, Mr Conner, I understand. As Euripides said, How dark are all the ways of God to man. Especially at a time such as this.

Blunt *and* **Gobbel** *exchange looks of dismay.*

Shandy   You will feel anger towards Him, Mrs Conner. You will wonder what purpose this tragedy serves in His Grand design –

Blunt   Yes, well, I was wondering that myself, weren't you?

Gobbel   Absolutely.

Blunt   What would the purpose of this tragedy be, do you think, Reverend?

Shandy   Well, that is for Him to know –

Gobbel   And us to find out.

Shandy   Yes, well – No: not for us to find out –

Blunt   So you don't know the purpose?

Shandy   No, but I know there is one –

Gobbel   How d'you know there's a purpose if you don't know what the purpose is?

Shandy   Because there's always a purpose, Constable – ?

Gobbel (*points to* **Blunt**)   Blunt.

Shandy (*to* **Gobbel**)   Blunt?

Blunt   No, I'm Blunt. He's Gobbel.

Shandy (*to* **Blunt**)   Gobbel?

Gobbel   No, that's me.

Blunt   Have you met Balthasar?

Shandy   No, how do you – no, yes, of course I've met him!

Blunt   Good, well, thanks for stopping by –

They try to bundle him out of the door.

Garson   My Baby! My Beautiful Baby!

Pause.

Gobbel (*to* **Shandy**)   So are you doing anything for Christmas?

Shandy   Step aside, Officer. That woman needs comfort.

He pushes past them. **Blunt** *and* **Gobbel** *watch in horror.* **Shandy** *takes her hand. This time she allows it.*

Shandy   There, my dear. There.

Garson   I felt her. Felt her leave this world.

Shandy   All flesh is grass, and all the goodliness thereof is as the flower of the field.

Garson *rests her head against him.*

Balthasar   See now, isn't that nice, dear? The Father's come all the way here just to offer his condolences about Miffy.

Blunt *and* **Gobbel** *look at each other: saved!*

Balthasar   I keep telling her the Church isn't just for believers but she / never listens, do you?

Shandy   Did you say Miffy?

Again, **Blunt** *and* **Gobbel** *look at each other: not saved.*

Balthasar   That's what we called her.

Shandy   Oh, a nickname . . . ?

Balthasar   No, just her name.

Shandy (*puzzled*)   Oh . . .

Balthasar   Why?

Shandy   No – just that wasn't the name the duty sergeant gave me.

Blunt   Duty sergeant?

Shandy   Yes, I was just calling the station to wish them a merry Christmas and she told me the unhappy news but I'm sure she gave another name –

Blunt   Oh, yes, well! The duty sergeant, she's just – always getting names wrong, isn't she?

Gobbel (*nods*)   Always!

Blunt   I wouldn't give any name she gave me a second thought if I were you. Would you?

Gobbel   If I were you?

Blunt   If you were him.

Gobbel   Not even if I was me!

Blunt   No, I'd just wipe it from my mind entirely and never even mention it! (*Pause.*) Now, Mr Conner, I don't

want to speak out of turn here, but I think Mrs Conner
should be resting, don't you? She looks very tired –

Balthasar   Oh – yes, dear – why don't you go back to
bed for a while? I'll wake you when Carol comes, I promise.

Shandy   Carol! That was / the name they –

Gobbel *coughs loudly to cover him and* **Blunt** *all but manhandles*
Balthasar *and* **Garson** *to the door.*

Blunt   No but I think you should go with her, don't you?
Just to make sure she gets safely to bed –

Balthasar   Safely – ?

Blunt   You can never be sure, not in that state, believe me
– I mean – she could be straight out the back door, couldn't
she?

Gobbel   Halfway down the road before you know it –

Blunt   Stark naked –

Balthasar   Stark naked?!

Blunt   Oh yes – !

Gobbel   Happens all the time.

Balthasar   Oh well, in that case, yes – will you excuse
me, Reverend?

Shandy   Would you like me to come and sit with her?

Balthasar   Oh – well, if you –

Blunt   No! No, we have – matters to discuss – with the
vicar, don't we?

Shandy   Do we?

Blunt   Yes, you know – community matters and –
bereavement – coordination. That sort of thing.

He ushers **Balthasar** *and* **Garson** *out of the door.*

You go on and get her to bed. And make sure she gets to sleep.

Garson   Night, night, Daddy.

Blunt   Night – night.

He closes the door behind them.

Shandy   Bereavement coordination?

Blunt   Yes – haven't you heard of it?

Shandy   No, I haven't.

Gobbel   Well, it's definitely something that exists, isn't it?

Blunt   Absolutely.

Shandy   Is it, indeed. (*Pause.*) Well, I have a very pressing engagement so it'll have to be quick. (*Pause.*) Though, frankly, the only thing that's worrying me at the moment is Mr Conner.

Blunt (*nods*)   I see. Take a note of that, Constable.

Gobbel   A real one?

Blunt   Yes, a real one! Now – what is it that's worrying you about Mr Conner?

Shandy   Well, I mean – he's just found out his only daughter's been killed on the motorway but frankly, he seems hardly at all.

Blunt (*nods*)   Hardly affected at all, yes, well now – you see, there may actually be a reason for that . . .

Shandy   Oh yes, undoubtedly. I've seen it before; total denial. The mind's defence mechanism. A refusal to even contemplate the truth.

Pause.

Blunt   Well, that's one possible reason . . .

Shandy   You think there's another?

Pause.

Like what?

Blunt   Well . . .

Pause. He looks at **Gobbel** *who urges him to tell.*

Blunt   Well . . . the other possible reason could be that . . . well, that he might somehow think . . . that it's not actually his daughter that's dead but . . . well . . . maybe . . .

Shandy   Maybe what?

Pause.

Gobbel   His dog!

Shandy   His dog?!

Blunt (*nods*)   Miffy.

Pause.

Shandy   Ah, I see! You mean, not so much denial as transference? Yes . . . I've never encountered it but I suppose it's possible. Are you schooled in psychology, Officer?

Blunt   Well . . . I dabble.

Shandy   Oh yes, it's fascinating, don't you think?! If I had my life to live again, that's what I'd be; a psychiatrist. I love the way it all seems to fit together so easily. I mean, religion's all very well but it doesn't stand up to analysis, does it?
So you're saying that the mind acknowledges the event but substitutes the life lost for one of lesser importance?

Pause. **Blunt** *looks at* **Gobbel**. *Pause.*

Gobbel   He thinks it's his dog!

Shandy *looks confused.*

Shandy   Yes, but –

Gobbel *goes to him.*

Gobbel   You have to help us, Father, please!

Shandy   Help you?

Shandy *looks at* **Blunt**.

Blunt   You see, there was a small misunderstanding . . .

Gobbel   Large!

Blunt   A large misunderstanding and – well, it's a long story – but basically . . .

Gobbel   They think it's their dog!

Blunt   They think it's their dog.

Shandy (*pause*)   What, you mean – both of them? They both – (*Pause.*) You told them it was their dog?!

Gobbel   No!
Blunt   Yes!

Shandy   Well, which?

Gobbel   No!

Blunt   Well, yes, but – we didn't know that's what we were telling them when we told them –

Shandy   But when you found out you hadn't told them what you'd told them – didn't you tell them then?

Blunt   We've been trying!

Shandy   Trying?! You mean they don't know that their daughter's dead?!

Gobbel   His heart's like a paper bag!

Blunt   He has a heart condition –

Shandy   And so?

Gobbel   So if we tell him he'll die!

Shandy   You don't know that; you can't possibly!

Gobbel   He's got tiny pills.

Blunt (*nods*)   Very small pills.

Shandy   But you can't just not tell him that his daughter's dead!

Gobbel   SSSHHH!

Shandy (*whispering*)   You can't not tell him his –

Catches himself.

Oh for goodness sake! I've never heard such a thing in my life! You're police officers! You have to tell them!

Gobbel   But what about his heart?

Shandy   His heart's in God's hands, not yours! Why, it's nothing short of immoral!

Pause.

Well?

Blunt   Now?

Shandy   Of course now! And not a moment longer!

Pause.

Blunt   It's actually not my turn . . .

Gobbel   I told them, fair and square!

Blunt   If you told them, why don't they know?

Gobbel   I don't know why they don't know but I know I told them!

Blunt   How can you tell someone something and then not know what they've been told?!

Gobbel   I don't know but I'll tell you this – !

Shandy   STOP THIS BICKERING RIGHT NOW!

Pause.

You're a disgrace to your office, both of you!

Gobbel (*pause*)   We don't have an office.

Blunt   We're going to tell him, Father, of course we are – We just need to tell him in the right way!

Shandy   In God's name, man – what right way is there to tell a man his child is dead?!

Gobbel   We could leave a note –

Shandy   A *NOTE*?!

Gobbel   Well, if you're so smart, you tell him!

Shandy   That's exactly what I'm going to do!

He heads for the door.

Blunt   No, wait – Father – let's just think about this a moment – !

They block the door.

Shandy   Stand away from the door.

Gobbel   The shock'll kill him!

Blunt   It'll be tantamount to murder!

Shandy   I'm warning you – You'll burn in Hell if you don't stand away from that door!

Gobbel   No we won't!

Shandy   You will; in the searing flames of Hell for all eternity!

Blunt   He's just trying to scare us! There's no such place!

Shandy   BE SURE, YOUR SIN SHALL FIND YOU OUT!

Gobbel   Stop shouting!

Shandy   ONLY THE TRUTH SHALL MAKE YOU FREE!

Blunt   You'll wake the neighbours!

Shandy   THE POWER OF CHRIST COMPELS YOU!

He tries to physically move them. There's a tussle; the three of them fall to the floor.

THE POWER OF CHRIST COMPELS YOU! THE POWER OF CHRIST COMPELS YOU!

Blunt *gets his hand over his mouth, muffling him.* **Shandy** *bites.*

Blunt   He's biting me!

Gobbel *tries to prise* **Shandy**'s *mouth open, to no avail.*

Blunt   Do something!

Shandy   THE POWER OF CHRIST COMPELS YOU!

Gobbel *takes out his truncheon –*

Shandy   THE POWER OF CHRIST COMP – !

– and whacks it over **Shandy**'s *head.*

Shandy *stands up.*

Shandy   What was that?

Gobbel *shows him the trunchon. Pause.* **Shandy** *nods.*

He goes limp and collapses.

Blunt *pulls free. The two of them stare at their handiwork. Pause.*

Blunt   What have you done?!

Pause. They both go to him. **Gobbel** *listens for his heart.*

Gobbel   There's no heartbeat!

Blunt   What?!

Gobbel   He's gone all hard!

Gobbel *thumps* **Shandy**'s *chest. It does, indeed, sound hard.* **Blunt** *feels* **Shandy**'s *chest, listens. Pause. He reaches inside his jacket and pulls out a Bible, which he throws at* **Gobbel**. **Blunt** *listens.*

Blunt   It's all right – he's alive!

The door starts to open. It's **Balthasar.**

Gobbel   Blunt!

Blunt *intercepts him at the door.*

Balthasar   Are you all right in there?

Blunt   Yes, of course we're all right, why wouldn't we be all right? What makes you think we're not all right?

Balthasar   What was all that shouting?

Blunt   What shouting? I didn't hear any shouting –

Balthasar   Someone was shouting –

Blunt   How's Mrs Conner? Is she sleeping?

Gobbel *looks around, panicked. He spots a cupboard and drags* **Shandy** *towards it.*

Balthasar   Well, not sleeping exactly . . .

Blunt   No, not sleeping but – resting?

Balthasar   Resting, yes; more resting than sleeping –

Blunt   Resting, absolutely, well, after all, they do say that a rest is as good as a – as a sleep, don't they?

Balthasar   As good as – ? Oh, yes, I suppose they do – do they?

Blunt   They do, they do – they're always saying it, yes –

Gobbel *gets the cupboard door open but has some difficulty lifting the body in.*

Pause.

Balthasar   Do you think I could come in, at all?

Blunt   Come in? Oh, you mean – in here?

Balthasar   Yes, the uh –

Blunt   The living room?

Balthasar   Yes –

Blunt   Well, I mean, of course, I mean; it's your living room, isn't it? At the end of the day. And you can come and go as you please – Was that Mrs Conner?

Balthasar   What?

Blunt   Just then. I thought I heard something – sounded like Mrs Conner?

Balthasar   I didn't hear anything . . .

Blunt   Really? I could've sworn I heard something . . .

Balthasar   Is there something wrong, Officer?

Blunt   Wrong? No –

Balthasar   It's just you seem like you don't want me to come in –

Gobbel *gives* **Blunt** *the thumbs up.* **Blunt** *steps away from the door.*

Blunt   No, not at all. Come right in.

Balthasar *enters.* **Gobbel** *leans against the cupboard door, trying to look nonchalant.*

Balthasar   Where's Reverend Shandy?

Blunt   Oh – Reverend Shandy, yes; he had to go, didn't he?

Gobbel *nods.*

Blunt   He said he's sorry but – he had to go to see someone else who's also had a bereavement – but a much worse one than yours.

Balthasar   Oh no, really?

Blunt   Sadly, yes. He said he was sorry but seeing as it's only a dog he couldn't wait and that he hoped you had a very happy Christmas.

Balthasar   Oh, I see. Well, that was very nice of him to come anyway, wasn't it? I must say I wouldn't have expected so many people to be so caring about all this; it's really very kind of you all . . .

They nod guiltily.

I just don't know what's happened to Carol. She should have been here by now. You don't think anything's happened, do you?

Pause.

I suppose it's probably just the roads. I'd call her on her mobile phone thing but I'm always worried she'll get distracted and have an accident.

Blunt (*nods*)   No, you're absolutely right. Lot of accidents happen like that, don't they?

Gobbel   Yes, they don't, I mean, do.

Blunt   No, I wouldn't bother with that.

Balthasar   No. And you never get a good line anyway. I did give her a call earlier this evening and right in the middle of talking to her, it just cut off, just like that.

Pause.

Blunt   Cut off?

Balthasar   Cut off. No – there was a terrible noise, like an explosion almost – and then it just cut off, just like that. Cut off dead.

Pause. **Gobbel** *totters slightly.*

Gobbel   Blunt – I feel a bit funny . . .

Balthasar   Are you all right, Officer?

Gobbel *totters towards* **Blunt**.

Blunt   He's fine, he's just a little – claustrophobic. Why
don't you have a seat, Constable? I'll take over here.

Blunt *takes his place blocking the cupboard, grins at* **Balthasar**.

Balthasar   Now, where are my manners? I didn't get you
that drink I promised, did I? What was it you were having
again?

Gobbel   Brandy!

Balthasar   Brandy, was it?

He heads towards the cupboard. **Blunt** *panics.*

Blunt   No! Something from the fridge.

Balthasar   Something from – ?

Blunt   Something cold, from the fridge.

Gobbel   Can't I have a brandy?

Blunt   Is the brandy in here?

Balthasar   Yes, it's –

Blunt   Then no; something from the fridge.

Gobbel   Why can't I have the brandy?

Blunt   Because it would be *good* – for Balthasar to *go* – and
get us something from the *fridge*.

Pause. **Gobbel** *twigs.*

Gobbel   *Ohhh . . . !*

Balthasar   I'm not sure what there is in the fridge . . .

Blunt   Whatever there is will be just fine.

Pause. They stare at him.

Balthasar   Yes, all right, I'll . . . go to the fridge.

Smiling inanely, they wait for him to go. As soon as he's gone, they leap into life.

Blunt We've got to get the vicar out of here before he comes round!

Gobbel He killed her, Blunt! Did you hear him? He phoned her up and she got distracted and that's why she's dead!

Blunt It could be worse.

Gobbel How could it be worse?!

Blunt She could be us! Now come and give me a hand!

Gobbel *drags himself up from the sofa.*

The small yap of a dog.

They both freeze. **Blunt** *turns to look at* **Gobbel**.

Pause.

Blunt That's not funny.

Gobbel I know.

Blunt Making that noise.

Gobbel I didn't.

Again, the yapping of a dog.

Pause.

They both turn, horrified, to look at the window. They run to the window and look out into the yard. The dog growls and yaps at them.

Blunt/Gobbel Miffy!

They try to quiet it down: Shoo! Go away! etc.

Gobbel What are we going to do?!

Blunt Get rid of it!

Gobbel Get rid of it?!

Blunt   Chase it away!

Gobbel   Chase it away how?!

Blunt   I don't know – throw a stick for it or something!

Gobbel   Me?!

Blunt   Oh, don't start that! Just get it away from here before they hear it!

Gobbel   How do I get out there?

Blunt   This way!

Gobbel *follows him to the door, but* **Blunt** *stops.*

Blunt   It's Balthasar! Quick – !

They run back to the window. **Blunt** *opens it, the yapping getting louder, and hurries* **Gobbel** *out.*

Gobbel   Blunt?

Blunt   What?!

Gobbel   I'm scared of dogs!

Blunt   It's a chihuahua!

Gobbel   I'm scared of them too!

Blunt   Just get out of there!

Gobbel   But how do I get (back in)?!

Blunt *shuts the window, just as* **Balthasar** *comes in.*

Balthasar   Now there's only one – Ah, there you are – now I'm afraid there's only one lager, but there's a bottle of cider if you'd care for a glass of that instead?

Blunt   That'd be dog.

Balthasar   Dog?

Blunt   Dog?!

Balthasar   Did you say dog?

Blunt   Dog? Why would I say dog? No, I said – fine. Cider would be fine. Thank you.

The sound of the dog yapping.

Balthasar   What was that?

Blunt   What?

Balthasar   Barking – outside . . .

The dog yaps and growls.

There! Didn't you hear it?

Pause. **Blunt** *shakes his head, feebly.*

It's there, behind you, at the window – !

Balthasar *starts towards the window.* **Blunt** *blocks him.*

Blunt   All right, Mr Conner, you're right; there is a barking noise.

Balthasar   There is, isn't there?

Blunt   Yes, but it's not a dog –

Balthasar   It's not?

Blunt   No, it's – children.

Balthasar   Oh – children?

Blunt   Yes – cruel, awful, delinquent children who think it's funny to make noises like a dog just to upset you!

Balthasar   Really? Doesn't sound like children . . .

Blunt   No, it's hard to believe, isn't it? But it is.

He turns back to the window.

This your idea of a joke, is it?! This your sick, twisted idea of a joke?! Taunting an old couple in their grief?! You sick and twisted little – delinquents!

He turns back to **Balthasar**.

Now, Mr Conner, don't you worry yourself – my colleague is out there as we speak, getting rid of them. I'm just sorry you had to hear it.

Balthasar   Oh, well, yes, I suppose that's . . . children, you say?

There's a terrible sound of dog yapping and growling and shrieks from **Gobbel**.

Balthasar   Goodness!

Blunt *looks out the window. He starts gesticulating to* **Gobbel**. *More noise.*

Balthasar   What's going on out there?!

He approaches the window again.

Blunt   No, now, Mr Conner, I must insist that you stay back – for your own safety. My colleague has everything in hand.

Yaps, shrieks, the clatter of dustbins. Pause.

I wonder if I could bother you for that cider you so kindly offered?

Balthasar   Oh yes – certainly –

A clatter. The yelping stops.

Do you think he's (all right) – ?

Blunt   CIDER! (*Pause.*) Please. Would be nice. Thank you.

Balthasar   Yes, of course.

He exits.

Blunt *opens the window and* **Gobbel** *climbs back in, looking scratched and beat up and traumatised.*

Blunt   What were you doing?!

Gobbel   It went for me!

Blunt   Did you get rid of it?

Gobbel   I was throwing sticks for it but it just kept staring at me with its teeth out and slavers coming out its mouth and I bent down and it just went for me, right at my face, all fur and teeth and claws!

Blunt   Yes, but it's gone?

Gobbel   Sort of.

Blunt   What do you mean, sort of? You mean it might come back?

Gobbel   No – that's not what I mean! That's not what I mean at all!

Pause.

Blunt   What have you done?

Gobbel   I had no choice! It came right at me! Look at my hands! They're torn to shreds!

Pause.

It was trying to bite my face, I swear! I had to defend myself, didn't I? So I grabbed it by the back of the neck – like they do on *Pet Rescue* except –

Blunt   Except what?

Gobbel   Except I didn't rescue it!

Pause.

Blunt   What are you saying?

Pause. **Gobbel** *lifts his helmet. Under it is a dead dog.*

Blunt   It's dead!

Gobbel   I know!

Blunt   You've killed it!

Gobbel   It was it or me, I swear!

Blunt   But you can't keep it there!

Gobbel I know, but I couldn't think! I was frightened someone might see me! What am I going to do?! I'm a murderer! Blunt – I'm a dog murderer!

Blunt Never mind that; we've got to get rid of it!

Gobbel I want to bury it! I have to take it somewhere and give it a decent burial.

Blunt Don't be ridiculous!

Gobbel You don't understand! I've killed a dog! But I did it for him, Blunt! I did it to save Beelzebub, didn't I? It was the right thing to do, wasn't it?

Blunt Yes, yes, whatever – just get the bloody thing out of here, quick!

Gobbel But what'll I do with it?!

Blunt I don't know, do I? Throw it in the bin or over the fence or something –

Gobbel The fence?

Blunt *pushes* **Gobbel** *towards the door.*

Blunt Put it in a cab and send it to the theatre! Anything, just for God's sake get it –

Balthasar *comes in just as they're going out.*

Balthasar Well, they're nice and cold anyway, that's for –

Blunt *and* **Gobbel** *do an immediate about-turn.*

Blunt That's it, just walk, keep walking –

Balthasar Are you all right, Officer?

Gobbel No!

Blunt He's fine, just a spot of cramp, isn't it?

Gobbel *nods, trying to keep his helmet balanced.*

Blunt   Adrenalin, you see, from all that fighting crime. Causes the muscles to lactate. So the best thing is to walk around for a while. There we go – better now?

Balthasar *hands* **Blunt** *the drinks.*

Blunt   Thank you very much.

Gobbel   Thank you.

Balthasar   You saw the children off then?

Gobbel   Eh?

Blunt   Yes, yes, it's all taken care of.

Balthasar   It's remarkable really; I could've sworn it was an actual dog.

Blunt   Yes, I know, well, that's kids these days; they have an amazing capacity for – imitating animals, don't they?

Gobbel   Do they?

Blunt   Yes, they do.

Balthasar   Well, yes, but it's just that it sounded so like –

Blunt   Miffy?! Oh, really, Mr Conner, please! Sounded like Miffy!

Gobbel   Ludicrous!

Blunt   Next you'll be saying she's alive!

Gobbel   Alive!

Blunt   Have you heard of such a thing!?

Gobbel   The very idea of it!

Blunt   What on earth made you think it was Miffy?!

Balthasar   Well, I *didn't* think it was Miffy . . .

Blunt   Oh – you didn't?

Balthasar   No, goodness, no – it sounded like a *small* dog –

Gobbel   A chihuahua!

Balthasar   Yes, exactly. Nothing like Miffy. Miffy was a Labrador.

The doorbell rings. **Blunt** *and* **Gobbel** *freeze.*

Balthasar   Now that *must* be Carol now! Seven hours that's taken from Bristol to here. Maybe you can be on your way at last.

He exits.

Pause. **Blunt** *looks at* **Gobbel**.

Blunt   A Labrador.

Gobbel   How was I to know?! It was you that told me to get rid of it!

Blunt   I meant scare it away! Not throttle it and stuff it in your hat!

Pause.

Gobbel   Maybe it's for the best.

Blunt   For the best? That you've strangled a chihuaha? How can that be for the best? How can any of this be for the best?!

Gobbel   Well, you'd never get a Labrador into a helmet, would you?

Blunt (*pause*)   Look – just get rid of it !

Blunt *goes to listen at the door.*

Gobbel   But where though?!

Blunt   Anywhere it can't be found!

Gobbel   How am I going to find somewhere that can't be found?!

Blunt   Because it's the same place they keep your brain!

He opens the door a bit and recoils in fright.

A young girl enters.

Blunt   Who are you?

Carol (*pause*)   Carol.

Pause. **Blunt** *and* **Gobbel** *look at each other.*

Blunt   Carol?!

Gobbel   But you're – ?

Blunt   But we –

Gobbel   Supposed to be . . .

Blunt   Thought you were . . .

They approach her slowly, in awe. She backs away.

Carol   Supposed to be what? Thought I was what?

Gobbel *touches her.*

Carol   Get off me!

Gobbel   She's real, Blunt! She's really real!

Carol   What d'you mean, I'm real? Course I'm real!

Blunt   But what about the accident?

Carol   What accident?

Gobbel   The one that killed you!

Carol   The one that killed me?!

Blunt   You didn't have an accident? On the way here?

Gobbel   Not even a small one?

Girl   I'm going to have a big one any minute, you keep on acting so creepy!

Gobbel   They must've made a mistake, at the station, like I said!

Blunt   But you're not thirty-four . . . ?!

Carol   No, I'm nineteen. Nearly.

Blunt   So you're eighteen?

Carol   Yeah. (*Pause.*) Nearly.

Blunt   They said she was thirty-four . . . ?

Gobbel   So?! It doesn't matter! All that matters is she's here and she's safe and it was all a big mistake and Blunderbuss isn't going to die and Christmas isn't ruined and we're saved, Blunt! We've got to tell him the good news!

Blunt   We haven't told him the bad news yet!

Gobbel   We can tell him that later!

Blunt   Carol, forgive us – this must all sound a bit odd. Where's your father?

Carol (*shrugs*)   Don't know. Don't care either.

Blunt (*pause*)   Is he bringing your stuff in?

Carol   I don't have any stuff, honest.

Blunt   No, but from the car –

Carol (*pause*)   I just want to get through the back. Can I go through?

Blunt   Oh – to see your mother?

Carol   Is she here?

Pause.

Blunt   There's something wrong here somewhere.

Balthasar *enters.*

Balthasar   Ah, there you are – have you looked out the back?

Carol   Not yet, no –

Balthasar   Oh well, anyway, he's not in the garage, far as I can see, but if you go through the back there, to the kitchen, that'll get you into the yard –

Carol   Through there?

Balthasar   Straight through, yes.

Eyeing them suspiciously, **Carol** *leaves.*

Blunt   That's Carol?

Balthasar   I know, it's odd, isn't it? There's me waiting for Carol and a Carol arrives, but the wrong one. I mean, what are the odds on that?

Pause. **Blunt** *looks at* **Gobbel***, who's deflated.*

Blunt   Astronomical.

Gobbel *looks heavenwards.*

Balthasar   That's not all; remember I said that sounded like a small dog and you said a chihuahua? Well, that's what she's lost – a chihuahua. I know you said it was children but maybe there was a dog as well, I don't know; anyway, she's been looking for it all night. Just got it yesterday, for Christmas, poor thing, so I said have a look. Not a good day for dogs all round, is it?

He looks out the window. He gesticulates at the girl in the yard.

I don't think it's there, if it ever was. Oh dear.

Pause. He gestures for her to come back round.

Still doesn't explain what's happened to my Carol. It's really getting late now. You don't think anything's happened, do you, Officer? You'd have heard, wouldn't you?

They can only hang their heads.

Oh dear, where's she going? That's not the way . . .

Balthasar *shuffles over to the door. Exits.*

Blunt   This is like some kind of nightmare!

Gobbel *takes off his helmet and looks inside.*

Gobbel   She just got it, Blunt! It was a Christmas present!
It was a Christmas present and we killed it!

Blunt   *We* killed it?!

Unbeknown to them, **Carol** – *confused about where she is – has
arrived at the window.*

Gobbel   I killed it, you killed it, what's the difference?! All
that matters is the poor thing's killed!

He pulls it out of the helmet in one gesture, holding it aloft. **Carol**
sees this and screams.

Shocked, **Blunt** *and* **Gobbel** *stare at her.*

She passes out on the spot.

Gobbel   Oh my God, she's dead!

Blunt   What do you mean, dead?!

Gobbel   Her heart's given out!

Blunt   Don't talk rubbish! She's just fainted! Quickly – get
her inside!

Gobbel *throws down the dead dog and heads out the hallway door.*

Blunt   Don't leave that there! (*Meaning the dog.*)

But **Gobbel** *rushes back in.*

Gobbel   Balderdash!

Panicked, **Blunt** *stuffs the dog into his own helmet and puts it on. He
rushes past* **Gobbel** *to the door.*

Blunt   Bring her in through the window – I'll stall him!

The door starts to open –

Balthasar (*off*)   I can't seem to –

Blunt *stops the door.*

Gobbel *opens the window and climbs out, shutting it behind him.*

Blunt Can't seem to what?

Balthasar (*pause*) I can't seem to find the young lady.

Gobbel *has lifted* **Carol** *up but now he can't get back in the window.*

Balthasar Is she in there with you at all?

Blunt With me?

Gobbel *knocks on the window.* **Blunt** *sees him and groans.*

Blunt No, unfortunately not.

Balthasar Oh . . .

Pause.

Is it possible to come in at all?

Pause.

Blunt Oh, wait a minute – I just saw her!

Balthasar Did you?

Blunt She's on her way to the back door! You better go and let her in!

Balthasar Oh no, I left it open for her . . .

Blunt Are you sure?

Balthasar Am I – ? Well, I think so, yes . . .

Blunt But I mean – with all due respect – you are getting on a bit; memory's probably not what it used to be –

Pause.

Balthasar I don't think it's too bad –

Blunt Well, that's not what you told me.

Balthasar When?

Blunt See what I mean? (*Pause.*) Better make sure.

Balthasar (*pause*) Oh, well – I suppose . . .

Pause. **Blunt** *checks he's going then rushes to the window, opens it.*

Blunt   Quickly!

Between the two of them they manhandle **Carol** *through the window.*

Gobbel *collapses, exhausted.* **Blunt** *struggles with her body.*

Gobbel   I can't go on with this, Blunt!

Blunt   Get up and help me!

Gobbel   Help you with what?

Blunt   Help me hide her!

Gobbel *takes her legs and backs towards the cupboard.*

Blunt   Not there!

Gobbel   Not there?!

Blunt   We can't put her in with the vicar!

Gobbel   Where then?!

Blunt   Over here! Quickly!

They carry her over to the chest and manage to put her in. **Blunt** *closes the lid.*

Gobbel   Can she breathe in there?

Blunt   It's mahogany, not tupperware! Right – now what?

The doorbell goes and they shriek with surprise.

Gobbel   Who's that?!

Blunt   How should I know?!

Balthasar *enters.*

Balthasar   Was that the doorbell again?

They nod, yes – weary with it.

I don't know what happened to that girl – she was going to the back door, you say? Just seems to have disappeared.

The doorbell goes again.

That surely must be Carol now; I'm terribly sorry about all
this.

Balthasar *exits.*

Blunt   Right – we've got to take control of this situation!
We've been at the mercy of events too long! Now's the time
to employ every facet of our training!

Gobbel   Right!

Blunt   Now! First – aims, in no particular order; revive
child, remove vicar, dispose of dog – what have I missed?

Pause.

There's something else we were meant to do; but what
was it?

Gobbel   Something else we were meant to do . . .

Pause.

Blunt   Never mind, it'll come back to me; you get rid of
the dog.

Gobbel   Right –

*He picks up his helmet and heads towards the hall. He stops in his
tracks –*

Blunt!

Blunt   What?!

Gobbel   It's gone!

Blunt   What?!

Gobbel   The chihuahua – it's gone!

Blunt   How can it be gone?!

Gobbel   Maybe it's a zombie, Blunt! A zombie
chihuahua!

Blunt   No, wait – I've got it under here!

Gobbel   What's it doing under there?!

Blunt   Not bloody much! Here –

He starts to take it off. Voices behind the door.

Gobbel   Blunt!

Blunt *hurriedly puts it back on.*

Balthasar *enters.*

Balthasar   No, no, not at all, I'm happy to help in any
way I can . . . Ah, Officers, allow me to introduce Miss . . .

To their horror, it's **Gronya**.

Gronya   That's Mrs.

Balthasar   Oh, I beg your pardon – Miss Gronya –

Gronya   Just Gronya.

Balthasar   She says there's some sort of child molester in
the area –

Blunt   We know.

Balthasar   Oh well – there you go. Who is it?

Blunt   No, we know what she's looking for –

Gronya   We've already met.

Balthasar   Oh, really, have you?

Gronya   Surprised you're still here.

Gobbel   So are we.

Pause. She looks up at the sash.

Gronya   Oh. (*Pause.*) So this is . . . ?

Blunt (*nods*)   Mr Conner.

Gronya   Oh, right, well – it's nothing for you to worry
about. Got enough on your plate. I'm just asking people to

keep their eyes open, let us know if you see or hear anything suspicious.

Balthasar   Oh, yes, well, of course I will – can't be having that sort of thing going on, can we?

Gronya   No. (*Pause.*) Well – I'll be on my way then.

She starts for the door. Stops.

I just want to say – I'm very sorry to hear about your loss.

Balthasar   About my – ? Oh, yes, well – thank you very much. I'm a little surprised you've heard about it, to be honest . . .

Gronya   It's a terrible thing, that sort of . . . thing.

Balthasar   Oh well, yes, of course, it is; but she had a fair innings, I think.

Gronya (*pause*)   Did she?

Blunt   I think it's probably best to let Mr Conner rest now.

Gronya   Shut it a minute – what do you mean, she had a fair innings?

Balthasar   Well, eight or nine years; that's not too bad, is it?

Gronya   Eight or nine?!

Balthasar   Yes, I think so, thereabouts. Why?

Gronya   Well – it's not my business, really; I just wouldn't say eight or nine was a fair innings . . .

Balthasar   No, but in dog years, what's that?

Gronya   Dog years?

Balthasar   Seven, is it, or is that cats? No, cats are shorter – it's seven so that's –

Gronya   But what's dog years got to do with your daughter?

Balthasar   My daughter? Nothing . . .

Blunt *and* **Gobbel** *are clutching their faces.*

Gronya   So who is it that died?

Balthasar   Who – ? Oh, Miffy was her name; my wife's dog. Labrador. Beautiful eyes, very sad.

Gronya *nods her head.*

Gronya   Oh very good. Very good. Everything worked out perfect; everything except the cover story. He thinks it's his dog, you say it's his daughter. I had you pegged as nellies from the off and I was bang on the money.

Pause.

Gobbel   What's she talking about?

Blunt   I don't know. What are you talking about?

She looks at **Balthasar**, *nodding.*

Gronya   So this is him, is it? The snake in the grass. It's always the same – look like butter wouldn't melt. The Mother Superior looked like that; like the kindest, frailest old granny you'd ever hope to have. But underneath the habit – a twisted, pie-fingering old Dyke.

Gobbel   What's a dyke?

Balthasar   I think I've missed something, have I? . . .

Gronya   You're going to be missing a whole lot more by the end of the night.

Blunt   You can't be serious – !

Gronya   You stay where you are, Dibble.

She takes out a mobile phone, dials.

Gobbel   What's going on?

Blunt She thinks he's the paedophile!

Balthasar I'm sorry, she thinks I'm the what?

Blunt Look, you've got this all wrong –

Gronya I said STAY WHERE YOU ARE!!
(*Into phone.*) Ballbreaker One here, who's that?
All right, well I've located King Rat. Repeat – I have
located King Rat. And a couple of collaborators, too.
Yup; red-handed where are you?
Right, well, position's secure for now but you should get
over pronto. It's Hobb Street.
What's the number here?

Blunt Thirty-seven.

Gobbel Fifty-eight, isn't it?

Gronya Fifty-eight. Yeah.
And Barry – bring the toolkit.

She shuts off the phone.

Gobbel Why's she bringing a toolkit?

Blunt Well, it's not to do the plumbing, is it?!

Gronya It is, actually.

Gobbel Well, that's a relief!

Gronya *Yours!*

Blunt Now, just look here a minute – first of all, this is a
total misunderstanding. Mr Conner isn't a paedophile and
we're not here to smuggle him out. Just give me a chance to
explain –

Gronya Go ahead.

Blunt No, not here – alone.

Gronya Bollocks, no. Explain or don't. Explain why I've
lived here all me life and never once clapped eyes on your
man here.

Blunt   I don't know – sometimes people just don't see each other. And anyway, what are you suggesting?

Gronya   That it's all a sham! That this is some kind of safe house!

Blunt   Well, that's just ridiculous!

Gronya   Prove it.

Blunt   Prove it?

Gronya   If you can.

The door opens. It's **Garson**.

Garson   What's going on here?

Blunt   And here's all the proof you need!

Gronya   Who's this?

Blunt   This – happens to be *Mrs Conner*!

Gobbel   Mr Conner's wife.

Blunt   Now – Mrs Conner – perhaps you could tell this lady how long you and Balthasar have been married?

She looks at them fearfully.

Garson   Well . . . about . . .

Pause. She looks at **Gronya**.

Gronya   It's all right. Just tell the truth.

Blunt   Yes – that's all we want; the truth.

Garson *goes to* **Gronya**.

Garson   I don't know who he is! They say he's here to help me but I don't trust him! Who is he?!

Blunt   No, you don't understand – !

Gronya   Shut it! This man's not your husband?

Garson   I don't have a husband!

Gronya   What have you sick bastards been up to?!

Blunt   You don't understand –

Groyna   Forcing an old woman into helping you with your sick charade? No, I don't understand!

Garson   Can't they just take him away? I'm scared!

Gronya   It's all right, love – you're safe now –

Blunt   She thinks she's on a boat!

Gronya   She what?

Blunt   She thinks she's on a boat! She's in shock or senile or something but she thinks she's on a boat, doesn't she?

Gobbel (*nods*)   She thinks I'm a Viscount!

Gronya   I don't care if she thinks you're a fucking Garibaldi! *He's* not her husband!

Blunt   She thinks she's on a cruise liner! Mrs Conner, tell her! You're on a ship, aren't you?

Garson   A ship . . . ?

Blunt   Yes – I'm the Captain, remember?

Garson   The Captain . . . ?

Gobbel   He's always starkers. In his cabin.

Gronya   Starkers in his cabin?!

Gobbel   Yeah, when the girls come in! But it's all right, though; they're all backwards.

Gronya   Starkers in his cabin with backward girls?! That's the most perverted thing I ever heard!

Blunt   No, look – ask her what year she thinks it is! Go on –

Gronya   What year is it? Can you hear me? D'you know what year it is?

Pause. She straightens.

Garson   Of course I know what year it is!

Gronya   Of course she knows what year it is!

Garson   It's 1961.

Gronya   It's Nineteen – it's what?

Garson   Martha, you know, if you're going to keep drinking that stuff, I suggest you invest in a diary. At least you'd keep track of the days.

Gronya   Did you call me Martha?

Garson   Oh, really! I don't see why you're in such a state! Anyone'd think it was you that'd just been publicly humiliated.

Blunt (*to* **Balthasar**)   What's she talking about?

Balthasar   I've really no idea! Garson, dear, what are you talking about? What's happening to you?

Pause. She hugs him.

Garson   Oh, Daddy! What am I going to do? How can I ever show my face again?

Gronya   He's her father?

Blunt   Course he's not! How could he be her father?

Gobbel   Maybe he had her at sixteen!

Gronya   He what?

Garson *turns to face* **Gobbel**.

Garson   You!

Gobbel   Me?

She advances on him, pointing.

Garson   How dare you show your face here! After what you've done! You absolute beast!

Gobbel   What have I done?

Garson   Don't you dare! Don't you dare act the innocent with me, Balthasar Conner!

Gobbel   *Who?*

Gronya (*pointing at* **Balthasar**)   I thought he was Balthasar?

Blunt   He is!

Balthasar   I am!

Garson   How could you do that to me?! How could you disgrace me like that, in front of all those people?!

Gobbel   All what people?

Garson   Our families, our friends, the vicar; all of them! Standing there in that stupid wedding dress, like an idiot!

Gobbel   Wedding dress?

Blunt   She thinks she's at a wedding!

Gronya   Someone stood her up. Is that what you're saying? Someone stood you up at your wedding?

Garson   Oh Martha, you know damn well he did! And you – !

She points at **Blunt***.*

Garson   You're no better.

Blunt   Me?!

Garson   Yes, you – messenger boy! If you were a man instead of his spineless stooge, you'd have refused to bring that letter and made him come to the church in person!

Gronya   What letter?

Gobbel   I'm confused!

Gronya   Shut it! What did it say, this letter?

Garson   What did it say?

Pause. Her confusion seems to lift.

That he couldn't marry me. That he had never truly loved me. That his heart was with another girl, a girl he could never have. He said he was sorry but that that . . . was that.

They all stare at **Balthasar**.

Gronya   Is that what you did?

Balthasar   Of course not – Garson, why are you saying this?

She turns to face him.

Garson   Because you make me sick, that's why! Nice old Balthasar! Gentle old Balthasar! What's he doing with that grumpy old bag? She cares more about that dog than him. He really deserves better. Such a gentleman. So patient. And so very, very kind!

She addresses the others.

So what do you think of that? Standing up your bride on her wedding day? Not very kind, is it? In fact, most people would say it was positively cruel. Wouldn't you agree, Officers? Wouldn't you say that it was positively cruel?

Pause.

Gobbel   Sounds fairly cruel to me . . .

Blunt   I'd say that was cruel, yes . . .

Garson   Yes. (*Pause.*) Well, so would my husband. Which is why he arrived at the church in good time, with not a hair out of place, and stood there before God, with his kind smile and eyes, and married a young woman that he didn't love and never would.

Balthasar   That's not fair, Garson. They were different days. I did what I thought was right.

Garson   Horseshit! You did what would cause the least embarrassment, the least fuss – !

Balthasar   The least hurt –

Garson   Balls! It was nothing to do with not hurting me! It was all about you; about how you would look, to me, to the neighbours, about how your damned family would look! You threw away both our lives and for what?! For the sake of appearances!

Pause.

Gronya   So he is your husband, then?

Garson   Yes. He's my husband. For better or for worse.

Gronya   Right. And you're sure he's not a paedo?

Garson   Oh, get a life!

She exits. Pause.

Balthasar   I'm terribly sorry about that. I don't know what's come over her these days.

Blunt   No, well, you know – women eh?

Gobbel   There's no pleasing them!

Gronya   You're a pair of wallies, you know that?

Her mobile phone rings. She takes it.

Ballbreaker One?
Yeah, I'm still here –
When was this?
So who is it?
You're joking – !
No, it's just bleedin' typical, isn't it?
But we don't have a name?
Well, it narrows the field, doesn't it?

Pause. She looks at **Blunt**.

Gronya   No. I was wrong about that. Better just return to base and we can go from there.
Right.

She shuts it. To all:

Well – looks like you're off the hook.

Blunt   How's that then?

Gronya   We got some new information.

Blunt   Like what?

Gronya   Wouldn't you like to know!

Blunt   Hold on a moment – You can't just go taking the law into your own hands! If you know something about a criminal in the area, you've got to tell us, hasn't she?

Gobbel   Or at least tell the police.

Blunt   Or at least – We *are* the bloody police!

Gobbel   *Language.*

Blunt   Never mind language – someone could end up dead!

Gronya   Not someone; a crawling, slimy nonce!

Blunt   Balthasar – tell her!

Balthasar   Tell her what?

Blunt   Tell her not to do it!

Balthasar   You know, he's right, dear. I can't see what good it'll do. Whoever this monster is, he'll have to answer to God.

Gronya   Answer to God?! That's a bloody laugh! He's the biggest nonce of the lot!

Gobbel   God's a nonce?

Balthasar   Oh now, you shouldn't say things like that . . .

Gronya   You don't know what you're talking about, old man! I was brought up by the so-called Sisters of Mercy and I'll say what I bleedin' well like!

Balthasar   No, but the Church does a lot of good
work . . .

Gronya   Good work? Good bleeding work? Well, here's
how much you know; he's a vicar!

Blunt   Who is?

She waves her mobile phone.

Gronya   The chicken-handler! The kiddie-fiddler! He's a
bloody vicar, surprise surprise! He's probably at the church
right now, having his bell rung! That's how much you know,
you old FOOL!

She goes to the door but **Gobbel** *has blocked it.*

Gobbel   No – we won't let you do it!

Blunt   What are you doing?

Gronya   Get out of my way, copper!

Gobbel   She's going to kill the vicar!

Blunt   No, let her go!

Gobbel   But we can't let her kill someone – remember
what the sarge said; don't let people – kill – other people.

Gronya   I'm going to count to three –

Blunt   Constable – let her go!

Gobbel   But it's tenterhook to murder!

Gronya   ONE!

Blunt   I'm sure the vicar is somewhere safe!

He indicates the cupboard.

Gronya   TWO!

Blunt   I'm sure he's locked away somewhere safe!

Gobbel   Are you going to three or five?

Gronya   THREE!

Pause.

Right!

She grabs him by the lapels.

Gobbel   Was that the three there?

Gronya   That was the three – and now you're out!

She retracts her fist to punch him and then there are three thumps from inside the wardrobe.

Pause. Everyone freezes.

Gronya   What was that?

Blunt *stamps his foot three times.*

Blunt   One, two, three!

Another three thumps from inside the wardrobe, and **Shandy**'s *voice –*

Shandy   Somebody open this door!

Gobbel   Ohhhh – somewhere safe!

Gronya *slowly approaches the wardrobe. She opens the door and* **Shandy** *rolls out.*

Balthasar   Reverend Shandy!

Shandy (*to* **Gronya**)   Who are you?!

Gronya   Who am I?!

Shandy *sees* **Blunt** *and* **Gobbel**.

Shandy   You! You'll pay for this! How dare you treat me this way?!

Blunt (*pause*)   Reverend! What are you doing in the cupboard?!

Shandy   Don't give me that! You know exactly why I was in the cupboard!

Gronya   And why's that?

Shandy   Because they put me in it! Hit me over the head and stuffed me in!

Gronya   Did they now?!

Shandy   It's nothing short of an outrage!

Gronya (*to* **Balthasar**)   Did you know he was in there?

Balthasar   No, I thought he'd gone!

Gronya   What do you mean, gone?

Balthasar   Well, I don't know – he came round to offer his condolences on Miffy dying (and then) –

Shandy   Miffy – that's right, the dog!

Gronya *grabs* **Shandy**.

Gronya   Shut it! (*To* **Balthasar**.) Go on.

Balthasar   Well, that's it, really – I took my wife through to her bed – and the Reverend stayed here because the officers wanted to talk to him about something –

Gronya   Did they now?

Shandy   What's going on here! Unhand me this instant!

Gronya   I'll un*cock* you if you don't shut up! Now sit down and don't move!

She pushes **Shandy** *towards the couch. She walks over to* **Blunt** *and* **Gobbel**.

Gronya   Well, now. Seems I underestimated you boys. Have to get the paedo out of town but you can't turn up on his doorstep, can you, case one of us clocks you. So you come here on the pretence of telling them their cat's dead and arrange for the so-called Father to meet you here. Not bad. Almost even clever.

Shandy   Will someone please tell me what's going on here?

Gronya   Oh, listen to it squeal! What's going on is you've been rumbled, mate!

Shandy   I've been what?

Gronya   We're on to you! You've been caught!

Shandy   Caught by who?

Gobbel   The PAPS.

Shandy   Caught by the PAPS!

Gronya (*to* **Balthasar**)   All right, old man. I'm giving you the benefit of the doubt. Off you go and sit with your wife; and stay there till I tell you otherwise.

Balthasar   But – what are you going to do?

Gronya   I don't know yet. But I'll try not to stain the sofa.

Blunt/Gobbel   Stain the sofa?

Shandy   Stain the sofa with what?!

Gronya   On you go now.

She ushers **Balthasar** *out, shuts the door behind him. She opens her mobile.*

Shandy   This place is a madhouse!

Gronya   Ballbreaker one – where are you?
Well, turn around – I was right all along.
I'm looking at him right now.
Yeah, I know. Maybe there is a God after all.
Have we still got that tarpaulin in the back?
Good. We'll need it.

She closes the phone.

All right, Gary Glitter – let's have your togs off!

Gronya *takes* **Gobbel**'s *truncheon from his belt.*

Shandy   I beg your pardon?!

Gronya   Clothes. Off. Now!

Shandy   Over my dead body!

Gronya   Fair enough.

She whacks **Shandy** *over the head. As before, he stands up straight.*

Shandy   Did you just hit me with that truncheon?

Gronya   I believe I did.

Pause. He nods.

Shandy   Right.

He collapses, unconscious. **Gronya** *sets about undressing him.*

Blunt   Now *that* – is definitely illegal!

Gobbel   Why's she taking his clothes off?

Blunt   Why are you taking his clothes off?

Gronya   It's Christmas, isn't it?

Blunt   So?

Gronya   So you pluck the turkey before you stuff it, don't you?

Gobbel (*pause*)   Where'd you get a turkey from? I couldn't get one anywhere . . .

Blunt   Shut up about the turkey!

Gronya   Up we get, Reverend.

She stands the semi-conscious reverend up, and starts to undo his trousers.

Shandy   Must we have cucumber again? It tastes of so very little.

Blunt   Look, you've got this all wrong, I swear! I know you've been told the paedophile is a vicar but there's no evidence to prove that Reverend Shandy's the one you're –

She pulls his trousers down. Surprisingly, **Shandy** *is wearing stockings, suspenders and little lacy panties.*

Gronya   Well – bloody – well!

Pause.

Blunt   All right, admittedly, that looks bad. But it doesn't mean he's a child molester!

Gronya   So what does it mean, then? A vicar wearing women's underwear?! What exactly does that mean?

Blunt   Well, it means that he's –

He looks desperately at **Gobbel**.

Gobbel   A woman!

Blunt   A woman?!

Gronya   He doesn't look like a woman.

Gobbel   You can talk!

Gronya   You what?

Blunt   No, what he means is that – he's not a woman – yet. But he wants to be.

Gronya   What are you talking about?!

Gobbel (*pause*)   He's a man trapped in a woman's body!

Blunt   No –

Gobbel   He's a *woman* trapped in a woman's body!

Blunt   No!

Gobbel   A man trapped in – ?

Blunt   He's a woman trapped in a *man's* body.

Gronya   And how d'you know this? Friend of yours, is he?

Blunt   No!
Gobbel   Yes!

Blunt   I mean, no, not so much a friend as . . .

Gobbel   A colleague!

Gronya   A colleague? What, so you're vicars, are you?

Blunt   No . . .

Gobbel   But neither's he!

Blunt   But neither's he!

Gronya   He's not a vicar?

Blunt   No, he's – he's –

Gobbel   He's a stripagram!

Gronya   Oh, he's a stripagram, is he?

Gobbel   We all are!

Gronya   You're all stripagrams, are you? Is that right, Reverend? You a stripagram, are you?

Shandy   Oh, yes please!

Gobbel   Yes; and that's why – we couldn't explain!

Blunt   Yes! Of course! That's why we couldn't explain! Because it's meant to be a surprise!

Gobbel   Because we're here – / for the daughter!

Blunt   For the daughter / exactly!

Gronya   What daughter?

Gobbel   The one that died!

Blunt   The one that didn't die – ! Mr and Mrs Conner's daughter –

Gobbel   Miffy –

Shandy   Carol!

Blunt   Carol, exactly – is coming home tonight, after a while away – and we've been hired to – strip. When she gets here, haven't we?

Gronya   Hired by who?

Pause.

Blunt   Well – by a friend of hers.

Gronya   Who?

Blunt   Who?

Gobbel   We don't know.

Blunt   That's right, we don't know.

Gronya   You don't know who hired you?

Blunt   Why would we? The agency just tells us where to go and that's where we go.

Gronya   And what agency's this?

Blunt   The agency we work for.

Gronya   Which is?

Pause.

Blunt   Stripper . . . vicars.

Gronya   Strippervicars?

They nod.

But you're not vicars.

Blunt   No, well, they don't just do vicars. That's just the name. They do all sorts – vicars, policemen –

Gobbel   That's us.

Blunt   Firemen . . .

Gobbel   Postmen . . .

Blunt   All sorts.

Gobbel   Taxi drivers –

Blunt   Yes, I think she's got the picture.

Pause.

Gronya   So let's say I was stupid enough to believe you –

Gobbel   Are you?

Gronya   No. But it still doesn't explain why he was in the cupboard.

Blunt   Ah, well, that's easy, isn't it?

Gobbel   Easy-peasy.

Pause.

Gronya   I'm waiting.

Blunt   You're not a very trusting person, are you?

Gronya   No, but I'm a very violent person if that's any incentive.

Blunt (*pause*)   Well, you see – it's all part of the surprise. It's what we call the – double surprise special. Yes, you see, the victim arrives – not the victim, I mean the um –

Gobbel   The deceased.

Blunt   The deceased – no! Not the deceased, the um – the client! Yes – that's what I mean, the client – the client arrives and we do, you know, our um . . . routine . . . and then they think that's it but then the doors open and out comes the vicar!

Gobbel   And that's the second surprise!

Blunt   Hence the name.

Gronya   Which doesn't explain why you sparked him out wih a truncheon.

Pause.

Gobbel   That's the third surprise.

Gronya   Is it now? (*Pause.*) So why didn't you tell me all this from the off?

Blunt   Well, we couldn't, could we? I mean, for all we knew, you might've been the girl or one of her friends even. We'd never work again, would we?

Gronya *nods. Pause. She takes out her mobile and starts to dial.* **Blunt** *and* **Gobbel** *barely contain their relief.*

Blunt   You're really making absolutely the right choice. If your friends come here, we'll all look stupid.

Gronya   I'm not calling them.

Blunt   Who are you calling?

Gronya   My daughter.

She puts the phone to her ear. But we can hear a phone ringing somewhere, muffled.

Pause. It's coming from the chest.

She follows the sound to the chest. She flings it open.

Gronya   Carol?!

She drags the girl out of the chest. She's barely conscious.

Carol   Mum . . . ?

Gronya   What the bollocks are you doing in here?! What have these bastards done to you?!

Now she's really angry. She turns to **Blunt** *and* **Gobbel**, *and advances on them.*

Gronya   What the fucking SHITE is going on here?! What is my Carol doing in that thing?!

Blunt   Now there's no need for bad language –

Gronya   Bad fucking language? Bad fucking cunty arse fucking language? WHAT HAVE YOU DONE TO MY DAUGHTER?!

Blunt   Nothing, I swear!

Gronya   Has that pervert touched her?

Gobbel   She fainted!

Blunt   That's right, she fainted!

Gronya   She fainted?! Why did she faint?! Because the pervert molested her?!

Carol   No, because they killed Chinkie!

Gronya   Chinkie the chihuahua? That we got you for your Christmas?

Carol   Yeah, he run away!

Gronya   How'd he get out the gift box?

Carol   He pissed it soft and ate his way out!

Gronya   I told you not to give him water, didn't I? So he run away?

Carol   And I went to look for him and the man said he was out there –

Gronya   What man?

Carol   The old cunt that lives here!

Gronya *slaps her.*

Gronya   Don't you swear, you cunt!

Carol   I didn't! But so he says he's out there, so I go through here and I go out there, but he's not there, these two cunts have killed him!

Gronya   Which two cunts?!

Carol   These two cunts!

Gronya *slaps her.*

Gronya   I said don't fucking swear!

Carol   I didn't!

Gronya   What's she talking about?! Did you kill my daughter's dog?!

They feign innocence.

Carol   He's under his hat!

Gronya   Under his hat?!

She points at **Gobbel**.

Carol   This cunt!

Gronya *slaps her.*

Carol   Ow! He's got Chinkie stuffed in his hat!

Gronya   Show me your helmet!

Gobbel   My – ?

Gronya   SHOW ME YOUR HELMET!

Quickly, he does. **Gronya** *snatches it and looks inside. Pause.*

There's nothing in here.

Carol   No, but it was, I promise! He must have got rid of it!

Gronya   Are you telling lies again, my girl?

Carol   No, I swear, on your life I'm not!

Gronya   Now, Carol – I want the truth now – I don't want any lies, you understand?

Carol   I'm not lying – !

Gronya   Shush, now – listen to me; did anybody touch you?

Carol   Touch me?

Gronya   You know what I mean; in a way they shouldn't have.

Pause.

Carol   Yes.

Blunt *and* **Gobbel** *are shocked.*

Blunt   Now just hold on a –

Gronya *shuts him up with a look.*

Gronya   You – had best be very, very quiet.

He takes this on board.

Now don't lie about this, babe – this is very important – this is like a matter of life and death. Who was it that touched you – in a way they shouldn't have touched you?

Pause.

Carol? Who was it?

Carol   I told you. It was Uncle Bernie!

Gronya *slaps her on the head.*

Gronya   You rotten little liar!

Carol   I'm not – he did it again tonight!

Gronya   Don't you dare talk that way! Your uncle Bernie's not laid a finger on you!

Carol   How do you know?

Gronya   Cos he's my brother, that's why, and I know he'd never lay a finger on you!

Carol   He makes me play lollies!

Gronya   Right, that's it, you cunt! You get back to the house this minute and go straight to your bed or Santa'll be getting a knife in his belly! On you go, right now! Run!

Carol *exits.* **Gronya** *turns to face them.*

Gronya   What did you two freaks think you were going to do?! Feed my daughter to your pervert pal?!

Blunt   Now just – control yourself –

Gronya   I am controlling myself, mate! You'll know when I'm not controlling myself because I'll be splashing around in your pervert guts like a sugar-rush kid in a paddling pool!

Blunt   But we're not perverts, we're stripagrams!

Gronya   Bollocks!

Gobbel   It might be bollocks, but it's true!

Gronya   All right then. If you're stripagrams – strip!!

Pause.

Blunt   Strip?

Gronya   Show me your routine! Come on!

Blunt   We can't.

Gronya   Why not?

Blunt   Because we –

Gobbel   We forgot the music.

Blunt   That's right! After all that, we forgot to bring the music! Can you believe it?

Gronya   There's a tape in the machine.

Blunt   Not ours.

Gronya   If it's music, you can strip to it.

Blunt   You'd think so, wouldn't you, but actually it's not –

Gronya   Now, you listen to me, skinbag – I don't care if it's Stephen fucking Fry reading *Harry bumboy Potter*; you'll be stripping to it. Or I'll be stripping the flesh from your nonce-loving bones! Now get on with it!

Pause. They shuffle nervously forward.

All of you.

She nods at **Shandy**.

Blunt   Him?

Gronya   You're a team, aren't you?

Shandy   Did you know – that there are actually skidmarks on the Turin Shroud?

Blunt   But he's . . .

It's not going to wash. **Blunt** *and* **Gobbel** *hoist the vicar to his feet.* **Gronya** *picks up a remote control and points it at the stereo.*

Gronya   This had better be good.

She clicks on the tape. It's an instrumental version of 'The Windmills of Your Mind'.

Almost weeping, they begin their strip. This should be improvised for maximum comic effect. They strip to their underwear.

Finally, the track ends. Pause. **Gronya** *nods.*

Gronya   If you're stripagrams, I'm Princess fucking Stephanie! Prepare to be vandalised!

Suddenly, there's the sound of snarling. **Blunt** *screams and flips backwards over the couch.*

Gobbel   What's wrong?!

He surfaces, clutching at his helmet.

Blunt   It's alive!

Gobbel   What is?!

Blunt   What do you think?!

Gobbel   It can't be!
(*To* **Gronya**.) It's alive!

Gronya   What's alive?!

Pause.

Gobbel   Nothing.

Gronya   What d'you mean, nothing?

Again, **Blunt** *screams and twists around.*

Gronya   What's under that helmet?

Blunt Nothing!

Gronya We'll see about that!

She jumps on top of him, trying to get his helmet off.

Blunt Help me!

Gobbel *jumps on too. The three of them roll around behind the sofa.* **Blunt** *manages to get free -* **Gobbel** *still grappling with* **Gronya**. **Blunt** *opens the window and tips the dog out of his helmet. It runs away.* **Gronya** *pulls him back down into the fray, which continues until . . . the phone starts ringing. Pause. The door opens and* **Garson** *comes in. She goes straight to it and picks it up.*

Garson Hello?

(*These italics heard only by her: 'Hello, Mum it's me. I'm really sorry the train got held up for hours at X but I'm on my way now.'*)

Right you are – so where are you now?

(*'I'm literally just minutes away, I'm in a taxi.'*)

Hearing this, **Blunt** *and* **Gobbel** *and* **Gronya** *stop fighting. They look up from behind the sofa.*

Garson All right, dear.

(*'I'll be there any minute now.'*)

Sheepishly, **Balthasar** *pokes his head round the door.* **Garson** *signals him to come in.*

Garson I'll put the kettle on, shall I?

(*'Oooh yes, I could do with a cup of tea, journey I've had.'*)

All right, dear. I daresay your father'll be there to meet you.

Balthasar *nods.*

(*'OK, bye!'*)

Garson See you soon.

She puts the phone down.

Blunt *and* **Gobbel** *stand.*

Balthasar   I'm sorry, it was just the phone was –

Garson   Oh, don't be so wet! If you've all finished behaving like lunatics, perhaps we could have our living room back?

Blunt   Who was that?

Garson   Who was what?

Blunt   On the phone?

Balthasar   Oh, that was Carol – wasn't it?

Garson *nods.*

Blunt   Carol?

Gronya   Whose Carol?

Gobbel   Carol Carol?

Balthasar   No, our Carol –

Gronya   Your Carol?

Blunt   Carol Carol?

Gobbel   Both Carols?

Balthasar   No, just Carol.

Shandy   Carol, that was the name! She's the one that's dead!

Garson   She's not dead. She's just been on the train.

Balthasar   What happened to her car?

Garson   She doesn't have a car.

Balthasar   She does, doesn't she?

Garson   I told you; she sold it.

Balthasar   She sold it!

Garson   Oh, she was worried about that greenhouse thing – you know what she's like – so she sold it to some friend of hers –

Gobbel   She sold it?

Blunt   To a friend!

Balthasar   When was this?

Garson   Oh, about a week ago. Sold it to a friend for next to nothing. I told you all this.

Balthasar   Did you?

Garson   I said to her, wait till after Christmas and drive here because the trains are always busy and getting held up, but no, no; she knew better, and then what happens? She gets held up for four hours near Crewe.

Blunt   So where is she now?

Garson   She's just on her way in a taxi. Say's she'll be here in a few minutes. I'm going to put the kettle on.

Balthasar   Oh, yes, a cup of tea – would anyone care for . . . ?

Garson   Not them. When I return I shall expect you all to be gone, thank you.

She picks up a glass of water and throws it on **Shandy**, *who splutters into full consciousness.*

Shandy   What in the name of – ?!

Garson   That includes you . . . Reverend.

She exits.

Balthasar   I'm terribly sorry, it's been a long day for her and she can get a bit . . . short. She doesn't mean to be rude.

Gobbel *grabs* **Blunt**.

Gobbel   Blunt! She's alive! She's really alive this time! She is, isn't she?

Blunt   Looks like it.

Gobbel   They got it wrong, didn't they?! Like I said! It must've been her friend that died – but they could only identify her from the car wreck?!

Blunt (*nods*)   That must be it.

Gobbel   I'm so happy, Blunt! I'm so happy! We're saved! It's all worked out! We were right not to tell them! We're saved!

*He hugs **Blunt**.*

Gobbel   Happy Christmas, Blunt!

*He hugs **Gronya**.*

Gobbel   Happy Christmas, PAPS woman, even though you were going to put fish up our todgers and paddle in our guts!

*He picks up a bunch of balloons and throws them in the air – taking two for himself. He then goes to **Balthasar** and hugs him.*

Gobbel   And Bulbousarse! Especially you! Your life's not ruined after all! Happy Christmas!

Balthasar   Oh – my life's not – ? Well, thank you, and to you . . .

*Next he goes to **Shandy** and attempts to embrace him.*

Gobbel   Happy Christmas, Father Shandy!

Shandy   Get away from me, you madman!

Blunt   He's only trying to be friendly.

Shandy   Friendly? Do you realise what you've done, you two idiots?

Gobbel   What?

Shandy   I was meant to be on stage fifteen minutes ago!

Gronya   On stage in what?

Shandy   We're doing *Cabaret* at the church hall. It was a fund-raiser for Barnardo's! Well, if you think you've heard the end of this, any of you – !

Gobbel   Don't be like that, it's Christmas! Have a balloon!

Gobbel *gives him a balloon.*

Shandy   A balloon! I'll show you what I think of your damnable balloon!!

He bursts it, with a bang! Suddenly, **Balthasar** *clutches his chest and collapses.*

Gronya   Jesus!

She runs to him. The door opens and **Garson** *comes in.*

Garson   What's happened?!

She sees **Balthasar** *on the floor.*

Garson   What the – ?!

Gronya *looks up at her, fingers on* **Balthasar**'s *pulse, her face telling the story.*

Garson   Oh no – No, Balthasar!

She drops to her knees beside him.

Oh, darling – oh, my darling –

Pause. The door opens. It's **Carol** – *their daughter* – *laden with presents.*

Carol   HAPPY CHRISTMAS, EVERY – !

She stops in her tracks: sees her father, attended by **Garson**. *Sees* **Shandy** *in his suspenders,* **Blunt** *and* **Gobbel** *in their underwear. Pause.*

Carol   What's going on?

Beat.

Blunt/Gobbel   Your dad's dead.

Lights out.

The Wonderful World of Dissocia

For Mum

The Wonderful World of Dissocia was first performed at the
Tron Theatre, Glasgow, and opened at the Royal Lyceum
Theatre as part of the 2004 Edinburgh International
Festival. It was revived by the National Theatre of Scotland
in 2007 for a tour throughout the UK. The cast for this
production was as follows:

Passenger 3, Oath-Taker Attendant, Goat, Biffer, Nurse 2	James Cunningham
Lisa	Christine Entwisle
Passenger 4, Oath-Taker, Ticket, Dr Clark	Alan Francis
Passenger 1, Oath-Taker Attendant, Jane, Violinist, Dot	Amanda Hadingue
Guard 1, Inhibitions, Vince	Jack James
Passenger 2, Oath-Taker Attendant, Britney, Nurse 1	Claire Little
Guard 2, Laughter, Dr Faraday	Matthew Pidgeon
Victor Hesse, Oath-Taker Attendant, Argument, Nurse 3	Barnaby Power

Director Anthony Neilson
Designer Miriam Buether
Lighting Designer Chahine Yavroyan
Sound Designer/Composer Nick Powell

Notes

What follows is a transcript of the original production of this play, including notes – where relevant – for translators. Stage directions, costume and design notes are therefore to be viewed as a guide only, and not as strict dictations. Nor, however, should they be dismissed out of hand. The set design, in particular, can be modified, but my advice would be to observe it to the extent that budget allows, as it is my belief that the overall concept serves the play well.

STAGE DESIGN

In Act One there is no scenery as such. Instead, the playing area is covered with domestic carpeting. Ideally, the stage should be raked. In venues with a proscenium arch it is suggested that the area in front of the safety curtain is also carpeted, that the first scene should be played in front of the curtain and that the curtain should be lifted after the elevator sequence, as Lisa enters Dissocia, to reveal the full expanse of carpet. This design concept is recommended for two reasons: firstly, it suggests that Act One is occurring in Lisa's 'interior'; secondly, such a large expanse of carpet mimics the view we have of the world in infancy – the hope being that the audience will be subconsciously more imaginative as a result.

COSTUME DESIGN

As the play begins, Lisa is meant to be going out somewhere with her boyfriend, so she would be wearing a party dress of some sort. This should be simple but bold in colour, indirectly suggesting the iconography of Dorothy's dress in the *The Wizard of Oz* or Alice's in *Alice in Wonderland*.

The emphasis in the first act is on colour, imagination and variety in all departments; but in costume terms this should be built up slowly. The elevator passengers will look quite normal; the Guards likewise, though one might begin to introduce some subtly odd elements. The first really outrageous costumes shouldn't appear until the Oathtaker team enters. This will serve to ease us into the world of Dissocia and maintain at least a tenuous link to the real world. In the 'Lost Property' sequence, Lisa is totally immersed and you can be as outrageous as you want (though you will find suggestions for costume in the stage directions).

SOUND DESIGN

The sound designer has two tasks in Act One: firstly, to help create the 'scenery' of Dissocia itself; secondly, to hint at what is actually happening in the real world. This 'real-life' narrative should only be suggested by occasional, subtle counterpoints to the action. A basic example is the 'elevator' scene – while Lisa perceives herself to be in a lift, the sound (and the actors' movements) suggest that she is actually in an underground train. Many other such possibilities exist, and will be suggested in the script where I feel them to be helpful.

In the original production, there was a continuous sound element in Act One, as a means of providing maximum contrast with Act Two. From the 'elevator' sequence on, stage microphones were used so we could give the actors' voices an unearthly quality, and also endow the stage space with a feeling of expansiveness.

In addition, there are three songs: 'Dissocia' was sung by the cast without accompaniment; 'What's an Hour' was sung by Lisa to a pre-recorded backing; and 'Who'll Hold Your Paw When You Die?' was pre-recorded. The chant of the Black Dog Army which ends Act One will be available on CD, but its use is entirely optional.

Characters

Lisa
Victor
Passenger 1
Passenger 2
Passenger 3
Passenger 4
Guard 1
Guard 2
Oathtaker
Oathtaker Attendants
Goat
Jane
Bear
Britney
Laughter
Ticket
Argument
Inhibitions
Biffer
Violinist
Nurse 1
Nurse 2
Nurse 3
Dr Clark
Dot
Dr Faraday
Vince

Act One

Lisa Jones — *a woman in her thirties* — *sits cross-legged onstage, absent-mindedly tuning the high E-string on an acoustic guitar.*

She tunes the string up and up until it reaches the correct note — and then continues on past it.

*The pitch of the string rises and rises, but **Lisa**'s face remains blank, her eyes distant.*

Higher and higher the note, the string growing ever more taut, the fretboard beginning to tremble under the strain, the tension rising — but still she winds the tuning peg, up and up and up and up until . . .

. . . the string snaps!

. . . and lolls away from the fretboard.

Lisa *stares at it impassively, a child who has senselessly broken her toy.*

She gets up to put the guitar away. As she does so, someone rattles her letter box.

She stops in her tracks and listens.

*Note: until his entrance, all **Victor**'s lines are either recorded or delivered, via mike, from offstage — a 'voice in her head'. The rattling letter box, however, is live.*

Victor   Miss Jones?

The letter box rattles again. **Lisa** *remains still, fearful.*

Victor   I know you're there, Miss Jones. I know you can hear me. It is vital that I speak to you.

The letter box rattles.

Please, Miss Jones. I have come a very long way to see you.

Lisa *doesn't know what to do.*

Lisa   If it's money you want, I don't have any! You can take me to court, see how far it gets you!

Victor   I am not here for money, Miss Jones. I'm here to discuss your wristwatch.

Lisa *touches her wrist.*

Lisa   My . . . wristwatch?

Victor   You recently handed in a 1972 Sekonda wristwatch for repair . . .

She nods.

Lisa   It was going slow. They said it had to be sent to a specialist.

Victor   A specialist in Switzerland, yes; that is who I represent.

Pause.

I assure you, Miss Jones, it is very much in your interests to hear what I have to say.

Pause.

Lisa   You'd best come in then.

Lisa *lets* **Victor** *in. He bears more than a passing resemblance to how we imagine Sigmund Freud: goatee beard, long coat, gloves, walking stick, hat, pocket watch.*

Victor   Thank you, Miss Jones. Crouching at a letter box does little for the lower back.

Lisa   Have you come all the way from Switzerland?

Victor   There would be little point in coming only part of the way, don't you think?

Lisa   There's no need to be arsey. It's you that wanted to see me.

Victor   No. Forgive me; I am tired and I have . . . precision issues.

He presents **Lisa** *with his card.*

Victor Victor Hesse. Of Hesse and Sons.

Lisa Has something happened to my watch? You haven't lost it, have you? It's just that my aunt passed it down to me and –

Victor Your watch is quite safe, I assure you. I wonder, though – before I explain – could I possibly trouble you for a small glass . . . ?

Lisa Oh, yes, of course –

She is about to get him some water . . .

Victor – of piss.

She stops.

Lisa Of piss?

Victor Yes – I drink a glass of urine every day. It's good for the system .

Lisa Really . . . ?

Victor I haven't managed it yet, today. Contrary to popular belief, they don't serve it on SwissAir.

Lisa (*reluctant to provide*) I don't know . . .

Victor You don't need?

Lisa It's not so much that . . .

Victor It's quite common. A lot of people do it.

Lisa Well, yes, I've heard of it. It's just it's usually . . . their own. That they drink.

Victor Their own? I don't think so . . .

Lisa (*nods*) Whenever I've heard of it.

Pause. For **Victor***, many things rattle into place.*

Lisa I'm sorry, I just –

Victor   No: that does . . . make sense, now that you say it.
My brothers *have* been . . . unusually *supportive* of the habit.

Pause.

Well – on to business: my father's name is Sylvester Hesse.
Have you heard of him?

Lisa   I don't think so . . .

Victor   I'd be surprised if you had. We operate from a
rather remote Alpine location and our clientele is . . .
exclusive, to say the least. However, my father's work in the
field of temporal mechanics has been instrumental in the
development of many technologies – from the alarm clock
to the internet.

Lisa   Do I have to pay extra for this? Because the man
said it'd be three, four pounds at the most or I'd just've –

Victor   This is not about money, Miss Jones. Your case is
of special interest to my father.

Lisa   But why, though? It's just a watch, isn't it?

Victor   To Sylvester Hesse there is no such thing as 'just a
watch'. Every clock face, every timepiece, reveals to him the
story of its owner; its hour hand mourns their losses, its
minute hand describes their lives, its second hand sings to
him of every moment spent in bliss.

Pause.

You don't believe me?

Lisa   I think you're exaggerating a bit . . .

Victor   No, Miss Jones, I am not! Quite the opposite. I
know how it sounds. But I have seen him *do* things;
beautiful, frightening, *maddening* things.

He sits down, cross-legged, on the floor and **Lisa** *joins him.*

Victor When I was a child, my mother told me that he had once made a watch so small, so ephemeral . . . that only a butterfly could wear it. The notion delighted me but I did not truly believe it. Until the day we found ourselves lost in the woods and I saw him, Lisa – with these eyes that see you now – I saw my father . . . take apart a spider . . . unspool its silk . . . and reassemble the creature as a timepiece . . . powered by its own tiny heart.

Lisa (*enchanted*) That's impossible . . .

Victor I cannot disagree. I only say that . . . I saw it.

He seems maudlin. **Lisa** *attempts to lighten the mood.*

Lisa So he's fixed my watch, then?

Victor Actually, no.

Lisa No?

Victor There was nothing to fix.

Lisa It was going slow!

Victor Was it?

Lisa Yes – it was always an hour slow!

Victor And you would reset it and wind it up but the next time you looked . . . ?

Lisa It'd gone slow again.

Victor And always by Exactly One Hour.

She nods.

Answer me honestly, Miss Jones: would you say that your life has recently been . . . out of balance?

Lisa Well . . . it hasn't been great . . .

Victor You've been finding it difficult to manage the . . . commitments of your life?

Lisa I suppose.

Victor   You've become sluggish, unfocused, apathetic.
You've neglected your friends, your family, your . . .
relationship?

Lisa   But what's this got to do with my watch?

Victor   At the start of British Summer Time, the clocks go
forward. You surrender an hour, correct?

She nods.

You surrender it in the belief that – when the clocks go back
– this hour will be returned to you. However – in October
last year – you returned from a trip to New York. British
Airways Flight 771. Scheduled to depart at 12.05 but
delayed by two hours. Of course, the time *here* is five hours
ahead of the time *there*. But to complicate matters further, at
the precise second you crossed the Greenwich meridian, the
clocks here went back . . . by *exactly one hour*.

Lisa   So?

Victor   Think about it, Miss Jones! A seven-hour flight on
BA from JFK with a two-hour delay on your UK ETA and
a five-hour lag from EST to GMT just as BST is ending?!

She thinks about it.

Victor   You didn't get it back! Somehow, in all the
temporal confusion of that instant, the hour that you
surrendered – the hour that was rightfully yours – went
astray! Do you see?

Pause.

Your watch is not an hour slow, Lisa. *You* are.

Over the next speech, a stage mike is used to add a hint of reverb to
Lisa*'s voice. Strange, discordant sounds can be heard on the*
soundtrack.

Lisa   Yes . . . yes, you know, that's right – I was really ill
after that flight. And ever since, I've had this sort of . . .
head cold, that I can't seem to shake off . . . And God, yes,

you know it *has* been since then! Everything was fine until
that trip to New York. But so . . . it's not just me, then? This
isn't just . . . how I am. Oh God and, you know, I *knew* that!
I told them! Everyone's been giving me such a hard time
about it – saying I don't care about anyone but myself, that
I was just being lazy and miserable, but I wasn't! It wasn't
my fault! I just lost an hour along the way!

Return to normal.

But, so – is there a way to get it back?

Victor   I am sure of it.

Lisa   And everything would be back . . . back to how it
was?

Victor   Yes. If you reassimilate the hour, balance will be
restored to your life.

Lisa   Balance will be restored to my life . . . God, you
know, that's just like me to go losing an hour! I'd lose my
head if it wasn't screwed on! So what do I have to do?

Victor   Your hour has been traced to a country called
Dissocia. Arrangements have been made for you to travel
there immediately. On the back of my card you will see a
number. Once I have gone, you must dial it and follow the
instructions you are given. When you arrive in Dissocia, you
must make your quest known. Our agents will find you and
assist you in your task.

Lisa   Wow . . . it's like being a spy or something!

Victor   This is no game, Miss Jones. A stray hour is a
source of tremendous energy. In the wrong hands, its
properties could be exploited to the most devastating ends.
There are those who will not take kindly to your efforts to
retrieve it; they will do what they can to obstruct and
mislead you.

He adopts the air of a hypnotist.

Just remember – the hour is yours. Never doubt it, never deny it. This will be your protection.

Lisa   I understand.

Victor   Good. The best of luck then, Lisa. My father is depending on you.

He exits.

Lisa *looks at the card. She takes out her mobile phone.*

Lisa   Balance will be restored to my life.

She dials the number. It rings, and then we hear an automated voice:

Automated Voice   Thank you for calling the Dissocian Embassy. If you wish to report a conspiracy, please press 1. If you think everyone would be better off without you, please press 2. If you wish to correct a temporal disturbance, please press 3. If you wish to press 4, please press 5.

Lisa *presses 3.*

Automated Voice   Thank you. You wish to correct a temporal disturbance. Your flat is now an elevator. To descend to Dissocia, please press 9.

Lisa   Balance will be restored to my life.

Decisively, she presses nine.

Immediately, there is a pinging sound.

From offstage, a voice:

Passenger 1   Hold the lift!

Lisa, *bewildered, has no idea how to do this.*

Suddenly (at least) four people have all cramped around her, as if in a small elevator. They look like fairly regular commuters.

Automated Voice   Doors closing. Going down.

The elevator begins its descent (although, curiously, it sounds more like an underground train).

Passenger 3 *makes a strange noise, like a groaning moose, but no one (save* **Lisa***) seems to notice. He does this a couple of times.*

Automated Voice   Going sideways.

Passenger 2 *takes out a mobile phone. She/he talks loudly and cheerfully:*

Passenger 2   Hi, it's me. Listen – I've been thinking about it, and I really think the easiest thing is to just push her down the stairs . . .

Lisa *can't believe what she's hearing.*

Passenger 2   Yeah. And I think you're right, she's almost bound to break her neck when she hits that landing. Yeah. And even if she doesn't, I think if you just prop her up and stamp on her chest . . . Exactly. I don't think anyone'll suspect us at all.

One of the **Passengers** *turns round to face a different direction. Slowly, the others do likewise.* **Lisa** *– thinking they must be turning to face the exit – does so too.*

Passenger 2   Exactly. Listen, I can't really talk about it now, I'm in a lift. What was that? I can't hear you, you're breaking up. I said you're breaking up. I'll see you tonight. Love you!

Passenger 2 *puts the phone away.*

Passenger 3 *groans.*

Automated Voice   Going down again.

Another **Passenger** *now turns back to the direction they were facing to begin with.* **Lisa***, getting a bit tired of all this, grudgingly follows.*

Passenger 3 *groans again, even more loudly than before.*

Lisa   Excuse me – are you all right?

This enquiry causes a ripple of disgust and embarrassment among the **Passengers***.*

Passenger 4   How rude!

Lisa   What? I was just asking if he was all right – he was making that noise . . .

They try to ignore her. **Lisa** *sulks.*

Passenger 3 *groans again.*

Passenger 4 – *who has been reading a paper* – *turns to face sideways. Once again, the other* **Passengers** *follow.* **Lisa**, *her arms folded, does not.*

A pinging sound.

Automated Voice   Dissocia. Arrivals.

Only now, as the doors open, does **Lisa** *turn. Just as abruptly, however, the* **Passengers** *about-face and leave the elevator in the opposite direction, leaving* **Lisa** *feeling stupid. Realising she should ask for directions,* **Lisa** *follows them* –

Lisa   Wait – excuse me! Excuse me – !

She follows the **Passengers** *offstage.*

By the ambient sound, the blinking lights and the airship that floats in the distance, it would seem that we are in some kind of airport arrivals lounge.

Two uniformed **Guards** *enter, mid-argument. They are both a mass of tics and twitches, bug-eyed and sweating with general paranoia.* **Guard 1** *is concerned about the length of his jacket.*

Guard 1   But does it cover my arse? Look –

Guard 2   Well, reasonably, I mean – most of it, yeah –

Guard 1   It only comes halfway down! You can see – there's such a steep drop from my arse to my legs – I've got such a fucking fat arse!

Guard 2   You haven't –

Guard 1   I have. It's womanly.

Guard 2   Womanly?!

Guard 1   Yeah, not so much fat as womanly –

Guard 2   There's nothing wrong with womanly!

Guard 1   Not on a woman, no, but on a man? It's grotesque! Men are meant to have small arses!

Guard 2   It looks fine, I'm telling you! I'd kill for an arse like yours: look at mine!

Lisa *is wandering around aimlessly when* **Guard 1** *sees her.*

Guard 1   Shit, look!

He grabs **Guard 2**, *stricken with fear.*

Guard 2   Bugger! And it's a woman too!

Guard 1   Should we go up to her?

Guard 2   We have to, don't we?! How do I look? Do I look terrible?!

Guard 1   No, you look fine – what about me? Does my breath smell?!

Guard 2   She's going to totally hate us!

Guard 1   I know – we're so fucking dull!

Lisa   Excuse me . . . . .

Guard 2   Um – hello – Um – can we help you?

He turns to **Guard 1**.

Guard 2   'Can we help you'! That's so fucking lame!

Guard 1   Yes, um – What we mean is – halt! Um – who goes there?!

Guard 2 *covers his face.*

Guard 2   Oh no . . . !

Guard 1   She thinks we're a right pair of twats!

Lisa   I just arrived, and I was wondering –

Guard 2   She's just arrived!

Guard 1   Oh – you mean you've just got here? (*To* **Guard 2**.) Of course she means that! What else would she mean?! I'm such a dick!

Lisa   I mean this is my first time here . . .

Guard 1   Ah, you mean you've never been here before!

He makes a 'duh' face at his own stupidity and immediately regrets it.

Shit, I shouldn't have made that face! I must've looked a right fucking prick! You do it!

He collapses to the ground. **Guard 2** *steps over him.*

Guard 2   Yes, sorry – you're saying you've never been here before?

Lisa   Not that I can remember.

Guard 2   Right. Because . . .

Guard 1   Because there are things . . .

Guard 2   There are things you have to do . . .

Guard 1   Things that *we* have to do . . .

Guard 2   Yes, to you –

Guard 1   Not *to* you, so much as –

Guard 2   – *with* you!

Guard 1   Exactly – *with* you –

Guard 2   There are things we have to do *with* you –

Guard 1   – if you haven't been here before.

Guard 2   Yes.

Pause.

Lisa   What sort of things?

Guard 1   Oh, it's nothing that bad, is it? I mean, it's not us, you understand –

Guard 2   No, I mean, we don't care –

Guard 1   We're quite easy-going, aren't we?

Guard 2   Yeah, I mean, we don't mind what anyone brings in, really –

Guard 1   No, I mean, as far as we're concerned you can bring in what you like, can't she?

Guard 2   Pretty much, yeah.

Guard 1   But, you know – the 'rules' say we've got to check, you know –

Guard 2   – that you're not, you know –

Guard 1   – bringing anything into the country that *we* wouldn't mind you bringing in –

Guard 2   – but that the *country* –

Guard 1   – that is, the *government* – um –

Both Guards   – would.

Lisa   It's all right, you know; I don't take it personally.

Guard 2   Are we boring you?

Guard 1   We are! We're boring her fucking rigid!

Lisa   No, really, you're not. I should think it's more boring for you.

Guard 2   Oh, it's not boring, is it?

Guard 1   Boring? No –

Guard 2   Not boring so much as –

Guard 1   – nerve-racking!

Guard 2   It's the war, you see.

Lisa   There's a war on?

Guard 1   There's always a war on.

Guard 2   We can't trust anyone. Not even a stranger like you.

Lisa   Oh dear. That must be awful for you.

Guard 1   Well, yes; but that is what we do.

Guard 2   Such is the lot . . . of an insecurity guard.

Pause.

Lisa   An *in*security guard?

Guard 2   Yes?

Lisa   Don't you mean a security guard?

The **Guards** *look at each other.*

Guard 2   What would be the point in that?

Guard 1   No, I mean, if it's *secure* –

Guard 2   – why would you have to guard it?!

Lisa   I suppose. (*Pause.*) Anyway, I don't want to be rude, but –

Guard 2   You want us to hurry up!

Lisa   I've just got something I have to find . . .

Guard 1   And you want us to get a bloody move on, of course you do! Of course she does!

Guard 2   You want us to stop dicking around like a couple of . . .

He looks to **Guard 1** *for support.*

Guard 1   Boring?

Guard 2   Ugly!

Guard 1   Fat-arsed –

Guards (*simultaneously*)   Pricks!

Guard 2   Of course you do!

Lisa What sort of things can I not bring in? You mean drugs, that sort of thing?

Guard 2 Drugs?!

Lisa Yes, you know – heroin, cocaine, cannabis –

Guard 1 Oh goodness, no!

Guard 2 We take a stack of them every day!

Guard 1 Couldn't function without them!

Guard 2 No, no, it's other things . . .

Lisa Like what?

The **Guards** *take out their notebooks.*

Guard 2 OK, well, do you have any . . . feathers?

Lisa Feathers?

Guard 1 From a pillow or a bird, say.

Lisa Why can't you bring in feathers?

Guard 1 Ah well, you see, a feather can be used to tickle a pilot's arse with –

Guard 2 Causing him to crash!

Lisa I'm not getting on a plane.

Guard 1 But that's exactly what a pilot-tickler would say, isn't it?

Guard 2 Can't take any chances.

Lisa Well, I don't have any feathers.

Guard 2 OK, well – have you got any . . . pants with –

Guard 1 Yes, with, like, clouds or – rabbits on them?

Lisa What's the problem with that?

Guard 2 They can very easily be used to strangle pilots!

Guard 1 So easily.

Lisa   No, I don't have any pants with . . . clouds or rabbits on them.

Guard 1   Right. Good.

Guard 2   Well, we're whizzing through these, aren't we?! God, that sounded so *gay*!

Guard 1   What about – any heart-shaped pebbles?

Lisa   No.

Guard 2   Dolls' heads?

Lisa   No.

Guard 1   Tonto facsimiles?

Lisa   No. Whatever they are . . .

Guard 2   Gum shields? Stick insects? Flump covers?

'No' to each.

Guard 1   Buckaroo? Haunted House? Fuzzy Pumper? (*All board games that would have been popular in* **Lisa***'s childhood.*)

Lisa   Nope.

Guard 2   Ping-pong tie-exfoliators?

Guard 1   She won't have one of *them*!

Guard 2   She might.

Offended, **Guard 2** *drags* **Guard 1** *aside.*

Guard 2   Don't undermine me!

Guard 1   I'm not!

Guard 2   You are! You're always undermining me!

Guard 1   What?! If anyone's being undermound round here, it's me!

Lisa *clears her throat.*

Guard 2   Sorry –

Guard 1 *throws himself around, like a child, at the injustice of it all.*

Guard 2   And no, like, really tiny houses or Knievel-shaped occupants . . . ?

Lisa   No.

Guard 2   And no donkey eggs?

Lisa   Definitely not.

Guard 2   All right – a couple of questions . . .

Guard 1   Has anybody other than yourself worn that dress today?

Lisa   Of course not.

Guard 1   OK – and have you left your hair unattended . . . for any period of time –

They become quite mesmerised by her hair.

– or allowed anyone else to . . . touch or stroke it recently?

Pause.

Lisa   No. No one.

A pause as they touch her hair – an almost sexual moment.

Lisa   Is that it?

Pause.

Guard 2   No!

Guard 1   No!

Guard 2   There's something else –

Guard 1   That's right! The oath!

Lisa   The oath?

Guard 1 *uses his walkie-talkie.*

Guard 1   Asshole 1 to control – this is Asshole 1. We need an Oath Team to Concourse 6 please. An Oath Team to Concourse 6 . . .

Guard 2   All new arrivals to Dissocia have to pledge allegiance to the Queen.

Lisa   You've got a Queen?!

Guard 2   Well, we did – sort of. I'm just telling her about the Queen.

Guard 1   Oh, right, yes.

Guard 2   You tell it better.

Guard 1   I so do not.

Guard 2   I always make an arse of it!

Guard 1   I'll start to cry if I tell it.

Lisa   Why, what happened?

Guard 1 (*tearful*)   Well, basically – we have a Queen . . . but she's missing.

Lisa   Oh dear . . .

Guard 2   Our Divine Queen has forsaken us!

Guard 1 *angrily grabs* **Guard 2** *by the lapels.*

Guard 1   She has not forsaken us! She is in hiding from the enemy! She'll return when it's safe to do so!

Guard 2 *puts up a fight.*

Guard 2   And when will that be, eh? When will it be safe?!

They wrestle each other to the ground.

Guard 1   Never!

Guard 2   It'll never be safe, ever!

Lisa *tries to intervene.*

Lisa   Safe from who?

Then there is the sound of a drum, and the two **Guards** *stop struggling, their mood suddenly changed.*

Guard 1   Oh, never mind that! It's the Oathtaker!

*An imposing figure – the **Oathtaker** – appears, comically grim, in robes and a ridiculous ceremonial wig. He has a round biscuit in one hand, and is attended by four ceremonial **Attendants**.*

*Of the two **Attendants** directly behind him, one carries an empty tray; the other carries a tray with a glass of water on it. Of the two behind them, one wears a drum; the other wears finger-cymbals.*

*As the procession takes a step, the **Oathtaker** intones these words in solemn fashion:*

Oathtaker   Oath-taker.

This is followed by a single beat of the drum.

*On the next step, as one, his **Attendants** reply:*

Attendants   Oatcake-eater.

*As they do, the **Oathtaker** takes a bite from the biscuit that he carries.*

This is followed by a single clash of the finger-cymbals.

And so it goes on, as they approach.

Oathtaker   Oath-taker.

Drum.

Attendants   Oatcake-eater.

Cymbal.

Oathtaker   Oath-taker.

Drum.

Attendants   Oatcake-eater.

Cymbal.

*The **Oathtaker** stops the procession for a moment and beckons his tray-carrying **Attendants**. The one with the glass of water steps up and kneels beside him. The **Oathtaker** lifts the glass from the tray and takes a drink of water. He clears his throat and returns the glass.*

The tray-carrying **Attendants** *return to their original positions, and then it begins again:*

Oathtaker   Oath-taker.

Drum.

Attendants   Oatcake-eater.

Cymbal.

And so on, until they arrive at **Lisa** *and the* **Guards**.

The **Oathtaker** *beckons his tray-carrying* **Attendants**. *The one with the empty tray steps up and kneels beside him.*

The **Oathtaker** *throws the biscuit down, and the* **Attendant** *returns to position.*

The **Guards** *position* **Lisa** *in front of the* **Oathtaker**.

Guard 2   Right – you stand there.

Lisa   Is this really necessary? I don't think I'll be here that long.

Guard 1   Look at her! She looks beautiful, doesn't she? You look beautiful!

Guard 2   I always cry at oath-takings!

Oathtaker   Will them that wants the oath taken step forward.

The **Guards** *prod* **Lisa** *forwards.*

Lisa   Um – yes, sir – that's me.

Oathtaker   Raise your wrong hand.

Lisa   My wrong hand?

Oathtaker   Sorry, your *right* hand.

She does so.

Now – repeat after me: I –

Lisa   I.

Oathtaker   And state your full name.

Lisa   Lisa Montgomery Jones.

Oathtaker   Lisa Montgomery Jones.

Pause.

Yes?

Lisa   It's you.

Oathtaker   Eh?

Lisa   It's you that's telling me.

Oathtaker   Is it?

Pause.

Where were we?

Lisa   I, Lisa Montgomery Jones –

Oathtaker (*nods*)   I, Lisa Montgomery Jones –

Pause.

Yes?

Lisa   It's you again. You're the Oathtaker.

Attendants   Oatcake-eater!

*The tray-carrying **Attendants** step up and kneel beside him.*

*Annoyed, the **Oathtaker** hurriedly takes a bite of the biscuit and follows it with a drink of water.*

*It catches in his throat, and he coughs and splutters for a while. His **Attendants** pat his back until he recovers.*

Oathtaker   Now – where were we?

Lisa   I, Lisa Montgomery Jones –

Oathtaker   Do hereby swear –

Lisa   Do hereby swear –

Oathtaker   My undying –

Lisa   My undying –

Oathtaker   Allegiance –

Lisa   Allegiance –

Oathtaker   To –

Lisa   To –

Oathtaker   Our –

Lisa   Our –

Oathtaker   Divine Queen Sarah –

Lisa   Divine Queen Sarah –

Oathtaker   Of the House of Tonin –

Lisa   Of the House of Tonin –

Oathtaker   Of the House of Tonin –

Lisa   Of the House of Tonin –

Oathtaker   Of the House of –

Lisa   Have you got lost again?

Oathtaker   No, they've got three houses.

Lisa   Of the House of Tonin –

Oathtaker   Sovereign of the East Wing of the Divided
States of Dissocia –

Lisa   Sovereign of the . . . East Wing . . . of the Divided
States of Dissocia –

Oathtaker   And pledge, in her absence –

Lisa   And pledge, in her absence –

Oathtaker   To defend her dominion –

Lisa   To defend her dominion –

Oathtaker   From the armies . . . of the Black Dog.

Lisa   From the –

*But everyone (except the **Oathtaker**) puts one hand on the top of their head, bows and murmurs this phrase:*

Guards/Attendants   Queen Sarah, protect us from the Black Dog King!

Pause.

Lisa   From the armies of the Black Dog –

They all repeat the action:

Guards/Attendants   Queen Sarah, protect us from the Black Dog King!

Oathtaker   And –

Lisa   And –

Oathtaker   In –

Lisa   In –

Oathtaker   So –

Lisa'*s beginning to get annoyed.*

Lisa   So –

Oathtaker   Doing –

Lisa *(sighs)*   Doing –

Oathtaker   Hereby make enemies of any other enemies, however many, if any, amen.

Pause.

Lisa   Hereby make enemies . . . of any . . . other enemies?

*She turns to the **Guards**, who mouth the words.*

Lisa   However many – if any – amen!

*The **Guards** applaud.*

Oathtaker   And now for the Ceremonial Song!

They all launch into the song 'Dissocia'.

All
Welcome to Dissocia
We're so pleased to meet both of ya
We already feel close to ya
Dissocia, Dissocia!

And though we'd never boast to ya
We'll be such damn good hosts to ya
We'll even make a roast for ya
Dissocia, Dissocia!

And now you are our friend we will
Defend you to the end remember
No one in the world above will
Love you like the people of
This wonderful new world.

And so we raise a toast to ya
We'll even give the vote to ya
We'll forward all your post to ya
Dissocia!

Lisa *ends up on one of the* **Guard**'s *shoulders, as cannons blast streamers all over her, the Dissocians arrayed around her Broadway-style. The jollity ends quite abruptly.*

Oathtaker   Right. I'm off for a shit.

But suddenly a siren starts up, and a mechanised voice:

Mechanised Voice   Incoming attack – assume safety posture! Incoming attack – assume safety posture!

Everyone starts running around in a panic, stuffing pieces of material into their mouths.

Lisa   What's going on?!

Guard 1 *tears a strip of material in two and hands her a piece.*

Guard 1   Put this between your teeth and bite down on it!

Lisa   What?!

Guard 1   Do it!

She does it. Everyone is lying down, the gags in their mouths, clutching the tops of their heads. The siren is deafening. **Lisa** *lies down.*

Guard 2   Press down on the top of your head!

But his voice is muffled by the gag, and **Lisa** *can't hear him. He pulls the gag out of his mouth.*

Guard 2   Press down hard on the top of your head! Don't let go until –

And then it hits: a wave of low-frequency sound that can be felt rather than heard.

The Dissocians seem to be in a state of seizure, their mouths crooked, their ears and noses bleeding. Some of them lose control of their bladders.

Guard 2 *– caught without his gag in – is bleeding from the mouth.*

Lisa *crawls over to him. Keeping one hand on her head, she manages to put the gag back in his mouth.*

And then, a huge and frightening voice seems to form out of the rumbling:

Voice
　　Citizens of Dissocia!
　　Surrender your Queen
　　Or live forever in the fist
　　Of the Black Dog King!

And then, abruptly, the attack ends.

Mechanised Voice   The attack is over – resume your business. The attack is over – resume your business.

Groaning, the Dissocians begin to pick themselves up.

Lisa   What on earth was that?!

Guard 1   It's happening every day now!

Lisa   I thought my head was going to explode . . .

Guard 2   It would've, if you hadn't been holding it down.

Lisa   But who was that voice?

Guard 1   That was him –

Guard 2   The Black Dog King!

Those within earshot cover their heads and repeat the mantra:

All   Queen Sarah, protect us from the Black Dog King!

Guard 2   Oh, I don't know why we bother with that! Queen Sarah's not going to save us! She's as scared as we are!

Guard 1   Keep your voice down!

Guard 2   Well, where is she then?! If she loves us so much, why hasn't she come back?! Why doesn't she do something?!

Guard 1   You know why! As long as she's alive, there's hope!

Guard 2   And how would we know?! Nobody even remembers what she looks like! For all we know, she could have been dead for years!

Suddenly, the **Oathtaker** *is there, in a fury.*

Oathtaker   Shut your blasphemous hole, boy! How dare you speak that way of your Queen?!

Guard 1   He's sorry, Oathtaker. He's just a bit tired, aren't you?

Oathtaker   We're all tired! But the very fact that he is able to speak such blasphemy is proof that our Queen still lives! And when the time is right, she will return to save us all!

Guard 2   Forgive me, Oathtaker.

Oathtaker   Take heed then. For if I hear such slander from you again, you'll be up before the Collective!

Guard 2   Yes, Oathtaker.

The **Oathtaker** *and his* **Attendants** *exit.*

Lisa *approaches the* **Guards***, still nursing their injuries.*

Lisa   He's a bit scary . . .

Guard 2   He hates my guts!

Guard 1   No he doesn't. If he hates anyone, it's me.

Guard 2   You're joking, aren't you? He loves you! You even get invited to his Twister evenings!

Guard 1   Only because I've got a new mat!

Lisa   Listen – I need to ask you something . . .

Guard 2   We probably won't know the answer. But you can try.

Lisa   OK, well, you see – I actually came here – to find something. Something I've lost.

Guard 1   Oh yes?

Guard 2   And what would that be?

Lisa   Well, it's . . . an hour. My hour, actually. I lost it.

The **Guards** *freeze in terror, staring at each other.*

Guard 2   An hour!

Guard 1   She's lost an hour!

Lisa   I know it sounds a bit odd but I was told it was here. I just don't know where . . .

Guard 1   Ah, right, yes, well –

Guard 2   An hour, yes –

Guard 1   Well, that's probably, that's probably – um –

Guard 2   I know!

Guard 1   Do you?

Guard 2   Yes – Lost Property!

Guard 1   Lost Property, of course!

Guard 2   It's the very place!

Lisa   So where's that? In here?

Pause. The **Guards** *seem confused.*

Guard 1   *In* here?

Only then does **Lisa** *realise that they are now outside. There are birds singing.*

Lisa   Oh. That's funny.

Pause.

Guard 1   OK, then. Bye!

Guard 2   Bye!

They almost fall over each other trying to get away, but **Lisa** *stops them.*

Lisa   You haven't told me how to get there!

Guard 1   Where?

Lisa   Lost Property.

Guard 1   Oh, right, yes. How does she get there?

Guard 2   How – ? Oh, yes, well – follow the sun?

Guard 1   That's right. Just – follow the sun and you'll get there.

Lisa *looks in the direction of the sun.*

Lisa   But it's setting . . . ?

Guard 1   No, it's set.

Guard 2   That's how it set –

Guard 1   Setting.

Lisa   Oh. All right, well – thank you. It was nice to meet you.

She shakes their hands (strangely, as during the song 'Dissocia', they also shake the hand of someone we can't see).

And I don't think you should be so insecure. You both seem like lovely people.

Sheepishly, they nod their thanks.

Guard 2   Be careful, won't you?

Lisa   I will.

Guard 1   Don't talk to strangers.

Lisa   I'll try not to. Bye.

They watch her walk off towards the setting sun. **Lisa** *exits.*

Guard 2   Did we do the right thing?

Guard 1   We did what we were told.

Guard 2   We're such fucking lackeys.

Guard 1 (*nods*)   We're pricks.

They exit.

Lisa *re-enters, the sun in her eyes. She sings to herself:*

Lisa
    Dissocia, Dissocia
    We're dum dum dum dum dum da ya
    We'll even roast a goat for ya
    Dissocia, Dissocia . . . . .

She comes to a stop.

Follow the sun. But it's just fields. Why would they have Lost Property in the middle of a field? That's the problem with insecure people; they just tell you what you want to hear.

Pause.

It does make for a beautiful sky, though, when the sun sets setting.

Pause. She has an idea: she takes out her mobile phone and dials a number. To her surprise, it works. (Here we might hear an effect similar to that outlined on page 10.)

Vince, it's me. Listen – I know I was supposed to be seeing you tonight and you probably think I'm messing you around, but something really important's come up. You know how I've been acting a bit funny recently? Well, it's because I lost an hour on the way back from New York. So you see, it isn't just me; I *do* know what love is and I *do* care about people. Anyway, my flat turned into an elevator and I've gone to this place called Dissocia. It's quite an odd place but the people are nice and the sky is really colourful and hopefully I'll be back soon with balance fully restored so don't worry about me. Give me a ring when you get this. Bye.

She puts the phone away. Pause.

I suppose that sounds a bit weird. I mean, it doesn't sound very much, an hour. Losing a year of your life, that's impressive – but an hour? I mean . . . what's an hour?

She makes a gesture as she says this:

An hour is just a sixty-second cycle –

She stops. A musical phrase has played under this.

Pause. She repeats the action:

An hour is –

The musical phrase occurs again. It seems to be connected to the gesture.

She makes the gesture on its own and, again, the musical phrase.

Obviously, this is a musical field. She giggles.

She makes a gesture like an orchestra conductor and the musical phrase plays again, in a classical style. This is not what she wants.

She thinks.

She makes a sexier gesture and the musical phrase plays again, in a swing style.

She shakes her head. She thinks. She decides.

Sweeping her arms up in a gentler motion, it's as if she lifts the music up from the ground, like flowers.

She sings 'What's an Hour'.

> An hour is a sixty-second cycle
> Dictated by our journey round the Sun
> It's frequently divided into quarters
> Like the hash we used to buy from Davy Dunn.
> An hour is a twenty-fourth of daytime
> If life's a bitch, an hour is a flea
> An hour doesn't mean
> So very much in itself
> But it's my hour
> And it means a lot
> To me.
>
> Of course I know an hour is just a construct
> Concocted by an order-hungry race
> I'm familiar with the work of Stephen Hawking
> (Though I'm not sure I would recognise his face).
> We could sit here and debate the implications
> Until our faces turned a funny shade of blue
> An hour is simply three thousand
> Six hundred seconds
> That I
> Could have spent
> With you.
>
> An hour is simply three thousand
> Six hundred seconds
> That I
> Should have spent
> With you.

Lisa *laughs, looking skywards, and a flurry of petals falls around her.*

She crouches down to play with them, but the petals become flies, which buzz around her. She runs away from them.

Go away! I hate flies! Go away!

But they persist, clustering around her bottom.

What are you doing around my arse?! You know that's very insulting! These pants were clean on this morning!

Goat   They're timeflies.

*A **Goat** is tethered nearby.*

Lisa   What?

Goat   Timeflies. Haven't you heard of them?

Lisa   Timeflies? Not really.

Goat   Never?

Lisa   Well, apart from as part of a phrase – 'Time flies when you're having fun.' I've heard that.

Goat   There you are, then.

Lisa   'Time flies when you're having fun'?

Goat   'Tend to cluster round your bum.'

Lisa   I've never heard that bit before.

Goat   And that's my fault, is it?

Lisa   No . . .

Goat   That's what you're implying.

Lisa   No, it's not.

*The **Goat** shrugs. Pause.*

Goat   They've gone now anyway.

Lisa *nods. The timeflies have, indeed, gone.*

Goat   That's because you're not having fun.

Lisa   If you say so.

Goat   I suppose that's my fault as well.

Lisa   Why would it be your fault?

Goat   It stands to reason: you were having fun − hence the timeflies − and then you met me, and now you're not. So it's obviously my fault.

Lisa   No, really, it isn't. I wasn't even having that much fun to begin with.

Goat   But you're having less now.

Lisa   Well . . .

Goat   And you're blaming me for it. You can, you know; it's all right.

Lisa   I don't want to blame you.

Goat   But I'm to blame.

Lisa   You're really not −

Goat   I am! I am to blame, I am!

The **Goat** *is very upset.* **Lisa** *sits beside him.*

Lisa   Oh no, what's wrong? Why are you crying?

Goat   I'm a miserable failure!

Lisa   Why are you saying that? How are you a failure?

Goat   Nobody ever blames me for anything! What's the point in being a scapegoat if you never get blamed for anything?!

Lisa   Oh . . . you're a *scapegoat*.

Goat   Isn't it obvious?

Lisa   Not really. I mean, you're obviously a goat . . .

Goat (*nods*)   But not obviously a scapegoat. I know. That's half the problem; people can't see the difference. And they're not likely to go around blaming ordinary goats for things. That'd be ridiculous; not to mention unfair.

Lisa   So you *want* me to blame you?

He nods.

But you really weren't to blame . . .

Goat   But that's good! There's no point in blaming me for things I'm to blame for. Anyone can be blamed for things they're to blame for. A scapegoat is blamed for things they had little, or nothing, to do with.

Lisa   Oh. Well, I suppose I could blame you for something . . .

Goat   Could you?

Lisa   If it'd make you feel better . . .

Goat   Oh, it would!

Lisa   All right, well . . .

Goat   Make it something big. Something that really upset you.

Lisa   OK –

She clears her throat and adopts a mock-angry tone.

Why did you put that mortice lock on? You know I lost my key! I had to sit outside for three hours until Mrs Cameron came back and it was really cold and raining!

Pause.

How was that?

Goat   I said something that really upset you.

Lisa   It did upset me! I was furious!

Goat   But something big though!

Lisa   Big like what?

Goat   How about your childhood? You could blame me for that.

Pause.

Lisa   There's nothing to blame you for.

Goat   Nothing?

Lisa   I had a very happy childhood, thank you. I was a very happy little girl.

[*In the original production, the second sentence was also pre-recorded and played simultaneously to the actor speaking the line.*]

Goat (*shrugs*)   If you say so.

Pause.

Lisa   This is stupid. I can't blame you for something I know you didn't do.

Goat   What about something I *might* have done?

Lisa   How d'you mean?

Goat   Well – something *somebody* did . . . but you don't know who. Something I could *possibly* have done – for all you know.

Lisa   Oh, yes, all right – Give me back my purse!

Goat   Eh?

Lisa   You stole my purse! You took it out of my bag in the cinema!

Goat   Did I fuck!

Lisa   Yes, you did! There wasn't even anything worth having in it – just a picture of my auntie and that was the only one I had, you sod!

Goat   I never stole your fucking purse! I've never even *been* to a fucking cinema!

Lisa   So you're going to deny it?

Goat   Of course I am! I didn't do it!

Pause. **Lisa** *doesn't understand.*

Lisa   Well, I know / you didn't, but –

Goat   But you don't know that for a fact! I *might* have done it – !

Lisa   Oh, I'm sure I'd have noticed a goat in the cinema!

He starts to cry again.

Goat   I thought you were trying to make me feel better!

Lisa   I know, I'm sorry.

Goat   It's not your fault. It's this war we're having. Everybody just blames the enemy for everything. There's nothing for a scapegoat to do!

Lisa *is at a loss. Then she has an idea.*

Lisa   Oh, wait a minute, of course, it's perfect! You stole my hour!

Slowly, the **Goat** *raises his head.*

Goat   What did you say?

Lisa   Well, I lost an hour, you see; that's why I'm here. But I reckon you stole it, you . . . thieving . . . goat, you! Give me back my hour!

The **Goat** *stands.*

Goat   Wait, wait – I wasn't ready. But that was good –

Lisa   Was it?

The **Goat** *positions* **Lisa** *so she's facing front. She doesn't understand why, but goes along with it.*

Goat   Yes, blame me for that. Blame me for the hour.

*The **Goat** pulls free the rope he was tethered with, and gathers it up.*

Lisa   All right – ready?

*He stands poised behind **Lisa**.*

Goat   Ready.

Lisa   Give me back my – !

*Suddenly, the **Goat** ensnares her with the rope.*

Goat   I've found her, Master! She's here! The girl that seeks the hour!

Lisa   What are you doing?! Let me go! You're hurting me!

*She tries to pull away, but the **Goat** has the rope firmly and starts to reel her in.*

Goat   I've got no choice, don't you see? He'll have to let me join him now.

Lisa   Who will? Join who?

Goat   The Master! He who will bring calamity to Dissocia! The Destroyer! The Black Dog King!

The sound of distant thunder.

*Having reeled **Lisa** in, the **Goat** winds the rope around her and ties it tight.*

Lisa   Listen, please – I really think you're making a mistake. I've never even been here before!

Goat   There's no mistake! A girl will come seeking an hour – she must be found! Oh, and I'll be rewarded with a lifetime of blame! I'll be the greatest scapegoat that ever lived!

*He forces **Lisa** to the ground and dances around her, in glee.*

Goat
  Rivers of bile will vein the land!
  Bones will twist inside the hand!
  Children will boil in mothers' wombs!
  Turning on lights will darken rooms!
  And heavy skies will teem with flocks
  Of tiny birds with human cocks!

Lisa   This is really horrible of you! And after all the things
I tried to blame you for!

The sound of passing cars, as if we're on a motorway lay-by.

The **Goat** *has become distracted by the sight of* **Lisa**'s *bottom, as she
struggles.*

He looks around, furtively. Decisively, he turns her over.

Lisa   What are you doing?

With one final glance behind him, the **Goat** *hitches up her dress.*

Goat   Just be quiet and you might enjoy yourself!

He starts to undo his trousers.

Lisa   Oh my God, what are you doing?!

The traffic is deafening now. The **Goat** *grunts as he tries to enter her.*

Lisa *lets out a shrill and chilling scream . . .*

And then, suddenly –

– the 'toot-toot' of a horn!

The **Goat** *stops what he's doing.*

*A woman drives on in a child's pedal car. She comes to a stop right
beside them.*

Jane   Hello there!

Jane *is dressed like a secretary, but she also wears an eyepatch, has
one of her arms in a sling, and has a support bandage on her leg: she's
in bad shape, but she covers it well with make-up and a thoroughly*

cheerful demeanour. She is one of those people whose sentences rise at the end, like questions.

My name's Jane and I'm from the CCS – the VCI – the CV – ? I'm from the Council.

Goat   I know where you're from.

Jane *consults her clipboard.*

Jane   Now – which one of you is Miss Lisa Montgomery Jones?

Lisa   Me! That's me, here.

Jane   Right – do you think you could maybe just untie Miss Jones for me?

The **Goat** *unties* **Lisa**.

Jane   All right, Miss Jones – Could you just confirm for me your date of birth?

Lisa   Um – 17th June 1969. (*Or as appropriate.*)

Jane   Right; and you've been a citizen of Dissocia for how long?

Lisa   Just a few hours really.

Now free, **Lisa** *tries for a kick at the* **Goat**, *who dodges it.*

Jane   A few hours. OK.

She notes this down.

So I take it you're Gavin Loxley?

The **Goat** *nods.*

Jane   And you're how old?

Goat   Six.

Lisa   Six?!

The **Goat** *nods.*

Lisa   You're a very, very, *very* bad goat!

Jane   Well, that all seems to be in order. D'you think you could just – help me out of this car?

Lisa *takes her arm.* **Jane** *shouts in pain.*

Jane   Not the arm, not the arm!

Lisa   Oh, I'm sorry –

She takes **Jane**'s *hand and helps her out.*

Jane   Anyway, as I said, my name is Jane? I'm from the Community Crime Initiative.

Lisa *nods.*

Jane   And I'm here to be beaten and anally raped for you.

Pause.

Lisa   You're what?

Jane   Right, well, what it is? Is what we call the Victim Concentration Scheme. Which is basically that Mr Loxley here was going to beat and anally rape you –

Lisa   He was what?!

Goat   I was going to piss on her as well.

Jane   Were you?

She looks at her clipboard.

Lisa   You dirty little sod!

Jane   Oh, I *am* sorry. It's been one of those days today.

She scrubs it out.

Right, so anyway; he was going to beat, anally rape and urinate on you –

Lisa *(shakes head)*   I can't believe that! I thought you just took the blame for things?

Goat *(shrugs)*   There's no smoke without fire.

Jane   But I'm here to be BAU'd on your behalf.

Lisa   Why would you want to do that?

Jane   Right, well, what it is? Is that under the previous Council? This borough had actually the highest crime rate in Dissocia. For example, over the last year, there were an average of *twenty-two* serious crimes per week.

Lisa   How many are there now?

Jane   Under the new scheme?

Lisa *nods.*

Jane   *Forty*-two.

Pause.

Lisa   So it's doubled?

Jane   Right, well, whilst it's true to say that, since the scheme began, statistics do show that serious crimes have increased – ?

Lisa   Doubled.

Jane   Doubled, yes, that's true, but actually what they don't tell you? Is that the number of *individual victims* of crime has, in fact, *fallen*.

Lisa   Fallen?

Jane   Yes, well, under the last administration? There was an average of *twelve hundred* individual victims of crime per year.

Lisa   And how many are there now?

Jane   Under the new scheme?

Lisa   Yes.

Jane   One.

Lisa   One?

Jane *suddenly gets a stabbing pain in her side.*

Jane   One!

She grabs hold of **Lisa** *as the pain passes.*

Lisa   And that's you.

Jane   And that's me.

Goat   I certainly feel safer than I used to.

Jane   So – shall we crack on with it, then?

Jane *hobbles to her pedal car. The* **Goat** *follows.*

Lisa   Wait a minute – I don't want you to get beaten and raped in my place!

Jane   Right, well; the only alternative would be for it to happen to you. And I don't think you'd want that. OK?

She takes a medical kit out of the car, and starts to pull on a pair of surgical gloves.

Lisa   But how's that the only alternative? I mean, you've stopped a crime. Why does it have to happen at all?

Pause. **Jane** *can't think of an answer to that.*

Jane   Right, well, I'm not actually in the position of deciding Council Policy? I'm just the victim. Mr Loxley?

She beckons to the **Goat**, *who follows her offstage.*

Lisa   No, listen, this is ridiculous, please –

She grabs the end of the **Goat**'s *rope.*

Lisa   This is really stupid! Please don't do this! You're only six and it's a really wicked thing to do!

With a grunt, the **Goat** *pulls it free and exits.*

Helplessly, **Lisa** *watches the offstage action: there is the sound of animal grunting,* **Jane** *screaming, the sound of blows.*

Lisa *can't watch any more.*

The awful sounds build and build.

(*Note: in the original production, the live offstage sounds were eventually swamped by a treated recording of a violent domestic argument.*)

Lisa *covers her ears and sings to herself:*

Lisa
   Dissocia, Dissocia! We'll even make a boat for ya!
   We'll dum dum dum dum dum for ya! Dissocia Dissocia!

She runs back and screams at them:

Leave her alone, d'you hear me? What's she ever done to you?! Leave her alone, you rotten horrible goat!

But the noise just gets louder. She starts to cry.

I hate this place, I hate it! I hate it and I want to go home! I want to go home! I want to go home!

She lies down and curls up, in a foetal position, her ears covered.

I want to go home I want to go home I want to go home.

Dissocia darkens around her, and the violent noises recede until finally she is just a small, lonely figure in the landscape. She makes little bleating pre-linguistic sounds.

Pause.

*A trapdoor opens near her head, hissing out icy smoke. A **Polar Bear** clambers out.*

*When **Lisa** sees him, she smiles.*

Bear   Hello, Lisa.

Lisa   Hello, bear. How are you?

Bear   Mmm. Not so bad.

Lisa   What've you got for me?

Bear   I've written a song.

Lisa   Have you?

Bear   Would you like to hear it?

Lisa   I would. I'd very much like to hear it. Is it nice?

Bear   It's quite nice, yes. Shall I begin?

Lisa   Please do.

*The **Bear** clears his throat. He sings 'Who'll Hold Your Paw When You Die?'*

> Who'll hold your paw when you die?
> Who'll hear you whisper goodbye?
> Who'll be beside you when brain death is declared?
> Who'll think about you and all we have shared?
> Some people call themselves friend
> But will they be there when you end?
> Life's full of clatter
> But none of it matters
> Only who'll hold your paw when you die.

*Delighted, **Lisa** applauds.*

Lisa   That was excellent!

Bear   It's not really finished yet.

Lisa   It was very good though.

Bear   Hmm. Thank you. D'you feel better now?

Lisa   I do. I really do. You've restored my faith in animals.

Bear   All right then. See you then.

Lisa   Bye.

*The **Bear** disappears back into the ground.*

*The light returns and, with it, the terrible sounds of the **Goat** assaulting **Jane**.*

*But now **Lisa** is smiling, still enchanted by the **Bear**'s song.*

After a time, the noises end.

Jane *reappears, badly beaten up, her clothes torn, but still clutching her clipboard; and still thoroughly cheerful.*

Jane   All right?

Lisa   Fine thanks. How are you?

Jane   Oh, I'm fine. I mean, a goat's penis; it's quite rough? But apart from that, I'm fine. So could you just sign here?

Lisa *signs.*

Jane   And could you just date it for me? Lovely. Thank you very much.

Lisa   No, thank *you*.

Jane   All right. Now Mr Loxley . . .

And then **Jane** *suddenly becomes hysterical, screaming at the top of her voice:*

Mr Loxley! Mr Loxley! Mr – !

Lisa *slaps her face. Pause.*

Jane   Thank you. Mr Loxley is actually napping at the moment.

The sound of the **Goat** *snoring, offstage.*

Jane   But I believe he does still intend to hand you over to the enemy –

Lisa   I'm sure he's got that wrong. What would the Black Dog Thingummybob want with me?

Jane *puts her hand on her head.*

Jane   Queen Sarah protect us from the Black Dog Thingummybob.

Lisa   Unless it's my hour he wants. Victor did say it was a source of great power. Maybe he thinks I know where it is.

Jane   Right, well, I wouldn't know about that. But what I'd suggest? is that I give you a lift to Lost Property. Would that suit you?

Lisa   That would be fantastic!

Jane   Righty-ho.

Lisa *helps* **Jane** *to the car. But then something strikes her.*

Lisa   How did you know I was going there?

Jane   Beg your pardon?

Lisa   How did you know I was going to Lost Property?

Pause.

Jane   Because you told me?

Lisa   I don't think I did . . .

Jane   Mmm. Well, what it is – is it was probably Mr Loxley that told me? He was saying quite a lot of things as you can imagine.

Lisa *nods, not quite convinced.*

Jane   Anyway, we should probably go now? It's just that I'm due to be carjacked at six.

Lisa *climbs into the small car behind* **Jane***.*

With a 'toot-toot', they drive off.

A sudden and thunderous blast of punky guitar music.

Jane *and* **Lisa** *are travelling at high speed around Dissocia's mountain roads.*

Lisa *(shouts)*   It's very fast this car, isn't it?!

Jane *(shouts)*   What?!

She turns down the music.

Lisa   I said it's very fast, this car!

Jane   What do you mean, car? It's not a car –

She seems to have become someone entirely different.

Lisa   Isn't it?

Jane   God, no!

She pulls on a pair of goggles.

Lisa   What is it, then, if it's not a – ?

Suddenly the car accelerates even faster, pressing them back into their seats.

– CAAAAAARRRRRR!

And then takes off into the sky, up and through the canopy of clouds.

She covers her eyes, terrified.

Oh no, listen, please – I'm not very good with flying and that's when I'm in a plane! Can we go back down, please?! Please can we go back down?!

Jane   Oh, nonsense: here, have a swig of this – that'll see you right.

Jane *swigs from a hip flask and passes it back.*

Lisa   Oh my God, you're drinking!

She looks over the side and screams.

Oh my God!

She takes the flask and drinks from it.

How is this thing flying? It doesn't even have any wings!

She looks down again – takes another swig.

Oh, we're so high up! – this is really . . .

But she continues to look (and continues to drink).

. . . quite beautiful. It's really quite beautiful!

Jane   What?!

Lisa   Dissocia – it's beautiful!

She whoops with joy.

It's *beautiful*!

She drinks from the hip flask again.

Jane   Yes, it is rather pretty, isn't it? The West was even prettier, once upon a time. But look up ahead!

Lisa   I think there's a storm brewing!

Jane   No – that's the West! The Black Dog reduced it to a wasteland in a matter of weeks! He'd do the same to us if he could!

Lisa   Why can't he?!

Jane   Because he wants Queen Sarah!

Lisa   But hasn't she gone missing?

Jane   Not exactly! The Collective sent her into hiding! Every single image of her was destroyed, even the money! Then they erased the memory of her face from every last citizen of Dissocia!

Lisa   So no one knows what she looks like?

Jane   Not a soul! So the Black Dog can't risk an all-out assault in case he kills her by accident!

Lisa   Here – you're not doing that thing! You know – Queen Sarah protect us – that thing.

Jane   Oh, that's just superstitious twaddle!

Lisa   You did it before!

Jane   I've never done it!

Lisa   You did, I saw you! After you were raped by the goat!

Jane   Have you gone fucking *mad*?!

Lisa   Don't shout at me – you were raped by a goat, I heard it!

Jane   It's hardly something I'd forget! Honestly, I don't know how you come up with these things, Lisa, I really don't.

[*In the original production, the second sentence was also pre-recorded and played simultaneously with the actor speaking the line.*]

An explosion goes off beside them, rocking the flying car.

Lisa Oh my God, what's that?!

Another explosion.

Someone's shooting at us!

She looks over the side.

We're flying over the West!

Jane Yes, sorry about that! Just a little detour – have to drop something off!

Lisa What are you dropping off?

Jane A bomb.

Lisa A bomb?!

The air is filled with anti-aircraft fire and explosions.

Oh my God! We're going to die!

Jane Well – got to do our bit, haven't we?

Another explosion.

Lisa No, wait a minute – this isn't my bit, this is your bit! And anyway – I don't want to drop bombs on people, whatever they've done!

Jane No, no, no: this is a novelty bomb!

Lisa A novelty bomb?!

Explosion.

What the hell is a novelty bomb?! You mean, it doesn't kill anyone?

Jane Oh no – it incinerates everything in a five-mile radius!

Lisa   So what's the novelty?

Jane   It leaves a scorch mark in the shape of a cat! Here we go –

She pulls a lever.

Bombs away!

The bombs whistle to the ground. Beneath them, explosions mushroom.

Lisa   Oh my God! There's people burning!

Jane   Good! Take that, you big bullies!

Lisa   No, it's horrible – all the houses are burning, look – those are children down there!

Jane   Yes, but look at that!

Lisa   Oooh, you're right – it's a cat!

Jane   Quite good, isn't it?!

Lisa   Have you got any other ones?!

Jane   I've got one shaped like a rhino?

Lisa   Oh, drop that one!

Jane *lets another bomb drop.*

Lisa   Wheeeeeeeeeeeee!

Another explosion beneath them. **Lisa** *looks back at it.*

That looks more like a walrus!

Jane   They're just prototypes. There's a good one that looks just like a little koala bear.

Lisa   Aww.

Simultaneously:

Jane   Die, you Black Dog scum!

Lisa   Die, you Black Dog . . . buggers!

More anti-aircraft fire on their tail.

Lisa *sits up and taunts them.*

Lisa   Come on, you want some?! You fucking want some?!

An explosion just behind them. **Lisa** *laughs.*

Jane   We're clear now!

Lisa   Well done! That was excellent!

Jane   You mustn't feel any sympathy for them, Lisa.
They're all slaves to the Black Dog King!

Lisa   I hate the Black Dog King!

Jane   So you should! I dread to think what he'd have done
if he'd caught you! I mean, you've heard that poem, haven't
you?

They start their descent.

Lisa
   Rivers of bile will vein the land?

Jane
   Bones will twist inside the hand!

Lisa
   Children will boil in mothers' wombs!

Jane
   Turning on lights will darken rooms!

Lisa
   And heavy skies will teem with flocks . . .

Both
   Of tiny birds with human – cocks!

The car rattles as they contact the ground and taxi towards a halt.

Jane   That's the one! Have you ever seen a penis bird?
Frightful things. Had one in the barn once. Came on my
hand while I was saddling up.

Lisa   Eeeuh!

The car comes to a stop.

Jane   Anyway, here we are: Lost Property. Over that hill.

Lisa *climbs out.*

Lisa   Well, thanks so much for the . . . flight.

Jane   Not at all.

Lisa   I've never been on a bombing mission before. It was very exciting.

Jane   Yes, it is rather jolly, isn't it? Anyway – toodle-oo!

With a last 'toot-toot', **Jane** *drives off.*

Lisa *waves goodbye. She walks up the hill towards Lost Property.*

As she climbs to the top of the rake, the other actors will set up for the next section. **Lisa** *watches them do so, making gestures with her hands that recall the gestures she made in her solo song, as if she is in some way conjuring the events. Over this, the following pre-recorded conversation plays.*

The sound of traffic. A conversation on the move:

Vince (*voice-over*)   Lisa! Lisa – where have you been?!

Lisa (*voice-over*)   What do you mean, 'where've I been'?

Vince (*voice-over*)   I thought I was meant to be seeing you tonight.

Lisa (*voice-over*)   Were you?

Vince (*voice-over*)   So what were you doing at the fucking airport?!

Lisa (*voice-over*)   Just leave me alone, Vince.

Vince (*voice-over*)   Is that what you want? Do you really want me to leave you alone? I can do that, if that's what you want. Because I'm telling you, I'm getting really fucking sick of this. Lisa, are you listening to me?

Lisa (*voice-over*)   Do what you like.

A hot-dog stand, with a sign that reads 'Lost Property'. Behind the stand is a mound of shoes and handbags.

At the stand, a trashy-looking Australian girl called **Britney** *is frying onions and splitting buns for the hot dogs.*

A muzak version of 'Who'll Hold Your Paw When You Die' is playing (or something similarly bland).

There are two outdoor café tables, with two people sitting at each. There are menus on the tables, showing nothing but hot dogs.

At table one sit two men we shall refer to as **Laughter** *and* **Ticket**. *They are respectably dressed.* **Ticket** *wears a panama hat. Every now and then* **Laughter** *will laugh loudly, and be hushed by* **Ticket**.

At table two sit another two men we shall refer to as **Argument** *and* **Inhibitions**. **Inhibitions** *wears a tweed suit and sports a bushy beard.* **Argument** *wears trousers and shoes – and no shirt, but a collar and bow tie, in the style favoured by male strippers.*

All of them are intently eating hot dogs from paper plates. There are no signs of water, or beverages of any kind.

Lisa *approaches* **Britney**, *who is now putting hot dogs into rolls.*

Lisa   Um – hello. I wonder if you could help me? I've lost something.

Britney *sets off around the tables, giving out hot dogs.* **Lisa** *follows her as she weaves inbetween them.*

Britney   What do you want me to do about it?

Lisa   Well – it's Lost Property, isn't it?

Britney   If it's lost then, yes, obviously.

Lisa   No, I mean – *this* is Lost Property. Isn't it?

Britney   Does it look like Lost Property?

Lisa   No, not really. But the sign says it is.

Britney   The sign?

Lisa *indicates the sign.* **Britney** *stops to look at it. She sighs heavily.*

Britney   I'm surrounded by bloody idiots! Biffer!

Biffer *hurries in. He is a chef and wears a grimy apron. He is dripping with sweat and carrying a tray full of hot dogs.*

Britney   Biffer, get that bloody sign fixed! Give me those.

Biffer *gives her the hot dogs. He replaces the sign with one that reads 'Lost Lost Property'. And then hurries back to the kitchen.*

Lisa   'Lost Lost Property'?

Britney *has put more hot dogs, in buns, on more plates. She sets off round the tables again. Although they have more hot dogs than they can possibly eat, the men are never less than grateful.*

Britney   Yes, well, that's why I was confused. You're looking for the Lost Property Office.

Lisa   Where's that?

Britney   We lost it.

Lisa   You lost the Lost Property Office?

Britney   There's no need to rub it in! We're obviously embarrassed about it.

Lisa   So what do you do here?

Britney   Well, if anyone finds the Lost Property Office, they'll hopefully bring it to us.

Lisa   So what's all that stuff behind the stall?

Lisa *indicates the pile of shoes and handbags.*

Britney *picks up the ketchup and mustard bottles and goes round the tables squirting it all over the men's hot dogs.*

Britney   Oh, that's lost property.

Lisa   So you've *got* lost property?

Britney   Well, yes and no.

Lisa   Yes and no.

Britney   Well, yes, people are constantly bringing us lost property. But ironically enough, the only lost property they never bring us is the actual Lost Property Office.

Lisa   Yes, but I don't understand. If you've got lots of lost property, surely you're the Lost Property Office anyway?

Britney   No, no, no. That doesn't follow at all.

Lisa   Of course it does – Why not?

As she answers this, a distracted **Britney** *squeezes a constant stream of mustard over* **Ticket**'s *hot dog.*

Britney   Well, you might have a lot of books in your house. But that doesn't make you a library, does it? You might have lots of hot dogs. But that doesn't make you a hot-dog stall, does it?

The flow of mustard ceases.

Everything all right for you?

Ticket   Delicious, thank you.

Britney *returns to the stall.* **Lisa** *follows.*

Britney   Actually, though, between you and me – the funny thing is . . . a couple of weeks back, someone actually *did* hand in a Lost Property Office; just not the one we lost. What are the odds on that? Anyway –

She tips a tray of hot dogs on to the floor.

BIFFER!

Biffer *appears with another load of hot dogs.*

Britney   Get those bloody hot dogs up!

Biffer *starts to gather up the hot dogs.*

Britney   Get the bloody fluff off them!

Lisa   Well, maybe I could visit that one?

*As **Biffer** hands **Britney** each hot dog, she throws it down again.*

Britney   What one?

Lisa   The Lost Property Office that someone found but that isn't the Lost Property Office you lost. Can I visit that one?

*Everybody stops what they're doing, frozen in fear. **Britney** doesn't know what to say.*

Britney   I don't know about that. I can't think of any reason why not . . . But I'm sure there must be one.

*Pause. **Laughter** suddenly stands.*

Laughter   I've got a question.

Britney   Yes?

Laughter *brandishes a menu.*

Laughter   It says here – 'Today's Special'.

Britney   Yes?

Laughter   What's so special about it?

A group murmur of appreciation for this question.

Britney   Well . . . it's Biffer's birthday!

*Apart from **Biffer** – who looks confused – they are all delighted by this and offer their congratulations. They sing him a well-known birthday song:*

They applaud. The applause dies down.

Lisa   That's very nice. So do you – ?

Britney   Hot dogs are on the house!

*Everyone is appreciative. **Britney**'s tone changes abruptly.*

Britney   BIFFER! HOT DOGS FOR EVERYONE! GET A BLOODY MOVE ON!

Biffer *scurries away for more hot dogs and the men go back to eating and chatting about how wonderful the hot dogs are.*

Lisa So can I visit the Lost Property now?

Britney (*frustrated*) It's highly irregular, you know!

Lisa It'll just be for a minute. I'll give it straight back, I promise.

Britney You promise?

Lisa I do, I promise.

Britney *disappears under the counter.*

Lisa *smiles at the diners.*

Britney *resurfaces, now wearing a false beard.*

Laughter *points at* **Britney** *and guffaws loudly. He is silenced by* **Ticket**.

Britney Lost Property, can I help you?

Pause. **Lisa**'s *patience is fraying.*

Lisa Yes, like I said – I've lost something.

Britney's *off round the tables again, this time throwing handfuls of fried onions over the ketchup-drenched hot dogs.*

Britney And what would that be?

Lisa An hour.

Britney Can you describe it?

Lisa Oh – I don't know. How do you describe an hour?

Britney Well, do you feel heavier since you lost it?

Lisa Actually, yes, I do.

Britney So it must be light. If it's light it's daytime. And if it's daytime, it must be big.

Lisa Why?

Britney   Because the small hours are at night. So it's a big hour, in the day – was it thick or thin?

Lisa   I can't answer that. Hours aren't thick or thin . . .

Britney   All right, then – was it dense or was it fine?

Lisa   That's just as stupid, if not more so.

Britney   Not at all. Have you never heard of someone's finest hour?

Lisa   Look – I can't believe there's been that many hours handed in. Can't you just see if my one's there?

Britney   Well, that's very selfish of you! I mean, there's a queue, you know.

The customers murmur their agreement.

Take a ticket and wait your turn. Biffer – where's those bloody hot dogs?!

Lisa *takes a ticket from the ticket roll on the stand.*

Britney   Number seventeen?

Ticket   Oh, that's me!

Argument   Good luck, old boy!

Biffer *rushes out with more hot dogs and collides with* **Ticket**, *spilling them all.*

Lisa   Oh dear!

Britney   Biffer, you idiot! Get them picked up!

Britney *and* **Ticket** *kick and beat* **Biffer**, *who crawls away.*

Britney *gets a cloth and wipes down* **Ticket**'s *jacket.*

Lisa (*to* **Laughter**)   I feel quite sorry for him.

Pause. **Laughter** *guffaws.*

Lisa   What's so funny?

Laughter *stops laughing.*

Laughter   I don't know – what you said?

Lisa   I just said I felt sorry for him.

Laughter *brays with laughter again.* **Lisa** *shakes her head.*

Britney   Now – how can I help you?

Ticket   Yes, you see – I was number three earlier.

Britney   Oh yes, I remember.

Ticket   But I lost my ticket.

Britney   I'm sorry, no one's handed in a number-three ticket.

Ticket   So what should I do?

Britney   I'm sure it'll turn up soon.

Ticket   I do hope so.

Ticket *takes another ticket and, munching on a hot dog, returns to his seat.*

Lisa   That's ridiculous.

Argument *stands.*

Argument   I disagree. I think it's eminently reasonable. I'd go so far as to say it was about the most reasonable thing I've either heard or seen ever. Do you concur?

Lisa   No, of course I don't.

Argument   Oh. Right.

Argument *sits down.* **Laughter** *brays out another laugh.*

Lisa   Why do you keep doing that?!

Ticket   He's lost his sense of humour.

Lisa   Oh, I'm sorry. That must be awful for you.

Laughter   Are you being sarcastic?

Lisa   No, not at all.

Laughter   I can't tell, you see. I tend to just laugh and hope it fits. It fits more things than not, I find.

Lisa   How did you lose it?

Ticket   He was the victim of a buse.

Lisa (*not smiling*)   Oh – that's . . . terrible.

Ticket   Isn't it? Especially as the buse has long been considered extinct.

Laughter   In the wild at least.

*This irritates **Lisa**. She watches them munch their hot dogs.*

Lisa   There's not much choice of food here, is there?

*At the other table, **Argument** stands, one foot on his chair.*

Argument   I disagree. I've never been anywhere with so much choice. I'm actually dizzy with the amount of choices on offer. I'd go so far as to say there is more choice here than in any other choice-based establishment I've ever visited ever. Would you concur?

Lisa   All they've got is hot dogs!

Argument   Yes. That's true.

He sits down again.

Inhibitions   There's no point arguing with *him*.

Laughter   That's what he's lost.

Lisa   What?

Inhibitions   The argument.

Lisa   Which one?

Argument   Which what?

Lisa   Which argument have you lost?

Argument   Any one you care to mention.

Lisa   But surely that could be fixed?

Argument   How so?

Lisa   Well – you say something and I'll agree with it.

Pause. This hasn't occurred to him.

Ticket   It's worth a try.

Argument   All right – let's give it a try!

There is much murmuring and excitement as **Argument** *approaches one side of the hot-dog stand.* **Britney**, *in turn, takes his seat at the table.* **Lisa** *stands at the opposite end of the stand, and the whole scene begins to resemble a session in Parliament.*

The hubbub dies down for **Argument**'s *opening statement.*

Argument   The wild-goose chase – is a cruel and barbaric sport – which should be banned outright!

Noise from all parties, some agreeing, some not.

Lisa   That's not a sport! It's a turn of phrase.

Noise.

Argument   Don't go telling me about wild-goose chases! I'll have you know I used to be a wild-goose-chase saboteur!

Noise.

Lisa   Don't be ridiculous. A wild-goose chase means you're hunting for nothing. How can you sabotage that?

Noise.

Argument   Easily!

Lisa   How?

The noise dies down. Everyone is curious.

Argument   You let loose – some geese!

Silence.

Inhibitions *suddenly becomes red-faced and angry, and shouts at the top of his voice:*

Inhibitions   You! – Are talking! – Absolute! – *Fucking*! – SHIT!

Pause. Everyone's a little taken aback by this.

Argument   Yes. Yes, I am.

He sits down.

Britney   Is everybody all right?!

Everyone nods.

*A **Violinist**, dressed as a giant hot dog (with 'Eat at Britney's' written on her front), appears and begins to play along with the muzak.*

[Note: it happened to be that in the original production the actress played the violin – it could be another instrument.]

Ticket   I must say – these hot dogs are absolutely delicious!

Argument   They are – they're excellent!

Britney *blushes with embarrassment.*

Ticket   And so you just put them in a roll . . . ?

Britney   We put them in a roll . . . with onions!

Argument   Ah, with onions!

Laughter   Onions, that's what it is!

Ticket   Well, they're absolutely top-notch.

Britney   Thank you!

Argument   You must give me the recipe.

Britney   Another round?

Argument   Well – I could have another round . . .

Laughter   Yes, why not?

Britney   Biffer – !

Lisa   No, wait a minute, hold on – I'm not all right
actually. Could you stop playing that? Could she stop
playing that?

*The **Violinist** carries on regardless.*

Lisa   Look – it's nice that you give people food while
they're waiting. But maybe if you didn't spend so much time
on the food, they wouldn't have to wait so long? I mean, it's
just a suggestion.

Britney   Biffer! Where's those bloody hot dogs?!

Lisa   This is so frustrating!

Britney   Ticket number *eighteen.*

Inhibitions   That's me!

Lisa   I don't even believe she's got –

*As **Inhibitions** stands, we realise that he's naked from the waist
down.*

Lisa *is shocked.*

Lisa   Oh my God – he's got no pants on!

Inhibitions   I've lost my inhibitions.

Argument *points at **Inhibition**'s genitals.*

Argument   Now that *is* funny!

Ticket *nudges **Laughter**.*

Ticket   He's right, it is!

Laughter *guffaws manically.*

Inhibitions *suddenly realises he's naked and drops to the floor in
shame, pulling a tablecloth down over him and tipping all the food on
to the floor.*

Biffer *comes out with more hot dogs and trips over **Inhibitions**,
spilling them all.*

Britney   Biffer, you clot!

262   The Wonderful World of Dissocia

She sets about **Biffer** *with a kitchen implement. Absolute chaos.*

Lisa *gets up in disgust.*

Lisa   Right, I've had enough of this! I don't even know what I'm doing here! You're all completely mad, the lot of you – and not in a good way!

She storms off.

There is laughter and screaming until she has gone and then –

– everybody starts retching and spitting out the hot dogs.

Ticket   I think I'm going to vomit!

Laughter   That was awful!

Britney's *accent seems to have changed.*

Britney   Listen everybody, I know it wasn't easy. But on behalf of the Dissocian Government, I'd just like to thank you for your contribution to the War Effort. It may seem like a small thing but believe me – anything that helps us stop Lisa finding her hour is extremely valuable. So give yourselves a round of applause . . .

A half-hearted round.

What they don't see is that **Lisa** *has heard it all .*

Britney   As a token of our gratitude, each of you is to be inducted into the Order of the Pulled-Up Socks, for your bravery in the line of –

Lisa   What's going on?

They fall silent.

Argument   Oh dear . . .

Lisa   Anything you can do to stop me finding my hour . . . ?

They all look ashamed.

This was all a fake?

Britney   Lisa –

Lisa   You haven't lost your sense of humour – And you haven't lost the argument – You haven't even lost your inhibitions!

Pause.

Why would you do this? Why don't you want me to find my hour?

Pause. **Britney** *gropes for an answer.*

Britney   Biffer!

Ticket   Biffer will explain.

Argument   Yes, Biffer.

Biffer *takes a central position. He speaks only in sounds and strange words.* **Lisa** *looks to the others for help in understanding him.*

Biffer *speaks.*

Britney   An hour is a source of tremendous energy. It generates life and it generates death.

Lisa   Yes, I know all that . . .

Biffer *continues.*

Britney   Dissocia is the life your hour generated.

Biffer *continues.*

Inhibitions   Your hour is like the sun to us.

Biffer *continues.*

Laughter   And if you reabsorb your hour –

Biffer *continues.*

Argument   – Dissocia will sweat?

Britney   Die.

Argument   Dissocia will die.

Lisa *absorbs this.*

Lisa   Oh look – you can't put that on me. I mean, I'm sorry I lost my hour, but you can't hold me responsible for what it got up to on its holidays.

Inhibitions   We're only trying to protect you, Lisa.

Lisa   No – you're trying to protect yourselves! And I understand that. I don't want you all to be destroyed. But I've got a life too and it's out of balance. I've got people that I care about – that I love and that love me – and I'm letting them down.

Britney   Nobody loves you more than us, Lisa. Don't you remember?

They gather around her, hemming her in, softly singing:

All
   And now you are our friend we will
   Protect you to the end remember
   No one in the world above will
   Love you like the people of
   This wonderful new world –

Britney   No! Because if you loved me, you'd help me! I mean, Victor said there'd be people trying to mislead me. But I didn't think it'd be you!

Biffer *starts again.*

Britney   Your hour contained much good, Lisa . . .

Biffer *continues.*

Argument   But it also contained clogs.

Britney   Evil.

Argument   Evil.

Biffer *continues.*

Violinist   The Destroyer is the embodiment of that evil.

Laughter   We fight him here so that you don't have to.

Biffer *continues.*

Ticket   In return you let us live.

Laughter   That is the agreement.

Lisa   I didn't agree to anything.

Pause. **Biffer** *walks away.*

Lisa   Where's he going?

Britney   Biffer is disappointed. He's said all he has to say.

Pause.

Lisa   I have to find my hour. I'm sorry but I do.

All   We beg you to reconsider, Lisa.

Britney   The Judas Goat has already made you known to the Destroyer. He has your scent now.

Lisa   But why would he want me? What use am I to him?

Suddenly, there is a rumbling in the distance. They all freeze in fear.

Violinist   INCOMING!

In a panic, they all stuff their gags in their mouths, cover the tops of their heads and assume the safety position.

The wave hits.

But **Lisa** *is still standing, left exposed.*

The others are all in convulsions around her.

Lisa *crouches at first, but slowly stands.*

Eventually, the wave passes. Groaning with discomfort, the others rise.

They see that **Lisa** *has stood there unaffected. A murmur of wonderment ripples through them.*

Inhibitions   She didn't cover her head! Did you see that?

Argument   But she's still alive!

Violinist   How is that possible? How did you withstand the attack?

Lisa   I don't know. It wasn't so bad really.

Britney   It had no effect on you at all?

Lisa   I've got a bit of a headache.

More murmurs of wonderment.

Biffer *has reappeared, bleeding from his ears and eyes.*

Argument   Biffer – Biffer will know!

Violinist   Yes, Biffer –

Inhibitions   Biffer knows!

They all agree that **Biffer** *will know.*

Biffer *points at* **Lisa** *and speaks.*

Britney   There is only one who could withstand an attack unprotected – ?

Biffer *proclaims something else. And then he,* **Britney**, **Argument** *and the* **Violinist** *rush to worship at* **Lisa**'s *feet.*

Britney   All hail, Queen Sarah. You have returned to save us all!

All   ALL HAIL, QUEEN –

Suddenly, **Laughter** *kicks over one of the tables.*

Laughter   Be silent, you fools!

Argument   How dare you, sir! Don't you know –

A collective gasp of shock.

Laughter *and* **Ticket** *have torn off their clothes to reveal that they are wearing dungarees over billowing silk shirts.*

They both have swords and the hats we associate with the musketeers of old France.

Violinist   It's the Three Mungarees!

Laughter   That's right, you cowardly curs! Mungarees! Defenders of the Realm and the Queen's own protectors!

They both sing this rousing ditty:

You take the M from Musketeers
The Ungarees from Dungarees
Put them both together –
The Three Mungarees – Ho!

Britney   I thought you'd been disbanded.

Ticket   We had! And we would happily have stayed that way had you not brought ruin on us all!

Lisa   Listen, there must be some mistake. I'm not the Queen of anywhere. I've never even been here before today!

Ticket   There's no mistake, M'Lady. We'll explain later – if we live out the day.

*Ticket takes **Laughter** aside.*

Ticket   My friend – we must send for reinforcements!

Laughter   It's too late, my friend. The Queen has been made aware. The Destroyer will be upon us in minutes!

*The Dissocians bow down before **Lisa**.*

All   Queen Sarah, protect us from the Black Dog King!

Lisa   I can't protect you – tell them!

Ticket   It's true. It is we that must protect our Queen!

Laughter   Quickly, all of you – seize whatever weapons you can!

Inhibitions   We don't stand a chance!

Argument   We'll be slaughtered like buses! (*As previously, in 'the victim of a buse'.*)

Laughter   Nonsense! We shall prevail!

Ticket   No, no, don't lie to them. It's true: we will all die in agony and live out the afterlife in excruciating torment!

No one is terribly enthusiastic about this.

But let us not forget why it is that we live!

As the Dissocians listen to this, they hum the tune of 'Dissocia'.

We are strong!

Laughter   And yet we cower in fear!

Ticket   We have one purpose!

Laughter   And yet we fight amongst ourselves!

Ticket   We must remember what we are – citizens of Dissocia, every one! We were born from the very stuff of courage! If we do not fight – we are less than nothing!

Laughter   Now is the time – here and now – that we fulfil our destiny! Now is the time that we fight!

Ticket   For the honour of our Divine Queen Sarah – !

Laughter   And the greater good – of Dissocia!

Ticket   Are you with us?!

Pause. The Dissocians reply as one – 'Yes!'

And then, in the distance, the sound of the Black Dog's approaching army, and their familiar chant:

Army
Rivers of blood will vein the land!
Bones will twist inside the hand!
Children will boil in mothers' wombs!
Turning on lights will darken rooms!
And heavy skies will teem with flocks
Of tiny birds with human cocks!

The Dissocians swallow their fear.

Ticket   Arm yourselves as best you can and prepare for the charge.

The Dissocians gather up implements from the hot-dog stand – a pathetic array of weaponry.

Lisa   No, wait – I don't want you to die for me! Let me face the Black Dog King alone!

Laughter   It may yet come to that, M'Lady. But not until we have spilled Black Dog blood by the pint!

The Mungarees move to the front. The Dissocians form a defence around **Lisa**, *their Queen.*

Together they face the approaching army, the chant growing ever louder.

Laughter   Still – it's good to be back in action, my friend.

Ticket   Indeed. And with our Queen at our side!

Laughter   A Mungaree once more!

Ticket   A Mungaree once more!

They perform the sword salute of the Mungarees.

CHARGE!

And set off towards the enemy, swords aloft.

The Dissocians follow, all of them shouting.

Lisa *watches them disappear into battle.*

The sound is deafening now – the sound of battle – which soon becomes the sound of death, as the Dissocians are slain by the Black Dog army.

Lisa *watches helplessly, in fear and sorrow.*

The sound of the battle finally ceases, and a shadowy figure emerges from the carnage.

Lisa *backs away from him as he walks towards her – backs away until there is nowhere left to go.*

Finally, the Black Dog King steps into the light and **Lisa** *sees his face for the first time.*

It is a face she knows only too well. She shakes her head in horror and disbelief.

Lisa   Oh my God – it's you!

For a moment, the lighting suggests we are back in her flat.

Vince *reaches out – his hands touch her shoulders.*

Blackness.

Act Two

Notes

The whole point of Act Two is that it is the polar opposite of Act One. There should be no overt colour used in set design, costume or lighting. The only sound effects should be the sound of footsteps, which occur only before and after scenes in which Lisa is given medication, and at no other point. The only exception to these two stipulations is in the final scene. Whereas the acting in Act One is stylised, in Act Two the style should be as naturalistic as possible. Accordingly, much of the dialogue in this act – especially in the first scenes – is little more than a sound effect, and the actors should be encouraged to improvise these scenes, using the dialogue as a guideline only, in order to achieve the maximum realism. In the original production, the hospital room was enclosed in a box, the front of which was clear perspex. This necessitated the use of radio mikes for the actors' dialogue. This allowed them to act on a much more intimate scale and was very effective. The set was lit with fluorescent lighting which flickered on and off (in stark contrast to the more fluid style of the first act). This is all very expensive, however, and I know that it will be beyond the reach of most companies. I don't expect fidelity to this design concept; I only mention it in the hope you might honour its spirit as best you can. The stipulations of no colour/no sound will mean that the hospital room will not be an accurate representation of modern psychiatric centres, which tend to be quite colourful places. It is important to me, however, that this play does not seem biased against the notion of psychiatric treatment; on some level, such treatment is always about the suppression of individuality which already loads the dramatic dice somewhat. In light of this, I would ask directors/designers to be careful not to tip the dice even further. For example, it's important that the room has a window: to omit a window would hint at an unacceptably inhumane environment. Similarly, the actors should endow the nurses, staff and relatives with a basic warmth, despite actions that may read as cold and impersonal. The play will be more interesting for it.

One

Lights up.

A room in a psychiatric hospital.

Lisa *lies, asleep, in a hospital bed.*

The sound of footsteps approaching.

The door opens.

Nurse 1 *enters. Gently, she nudges* **Lisa** *awake. She helps* **Lisa**, *who is very drowsy, into a sitting position.*

She puts two pills in the palm of **Lisa**'s *hand and helps them to her mouth.*

She pours a glass of water and holds it to **Lisa**'s *mouth.*

Lisa *manages to swallow the pills.* **Nurse 1** *makes sure of this.*

Lisa *lies down again, goes back to sleep.*

Nurse 1 *covers her shoulder with the sheet, then leaves.*

The sound of her footsteps as she walks away, down the corridor.

Lights down.

Two

Lights up.

Lisa *is asleep.*

The sound of footsteps approaching.

Nurse 2 *enters.*

Gently, he nudges **Lisa** *awake.*

Nurse 2 *helps her into a sitting position, gives her some pills and some water to wash them down with.*

Lisa *lies down again, goes back to sleep.*

Nurse 2 *covers her shoulder with the sheet, then leaves.*

The sound of his footsteps as he walks away.

Lights down.

Three

Lisa *is slumped in bed, awake.*

Decisively, she gets up, gathers her belongings and leaves the room.

Pause.

The sound of muffled voices.

She re-enters, ushered in by **Nurse 3**.

Lisa   I just want to use the phone –

Nurse 3   That's fine, you can use the phone.

Lisa   I've got a right to use the phone.

Nurse 3   Right, well, you leave your stuff here and I'll take you to the phone, fair enough?

Pause. Reluctantly, **Lisa** *hands over her armful of belongings.*

Lisa   And I want to have a cigarette.

Nurse 3   Do you smoke?

Pause.

Lisa   Sometimes.

Pause.

Look, I don't need this, I'm fine now. I'd be better off at home –

Nurse 3   You'll be home soon enough.

Lisa   But it's not doing me any good here, I'd feel much better at home, you know – with all my things around me . . .

Nurse 3   Why don't you get back into bed?

Lisa   I don't want to go back to bed! I'm fine now, I'm ready, I'll take my medication, I swear – !

Nurse 3   Come on, back to bed.

Reluctantly, **Lisa** *gets back in.* **Nurse 3** *puts her belongings back where they came from.*

Nurse 3   That's a girl. Listen – as soon as you're better, you'll be turfed out, believe me. We need the beds.

Lisa *sulks.*

Nurse 3   Now don't be creeping around cos I'll be watching.

She exits.

Lisa *fumes for a while, then tears get the better of her.*

She puts the pillow over her head.

Lights down.

Four

Lights up.

Lisa *is asleep. The pillow is on the floor.*

The sound of footsteps.

Nurse 1 *enters and jostles her awake.*

She helps **Lisa** *into a sitting position and administers medication.*

Lisa *goes back to sleep.*

Lights down.

Five

Lights up.

The sound of footsteps.

Lisa *lies in bed, slumped but awake. She looks hostile.*

Nurse 2 *enters.*

Nurse 2   Hi there.

He empties some pills into **Lisa**'s *hand and pours her a glass of water.*

Here we go.

Resentfully, she takes the pills.

Nurse 2 *exits.*

Lisa *puts her Walkman on.*

She listens.

The tinny sound of music, which we might just be able to recognise as the punky music from the flying car sequence in Act One.

She nods her head.

Lights down.

Six

The sound of **Lisa** *singing raucously.*

Lights up.

Lisa *is dancing manically around the room, on the bed, everywhere, Walkman in her hand.*

Nurse 1 *enters accompanied by* **Nurse 3**, *and attempts to take the Walkman away from* **Lisa**, *who resists.*

Lisa   No!

Nurse 3 *restrains her, with as little contact as possible, and manages to get the Walkman. She wraps the headphone cable around it.*

Lisa   What are you doing?

Nurse 1   You're supposed to be resting, Lisa.

Lisa   You can't take that, it's mine!

Nurse 1   You can have it back when you've calmed down.

Lisa   Right, I'm calm, I'm totally calm, see? I was just dancing, but now I'm totally calm, so you can give it back to me.

Nurse 1   Later.

Lisa   No, listen, you don't understand – I need it, I really need it –

Nurse 1   You'll get it back when you've calmed down.

Lisa   Give it back to me, you fucking cow!

Nurse 1 *exits, followed by* **Nurse 3**.

Lisa   Give it fucking back !

Pause.

Like a petulant child, **Lisa** *continues to dance and sing, but soon she is tired out, and she crumples to the floor, in tears.*

Lights down.

Seven

Lights up.

Lisa *is asleep on the floor, where she fell.*

The sound of footsteps.

Nurse 3 *enters, helps her up.*

Nurse 3   Oh dear, come on – up we get.

Nurse 3 *helps a compliant* **Lisa** *up into the bed.*

Lisa *adopts a sleeping position immediately, but* **Nurse 3** *interrupts her, sitting her up and giving* **Lisa** *her medication, which she takes obediently.*

Lisa *lies down again.*

Nurse 3 *exits.*

The sound of footsteps as he walks away.

Lights down.

Eight

Lights up.

Lisa *sits in bed, waiting.*

The door opens and a doctor enters.

Dr Clark   Lisa? I'm Dr Clark.

She shakes **Dr Clark***'s hand.*

Lisa   I've actually got a doctor.

Dr Clark   Dr Spence, I know. But you'll be seeing me for a while if that's all right?

Pause.

He sits down and opens her notes.

So – you've been having a bit of a time, haven't you?

Pause.

Lights down.

Nine

Lights up.

Lisa *is in bed, reading – but the movement of her feet beneath the sheets betrays her lack of concentration. She has to keep turning the page back and starting again.*

Nurse 2 *enters.*

Nurse 2   Hello again.

He empties the pills into **Lisa**'s *hand and pours her a glass of water.*

Lisa *stares at them.*

Lisa   Are these the same ones as before?

Nurse 2   Before when?

Lisa   It's just I asked Dr Clark about some other pills. He said he'd see if there was anything less heavy.

Pause.

Nurse 2   These are what it says on your sheet.

Lisa   Yes, but he said he'd try find something lighter because these ones make me feel really dopey?

Nurse 2 *(nods)*   Right . . .

Pause.

But these are what it says on the sheet.

Pause.

Lisa *takes them.*

Nurse 2 *points at* **Lisa**'s *book.*

Nurse 2   What's that like?

Lisa   I don't know. I can't focus on it, on the words.

Nurse 2   Oh, right . . .

Lisa   That's another thing about them.

Nurse 2   Yeah – oh well; heard it's not that good anyway. Just wait for the film, maybe. Bye then.

Nurse 2 *exits.*

It's an insensitive comment but, for the first time in this act, **Lisa** *smiles.*

Lights down.

Ten

Lisa *is asleep.*

The door of **Lisa**'s *room has a window in it, so nurses can look in.*

The curtain pulls back and **Nurse 1** *does exactly this.*

All is well. **Nurse 1** *continues with her rounds, leaving the curtain drawn.*

Eleven

Lisa's *sister,* **Dot**, *sits in the chair by her bed.*

Dot   The thing is, in the end of the day, it's just selfishness, Lisa, it really is.

Lisa *is slumped in bed, feeling a bit nauseous.*

Dot   You know what happened to Auntie Liz. You want to end up like that? How d'you think that'd make Mum feel?

Pause.

I mean, do you want everyone to think you're some sort of nutcase? I know you're not but that's what people think and you can't blame them.

Pause.

I mean, I can help you out now and then but I've got a mortgage to pay.

Pause.

And meanwhile, you're out there merrily buying shoes and handbags and things you'll never use –

Pause.

I've tried being nice. I've tried everything.

Pause.

A few pills, twice a day, that's all you've got to manage. I take four myself and they're only vitamins; I don't end up scribbling on the walls if I miss a day, but I still manage to take them.

Pause.

And if you don't care enough about yourself, then at least do it for Mum or for Mark or for me.

Lisa   Dot, I'm sorry but I'm really feeling sick . . .

Dot   You haven't heard a thing I've said, have you ?

Lisa   No, I have, I just – need to rest now.

Angrily, **Dot** *gets up.*

Dot   Yeah well – I know how you feel .

She exits.

Lights down.

Twelve

Lights up.

Lisa *looks down at the Walkman in her hand.*

She puts the headphones on, presses play.

The same tinny music.

But this time, there is no movement.

She just listens.

Lights down.

Thirteen

Lights up.

Lisa *sits up in bed, reading.*

She seems more concentrated now.

The door opens and a doctor comes in, holding **Lisa***'s notes.*

Dr Faraday   Sorry about the wait – Lisa, is it?

She sits up. He offers his hand, which she shakes.

Dr Faraday   Dr Faraday. But call me Peter.

Pause.

Lisa   What happened to Dr Clark?

Lights snap out.

Fourteen

Lights up.

Lisa *is reading. She's almost finished her book.*

The sound of footsteps approaching.

She marks her place in the book, puts it down on the bedside cabinet.

She pours herself some water.

Nurse 1 *enters.*

Nurse 1   Hi there.

Lisa   Hello.

Nurse 1 *hands the pill container to* **Lisa***, then goes to draw the curtains.*

Lisa *takes her pills.*

Nurse 1   Lovely weather out there.

Lisa   Yes, I was out for a while.

Nurse 1   Indian summer.

Lisa   Yeah. Probably be pissing down by the weekend.

Nurse 1   Well – as long as it doesn't rain on Thursday.

Lisa   What's happening Thursday?

Nurse 1   Friend of mine's getting married.

Lisa   Oh, that's nice.

Nurse 1   Yes, well – good excuse for a party, isn't it?

Lisa   Yeah. Well – don't get *too* drunk.

Nurse 1   I'll try. All right then –

Lisa   See you then.

Nurse 1 *exits.*

Lisa *looks at the sunlight pouring through the window.*

She sighs.

Lights down.

Fifteen

Lights up.

Lisa *is sitting, fully upright, in bed.*

She looks at herself in a compact mirror, adjusts her hair, puts the mirror away.

She takes a deep breath.

Vince *enters. He's carrying a plastic bag full of things.*

He hugs her, but there's a lack of affection in it.

He sits in the chair.

Vince   How are you?

Lisa   Fine. Good, actually.

Vince   Good.

Pause.

Lisa   How's work?

Vince   Oh, you know – hectic. Same as ever.

Pause.

I'm sorry I couldn't get away –

Lisa   It's fine.

Pause.

Vince   I mean, I probably could've but –

Lisa   Honestly, it's fine. I don't want you to mess up your work because of me. I feel bad enough as it is.

Pause.

Vince   You don't have to feel bad.

Pause.

But you're feeling better now?

Lisa   Much.

Vince   Good.

Pause.

Lisa   Roll on Sunday is all.

He nods, smiling humourlessly. Pause.

Simultaneously:

Vince   Lisa, I –

Lisa   Vince, I –

Pause.

Lisa   You first.

Vince   No – you.

Pause.

Lisa   I just want to say that I'm sorry for all the trouble I've caused. I don't mean to. I just . . .

He nods. Pause.

Vince   But it's difficult, you know – ?

Lisa (*nods*)   I know.

Vince   I mean, you say you don't mean to. But you know what happens when you come off the medication. This happens. Sooner or later you end up here.

Lisa (*nods*)   I know.

Vince   Yeah, but it's not *enough* to say that you know! I mean, why – ?

Pause.

I thought you wanted to get better.

Lisa   I *do* want to get better.

Vince   Well, yes, you say that but then you don't take your *medication* –

Lisa *sighs heavily.*

Vince   Yeah, well, you can fucking sigh, but what can I do? All I can do is nag you to take the fucking pills and then you resent me for nagging you, I just –

Pause.

I don't know if I can do this any more, I really don't –

Lisa   Vince – I'm really going to try –

Vince   You say that / *every* time!

Lisa   I know! I know I do, but you don't understand –

Vince   That's not my fault! It's not my fault that I don't understand!

Lisa   I'm not saying / it is –

Vince   I mean, I've got a message from you on my phone. Do you want to hear it?

He takes out his mobile phone and pushes it at her.

She doesn't want to hear.

Because it's just nonsense. You're just, you're saying – nonsense!

Pause.

Lisa   So what are you saying? You want to leave me?

Vince   *Leave* you . . .

Lisa   Split up with me.

Long pause.

What it is: it's like the Sirens.

Pause.

Vince   The Sirens?

Lisa   You know. They sit on the rocks and they sing to the sailors. And what they sing is so lovely it's like . . . they're hypnotised. They know if they sail to them their ship's going to get all smashed up. But they think it's worth it, you know – for the song.

Long pause.

Vince   I should go.

Pause. She nods.

Got to finish this proposal. Here's your stuff.

He hands her the plastic bag. She nods her thanks.

Pause.

Lisa   Will you come for me on Sunday?

Pause.

Or should I make other plans?

Pause.

Vince   That thing you said. About the Sirens.

Pause.

I understand that.

Pause.

I'll see you Sunday.

He exits.

Pause.

Lisa *lifts things out of the plastic bag: a jumper, another book, some bills from home.*

Then she sees something at the bottom of the bag.

She smiles affectionately.

Lights down.

Sixteen

Night. **Lisa** *is asleep. She looks at peace. In her arms she holds a small polar bear.*

We hear music at last.

Coloured lights play on her face, swirling around her head.

Dissocia still exists, caged within her head.

There is little doubt that she will return to her kingdom.

The music ends.

Lights down.

Realism

For Amy

Realism was first performed on 14 August 2006 by the
National Theatre of Scotland at the Royal Lyceum Theatre,
Edinburgh, as part of the Edinburgh International Festival.
The cast was as follows:

Paul; Galloway,	
Independent Politician;	
Minstrel, Bystander	Paul Blair
Angie, Presenter, Bystander	Louise Ludgate
Laura, Right-Wing Politician	Shauna Macdonald
Stuart McQuarrie	Stuart McQuarrie
Father, Pundit, Simon, Minstrel	Sandy Neilson
Mother; Left-Wing Politician	Jan Pearson
Mullet, Minstrel	Matthew Pidgeon

Director Anthony Neilson
Designer Miriam Buether
Lighting Designer Chahine Yavroyan
Sound Designer/Composer Nick Powell

Notes

While the dialogue in this play is largely my own, the material herein was hugely influenced by the suggestions, criticisms and improvisations of the actors and creative team, whose names are listed in the text.

As ever, what follows is a record of a show that was presented in 2006. Elements of the sound or production design may be described, but should only be taken into account; they represent no stipulation on my part (except where indicated).

The play contains references to topical events, localised matters and personal issues that may limit its relevance in other territories or times. Where possible, I have attempted to explain the dramatic relevance of these moments so that the imaginative translator may find a way to adapt them.

Though *Realism* is divided into acts, it should be presented without an interval.

Please note that though there are several phone conversations during the play, at no point should a phone ever be present (or represented) onstage.

THE SET

In the original production, the stage was raked from front to back with a slight imbalance upstage left.

All the elements of a normal home were present. From front of stage to back: a sofa, a fridge with work surface, a washing machine, a toilet, a bed, a dining table and chairs, an armchair, etc. Various practical lights (both standing and hanging) were also arranged around the set.

However, the stage itself was covered with several tons of off-white sand. All of the aforementioned furniture was cut off to varying degrees (and at varying angles) so as to appear 'sunk' into this sand. The television was placed at the very front of the stage, seeming almost completely submerged, allowing only enough space to use it as a lighting source for the sofa.

The walls on all three sides consisted of large pillars, grey and textured, which hinted at concrete. Actors entered and exited between them.

PRE-SHOW

As the audience arrived, we played a medley of UK traditional tunes which was famously (until 2006) used as the opening music for BBC Radio 4. It not only set the play's beginning firmly in the morning; it also inspired a spirit of joviality, which I would recommend – as *Realism* is, to all intents and purposes, a comedy. If you have any kind of equivalent – a light tune that your audience finds synonymous with morning – I would respectfully suggest that you consider its use.

'Breakdowns' are presented in square brackets at the scene beginnings. These describe what is actually occurring in the play's 'real' time-line. I wrote them for my own benefit and present them for your interest only. You may prefer not to read them, and experience the show in the same vague sense of confusion that the audience did.

Characters

Stuart
Paul
Mother
Father
Mullet
Angie
Presenter
Pundit
Right-Wing Politician
Left-Wing Politician
Independent Politician
Audience Member
Laura
Minstrel 1
Minstrel 2
Minstrel 3
Simon
Cat
Bystanders

Act One: Morning

One

[*In which . . .* **Stuart** *gets a phone call from his friend* **Paul***.* **Paul** *wants him to come and play football.* **Stuart** *declines the offer. He puts out some food for the cat. He remembers a dream he had the previous night. He goes back to bed.*]

Stuart *sits on the couch, in his bedclothes. He has one hand down his pants, absent-mindedly squeezing himself – it is not a sexual gesture. He looks very tired.*

Paul, *wearing a suit, is looking in the fridge. (Note: at no point in the following scene do the actors make eye contact.)*

Paul   Did I wake you?

Stuart   No, not really.

Paul   Not really?

Stuart   I was awake.

Paul   Were you still in bed?

Stuart *smells his fingers.*

Stuart   Yeah, well, it's Saturday morning so . . .

Paul   So I woke you up. I'm sorry.

Pause.

Stuart   What's going on?

Paul   Were you out last night?

Stuart   For a while.

He tries to look at a birthmark on his shoulder. It's itching.

Paul   D'you get pissed?

Stuart   A bit.

Paul   A bit?

Stuart   Paul – I've not even had a cup of tea –

Paul   I was just wondering what you're up to. You playing fives later?

He starts dribbling a football back and forward.

Stuart   I don't know. I don't think so.

Paul   You've got to.

Stuart   Why have I got to?

Paul   We're already a man down.

Stuart   I don't think I can.

Paul   Why not?

Stuart   I just – I don't really feel like it.

Pause.

Paul   What do you feel like, then?

Stuart   What?

Paul   What do you feel like doing?

Stuart   Not much.

Paul   Aw, come on – come and play footie. We'll have a few pints.

For the first time we see **Paul** *from the front. His shirt is half open and his suit jacket has vomit down it.*

Stuart   I really don't feel like it.

Paul   So what are you going to do? Just mope about your flat all day?

Stuart   I've got stuff to do.

Paul   Like what?

Stuart   Just boring things.

Paul   Like what?

Stuart   For fuck's sake . . .

Paul   I'm just asking.

Stuart   Like washing, cleaning up – domestic shit.

Paul   You can do that tomorrow.

Stuart   I can't.

Paul   Why not?

Stuart   Cos I just – I haven't got any clean clothes . . . I just need to get myself together.

Paul *crosses to the couch and sits beside* **Stuart***.*

Paul   I could come over after. Get a few cans in. Get a DVD out.

He instantly falls asleep. During the next exchange, he nods in and out of consciousness.

Stuart   Paul, I really – I just want to do nothing.

Paul   You want to do nothing?

Stuart   Yeah, I just –

Paul   We don't have to do anything. We can just kiss and cuddle a bit; there's no pressure.

Stuart   That's tempting.

Pause.

No, really, I just – I said to myself I was just going to do nothing today. It's been a fucking hellish week at work and I'm just knackered; just want to chill out.

Paul   What good – do you?

Stuart   Eh?

Paul   That going to – ?

Pause. Annoyed, **Stuart** *stands. Damned reception.*

Stuart   Fucking things.

Paul   I said what good's it going to do you, moping about your flat all day?

Stuart   I'm not going to be moping.

Paul   You are – you're going to mope.

Stuart   I'm not going to mope.

Paul   Mope, mope, mope; that'll be you.

Stuart   Right, well, so if I want to mope I can fucking mope, can't I? I mean, I'm not planning on moping but I reserve the right to mope in my own fucking house.

Paul   All right, all right; calm down, calm down. I just don't want you getting all depressed.

Stuart   I'm not, I'm fine.

Paul   All right.

Stuart   Just want to spend a bit of time on my own.

Paul   Fair enough.

He staggers to his feet.

Will I give you – tomorrow?

Stuart   Will you give me tomorrow?

Paul (*louder*)   Will I give you a *shout* tomorrow?

Stuart   Yeah, give me a shout tomorrow.

Paul   If you change your mind –

Stuart   I'll give you a bell.

Paul   Give us a bell. We'll be in the Duck's Arse from about five.

Stuart   All right, cheers.

Paul *exits.*

Pause. **Stuart** *yawns.*

Stuart *goes to the fridge, opens it. He takes out a tin of cat food and prises back the lid. He fills a bowl with food. Some of it drops onto the floor. At the top of his voice he shouts:*

Here, kitty kitty kitty kitty!

He considers staying awake, but then walks back towards his bedroom.

On the way, his **Mother** *appears. He stops.*

Mother   Have you seen the sky?

Stuart   What do you mean?

Mother   It's full of bombers.

Stuart   Where from?

Mother   Israel? [*At the time of writing, in 2006, Israel had invaded Lebanon. Substitute a more topical/timeless reference if necessary.*]

Pause. **Stuart** *continues on his way.*

Mother *takes a seat at the dining table.*

Stuart *climbs back into bed.*

Lights fade. Music – during which **Father** *enters, carrying a morning paper. He takes a seat at the dining table, handing part of the paper to* **Mother**. *They read.*

Two

[**Stuart** *gets up again. He remembers another fragment of a dream. He makes himself a cup of tea, and gets a mild electric shock from the toaster. Feeling bad about himself, he attempts to exercise but ends up pretending to be a rabbit. He remembers a friend chasing him with a shit-covered stick. The same friend got him to taste a crayon, which was horrible. He watches a news report about the Middle East crisis.*]

Stuart *wakes up with cramp. He hits the side of his leg. The pain passes. Pause.*

Paul *enters behind* **Stuart***, carrying a huge carrot.* **Stuart** *doesn't see him.*

Paul   Stuart.

Stuart   What?

Paul   That fucking squirrel's back.

Stuart   What does he want?

Paul   He wants his guts back in.

Stuart   That'll cost a fortune.

Paul   Yeah, but Angie'll pay for it. She's on her way out.

Paul *sits in the armchair.*

Stuart *gets up and collects a cup from the cupboard.*

Father   Stuart, don't bother me.

On his way to the fridge, **Stuart** *looks inside the cup, checking that it's clean. He turns on the electric kettle.*

Mother   Can you see it? There – a castle, look. The tea leaves make a turret, and the tea's like a moat at the bottom.

Stuart   What's a moat?

Mother   It's the water round a castle, to keep the folk from getting in.

Simultaneously, **Mother** *and* **Stuart** *sing a fairly buoyant, very British wartime song – the sort of song a mother used to sing:*

I like a nice cup of tea in the morning,
I like a nice cup of tea with my tea . . .

But **Mother***'s voice fades away, leaving* **Stuart** *groping for the lyrics. A sound arrives, punching into him the realisation of her absence.*

Stuart *takes a moment to recover, then puts the cup down. He looks at the jars in front of him.*

Stuart   Coffee – tea? Tea – coffee?

Stuart *opens a box of tea bags. He drops a tea bag into the cup.*

He opens the fridge.

He takes out a packet of bread. He snaps off two pieces and pushes them into the toaster. He takes some milk out of the fridge. He smells the milk.

The sound of children playing

The sound of the water boiling in the kettle becomes the sound of horses galloping. It reaches a crescendo . . . then stops.

He pours the hot water into the mug.

Smoke is beginning to rise from the toaster. The bread is trapped in there.

Stuart *tries to get the toaster to eject the toast but it isn't working. He's beginning to panic.*

Mullet *appears behind the couch. He looks like a child from the seventies. He is hyperactive and extremely irritating.*

Mullet (*in an annoying sing-song voice*)   Stewpot! Stewpot! Stewpot! [*This is what many children called Stuart were nicknamed in the seventies.*]

Stuart   For fuck's sake, what?!

Mullet   The toast's burning!

Stuart   I know! I can't get it out.

Mullet   Use a knife!

Stuart   I'll get electrocuted.

Mullet   You won't.

Panicked, **Stuart** *runs to the cutlery drawer and runs back to the toaster.*

He plunges the knife into the toaster and is immediately thrown on to his back by the resulting shock. **Mullet** *finds this hilarious.*

Mullet (*gleeful*)   You fucking knob!

Angrily, **Stuart** *smacks the toaster off the surface.*

Mullet   That was a fucking beauty!

Stuart   My heart's going like the clappers!

Pause.

Fucking hell.

He picks up the toaster and the burnt toast. He takes a knife to the toast and starts to scrape off the burnt bits.

Angie *appears behind him, wearing a dressing gown. She stops, annoyed.*

Angie   Why do you do that?

Stuart   What?

Angie   Scrape the fucking toast into the sink?

Stuart   I don't like burnt toast.

Angie   So scrape it into the fucking bin! It just clogs the sink up. And then you smear it on the side of the Flora [*a type of margarine*]. You're a dirty bastard.

She continues across the stage.

Stuart   I thought you were going to call me?

She exits.

Pause. **Stuart** *throws the toast into the pedal bin.*

He walks over to the sofa, sits down.

Stuart   I've broke out in a sweat from that shock.

Mullet   That was a beauty. You went fucking flying!

Stuart *tries to look at his mole.*

Mullet   What's wrong?

Stuart   That birthmark's itching.

Mullet   Let's see.

He takes a look at it.

I'm not joking, man; that's cancer.

Stuart   It's not cancer. I'm too young to have cancer.

Mullet   You're joking, aren't you? Fucking Kylie's got cancer – look how young she is! If someone with all that money and an arse like that can get cancer, you think you can't? What else is wrong with you?

Stuart   My left eye's still funny.

Mullet   That's diabetes.

Stuart   It's not diabetes!

He goes to the mirror, distressed. Behind him, **Mullet** *makes faces and rude signs.*

Mullet   Why not? Your uncle had it.

Stuart   Doesn't mean I've got it.

Mullet   So why are you thirsty all the time?

Stuart   Am I thirsty all the time?

He thinks about it.

I'm thirsty a lot of the time. And I keep getting cramp. Is that diabetes?

Mullet (*mimics*)   'Is that diabetes?' You're such a fucking jessie.

Stuart   Fuck you.

Mullet   What's happened to you, man? You were going to be a choo-choo driver. You were going to be an astronaut. What's happened to that guy? What's happened to the guy who was going to build a rocket and fly to fucking Mars? I mean, look at yourself. What do you see?

Pause.

Stuart   A fat fucking shite.

Mullet   A fat fucking shite. And how do you feel?

Stuart   Like shite.

Mullet   Like shite. And what are you going to do about it?

Stuart   Fuck all.

Mullet   You're going to do fuck all. You could have gone out to play footie but you're going to sit around the house all day moping and why? Because of a girl! Because you're waiting for a girl to call you!

Stuart   I can't help it. I love her.

Mullet (*mimics*)   'I loooove her'! So why did you dump her then?

Stuart   I didn't.

Mullet   You did. You dumped her because she had horrible, wobbly thighs and a wonky fucking nose.

Stuart   Shut your stupid face.

Mullet   It's true.

Stuart   It's not!

Pause.

Mullet   Hey, Stu – do that thing with your pants!

Pause. **Stuart** *pulls his pants up over his belly. Cranking one arm, he lets his belly extend to its full size, as if pumping it up. Then he removes an imaginary cork from his belly and lets it deflate.*

Mullet   *That* – is fucking *genius*.

Stuart   I'm a fat sack of shit.

Mullet   So what? So's Tony Soprano and he gets shags. And you know why? Because only poofs care what they look like. And women know that.

Stuart *gets on to the floor.*

Mullet   What are you doing? Are you going to do press-ups? Only wanks do press-ups.

Stuart *starts doing press-ups.*

Stuart   I'm not listening to you.

Mullet *gets down beside him and moves and talks in rhythm with* **Stuart**'s *increasingly laboured exercises.*

Mullet   Good. So you won't hear me say how *boring* they are, and what a *poof* you are, and how *boring* they are, and what a *wank* you are, and how boring they are, and how *fat* you are, and what a *weakling* you are –

Stuart *gives up, knackered and exasperated, and strangely amused.*

Mullet   How many was that?

Stuart   Four. (*Or however many he managed.*)

Mullet *derides him.*

Mullet   Four! You only managed four?!

Stuart   I'm going to build them up over time.

He stands up and starts to jump up and down, on the spot.

Mullet   Look at you now! You look like a fucking rabbit!

Stuart   Do I?

Mullet (*excited*)   Do this – Stu – do this.

Hopping alongside **Stuart**, **Mullet** *makes paws with his hands and sticks his teeth out.*

Mullet   Like a rabbit!

Stuart *does it.*

Mullet   Are you hungry, rabbit?

Stuart *nods.*

Mullet   You want some carrots?

Stuart *nods.*

Mullet   Say, 'I want some carrots, Mr Farmer.'

Stuart　'I want some carrots, Mr Farmer.'

Mullet *offers his crayons.*

Mullet　Right – Imagine these are carrots! Come and get the carrots.

Stuart *follows after* **Mullet**.

Mullet　No, but you have to hop.

Stuart *hops after him.*

Mullet　That's it – come and get the carrots, Thumper!

Stuart *reaches him but* **Mullet** *suddenly produces a stick.*

Stuart　What's that?

Mullet　It's a stick!

Stuart　What's on the end of it?

Mullet　Keich! [*Scottish slang for shit.*]

Stuart　Fuck off – is it?

Mullet　Smell it.

Tentatively **Stuart** *does – he gags.*

Stuart　Aw, fuck off!

Grinning, **Mullet** *chases after him.*

Stuart　Fuck off! Fuck off, ya dirty bastard!

They run around laughing, and occasionally gagging.

Mullet *whoops like a Red Indian and suddenly lots of others appear, as if in a playground. He chases them all around and for a moment the stage is full of noise and activity. One by one they claim sanctuary by the walls. Finally, out of breath,* **Stuart** *is cornered.*

Stuart　Put that down.

Mullet　Why?

Stuart　*(gags)* Just put it down. I'm telling you.

Mullet　Telling me what?

Stuart   Telling you to put it down.

Mullet *thrusts the shitty stick at him.*

Stuart   You better fucking not – I'm telling you.

Mullet   You want the carrots? Are you going to hop to the carrots?

Stuart   I'll hop to the carrots if you put it down.

Pause. **Mullet** *puts the stick down.*

Stuart *advances a little.* **Mullet** *quickly picks the stick up and thrusts it at him again.*

Stuart   Put the fucking thing down!

Mullet   All right, all right – I'm putting it down.

He puts it down, then throws the orange crayons.

Hop to the carrots, rabbit.

Stuart *hops over to the carrots.*

Mullet   Eat one.

Pause. **Stuart** *eats the end of one. He spits it out in disgust.*

Stuart   That's fucking awful!

The game's over – **Stuart** *sits on the couch.*

Mullet   Stewpot! Stuart! Stuart.

Stuart *ignores him.*

He picks up his tea and sips it. He turns the TV on – its light plays on his face.

Dejected, **Mullet** *gathers up his things and leaves, dragging his stick behind him.*

The sounds of war.

Behind him, people run screaming as if under heavy fire, taking shelter behind the appliances.

Oblivious to them, **Stuart** *crosses to the fridge and fixes himself a bowl of cereal.*

He arrives back at the couch as the same time as the others, who assemble themselves around him.

Three

[**Stuart** *gets annoyed by a radio discussion show in which the guests all seem to be in favour of the smoking ban (introduced in Scotland in 2006). a pirate radio station interferes with the reception. He imagines himself a member of the panel. He considers how to get* **Angie** *to call him.*]

Pundit   The simple fact is that this is a blight on our society and a drain on the already stretched resources of the Health Service; and if the pitiful souls that participate in it do not have either the ability or the moral fibre to control themselves, then it's actually our societal *duty* to make sure they can do as little harm to others as possible.

Applause.

Presenter   Remind me what your party's position on the ban is, Right-Wing Politician McDonald?

Right-Wing Politician   My party's position –

Left-Wing Politician   I don't think the Conservatives have a position.

A spattering of laughter and applause from the audience. **Stuart**, *sandwiched between them, continues to eat his breakfast.*

Right-Wing Politician   No, actually, our position is that we're broadly in favour of the ban –

Left-Wing Politician   Broadly.

Right-Wing Politician   But that we argued for certain exemptions, such as private clubs.

Left-Wing Politician   Conservative clubs by any chance?

Some laughter.

Presenter   And what's your personal view?

Right-Wing Politician   My personal view –

Presenter   Given that the question was whether the current smoking ban is an infringement of civil liberties.

Right-Wing Politician   Right, well – it obviously is an infringement on the civil liberties of smokers –

The sound of a pirate radio station cuts in – booming dance music.

Stuart   Oh fuck –

In unison, the panel members all get up and crab-walk across the stage, stopping here and there, until, finally, the reception returns.

Right-Wing Politician   But is their right to smoke more important than the rights of those who don't?

And then cautiously – so as not to lose reception – they back on to the couch, as one.

Independent Politician   So it's a question of whose rights are more important?

Right-Wing Politician   Exactly.

Independent Politician   Which is exactly the Labour Party's position.

Right-Wing Politician   I was asked what *my* opinion was.

Pundit   A more important question is why should the general public have to pay billions of pounds a year to help cure these wretched individuals of their self-inflicted ailments?

Applause.

Stuart   I'm sorry but the hypocrisy here is absolutely stunning. I mean, they've banned smoking at bus stops!

Pundit   I should think so.

Stuart   All right, well, tell me this: if cigarettes are *so toxic* that it's dangerous even to *stand near a smoker at a bus-stop* . . . why are we selling them at all? Why not ban them altogether?

Presenter   That's a good point, isn't it, Jan Pearson? Why not ban them altogether?

Left-Wing Politician   Well, that really *would* be an infringement on civil liberties –

Stuart   Oh, what bollocks! If you were concerned about civil liberties you wouldn't have banned the right to demonstrate outside Parliament!

A solitary cheer from the audience.

Thank you. I mean, let's say we suddenly found out that fucking – Pot Noodle – was so horrendously poisonous – that just being in the same *building* as someone eating it was potentially fatal: are you saying we'd keep it on the shelves?

Left-Wing Politician   A slightly different thing.

Stuart   Yes, it is, and we all know why; because the government isn't making £3.50 worth of taxes on every Pot Noodle sold!

Some applause. He gets up and crosses to the fridge to get more milk for his cereal.

All I'm saying is, make your minds up: if smoking's legal, then let people do it. Let the pubs and the restaurants and the workplaces decide whether they allow it or not. But if it's as dangerous as you say it is – and you're genuinely concerned about the health of the nation – then have the guts to ban it outright . . .

Applause. Warming to his theme (and still eating his cereal):

. . . but you won't, will you? because you don't want everyone to suddenly stop smoking. Because if everyone stopped smoking, they'd have to raise income tax by about two pence in the pound; and the people that'd shout loudest

about it are the same wankers that are shouting about
having to pay smokers' health bills.

Hitting his stride now, he adopts the manner of a lawyer.

You see, what we have in the smoking ban is an unholy
alliance between –

*He stands in the spilled cat food. Disgusted, he scrapes it off his bare
foot while continuing:*

What we have in the smoking ban is an unholy alliance
between the hypocritical and the sanctimonious. On the one
hand, we've got a government who want the nation to get
healthier, but not so suddenly that it jeopardises their
chances of re-election. And on the other hand, we've got a
society – a post-Thatcherite society – that is so fractured
and dysfunctional that the only way a semblance of unity
can be preserved is to feed it a constant stream of state-
approved scapegoats for us to mutually fear or disdain.

Now to the audience:

In summing up, I can put it no better than the famous poem
written by some Jewish guy or possibly a German:

> When they came for the gays
> I did not speak out
> Because I was not . . . a gayboy. Or something.
>
> When they came for the fox-hunters
> I did not speak out,
> Because I was not a toffee-nosed twat on a horse,
>   with a little trumpet.
>
> When they came for the smokers
> I did not speak out –
> Because I was not a yellow-fingered ashtray weasel.
>
> But then they came for me.
> And there was no one left to speak out.

And with this, **Stuart** *passes his empty cereal bowl to the* **Right-
Wing Politician** *and makes his way to the bed.*

A stunned pause and then, one by one, the panellists begin to clap, and the audience begins to clap, and then the panellists stand, and so does the audience. The response is tumultuous.

Right-Wing Politician   Who was that man?

Pundit   I don't know, but he's turned my head around, I'll tell you that!

Independent Politician   He's turned everyone's head around!

The **Presenter** *attempts to get the audience to calm down.*

Presenter   All right, thank you, ladies and gentlemen, can we – ?

But now there is a thumping of chairs.

No please – please put down the furniture –

At this point, someone from the audience rushes up to the stage and throws a chair at the **Presenter**.

Audience Member   Fascist bastards!

The chair just misses her. The **Audience Member** *runs out of the doors.*

Presenter   Ladies and gentlemen, please stay calm! Please, no smoking, please – please don't light those – don't light that cigarette!

Smoke begins to curl onto the stage. The panellists begin to cough and splutter.

(*To panellists.*) I think we should go. (*To the audience.*) Ladies and gentlemen – listeners at home – I'm afraid we have no choice but to abandon this week's *Any Questions* due to a stunningly lucid intervention from a member of the public!

Left-Wing Politician (*into mobile*)   Get me the Prime Minister. (*Pause.*) I don't care about that – get him on the phone right now!

Pundit   Keep to the floor where there's air!

They drop to the floor and start to crawl away, a riot occurring in the audience.

Presenter   Next week we'll be in Stevenage – so if you want tickets for that visit our website or call us on 0800-777-444 –

A fireman enters (the actor playing **Mullet***), his torchlight casting a beam through the smoke.*

Mullet   We've got to go now!

He lifts the **Presenter** *over his shoulder and carries her out.*

Presenter   And don't forget *Any Answers* after the break –

She is taken away.

Through the smoke, **Stuart** *is illuminated, sitting cross-legged on the end of his bed. His pot belly makes him look like Buddha.*

The sounds of the audience riot fade.

As the smoke clears, he stands and walks to the front of the stage.

He peers out at the audience, as if looking in a mirror.

Stuart *says only a few of the following statements out loud. The rest are played on tape, creating a collage of sound. During this,* **Angie** *crosses the stage at the back in her dressing gown, towelling her hair; and the* **Right-Wing Politician** *takes her clothes off – she is wearing a nightdress underneath, and now becomes* **Laura**.

Stuart   It's me.
It's Stuart.
It's me again.
I know you're ignoring me.
I know you don't want to speak to me.
I need to speak to you.
I've got some things of yours.
You've got some things of mine.
You should come and get them.
I should come and collect them.
Please call me.

Will you call me?
As soon as you get this.
When you've got the time.
Today if possible.
I'll be in.
Or try my mobile.
But we need to talk.
I'd like to talk.
It'd be good to talk.
I miss you.
I love you.
I made a mistake.
It won't take long.
It's really urgent.
Please.
Please call me.

The smoke clears to reveal **Laura**, *sitting on the toilet.*

Four

[**Stuart** *lies in bed thinking. He tries to masturbate. He hears an ice-cream van outside and contemplates buying one; instead he opens some mail. It is a bill for the council tax. He makes up a little song. He takes a shit. He takes a shower.*]

Stuart   What are you doing?

Laura   What does it look like I'm doing?

Stuart   Number twos?

Laura   No.

Stuart   Number threes?

Laura   What's number threes?

Stuart   Both.

Laura   No, just number ones.

Pause.

Get out then.

Stuart   Why?

Laura   What do you mean, why? Cos I can't pee with you
. . . standing there.

Stuart   Why not?

Laura   Cos I just can't. I can't pee with anyone in the
room.

Stuart   Try.

Laura   No!

Stuart (*mimics*)   'No!'

Laura   Stuart . . .

Stuart   Do you not love me?

Laura   Yes. What's that got to do with it?

Stuart   'What's love got to do, got to do with it?'

Laura   'What's love but a second-hand emotion?'

Stuart   Do you not trust me?

Laura   Yes. Sort of.

Stuart   Sort of?

Laura   Look, it doesn't matter if I trust you or not, I still
can't do the toilet with you sitting there! I can't even do it
with my sister in the room.

Stuart   There's lots of stuff you do with me that you
wouldn't do with your sister. Well – outside of my
masturbatory fantasies.

Laura   You're disgusting. Do you really think about that?

Stuart   What?

Laura   About me doing things with my sister?

Stuart *shrugs.*

Laura   What sort of things?

Stuart   Just being tender and sisterly with each other. Sometimes using a double-ended dildo.

Laura   That's disgusting. You're a dirty old perv.

Pause. He's not leaving.

Please – I'm really desperate.

Stuart   Can't be that desperate.

Pause.

Two people that love each other – they should be able to pee in the same room.

Laura   See that's where we differ. I don't think peeing has anything to do with love.

Stuart   I don't want you to piss on my face. I just want you to pee with me here in the room.

Laura   But why, though?

Stuart   I don't know. Because it's something you've never done with anyone else.

Pause.

Laura   I don't think I can.

Stuart   Try.

Pause. He makes a peeing sound.

Laura   I don't think I can.

Stuart   Are you worried you'll fart?

Laura   No!

Stuart   It's all right. Sometimes you need to kick-start the bike. I understand.

Laura   I'm not worried I'm going to fart!

Pause.

Stuart Just think of cool, clear water. Flowing. A rushing brook. Niagara Falls. Waves crashing against the pier.

She tries. Pause. A trickle.

Oh – something's happening . . .

Pause. He puts his hand between her legs.

Laura No, it'll stop.

Stuart I just want to feel it.

Pause.

I love everything that comes out of you.

He starts to touch her. She hugs him.

Enter **Angie**.

Angie What's going on here then?

Music. Bad porn music.

They stop, startled. **Laura** *is still aroused.*

Angie You don't have a fucking clue what you're doing. Get out of the way.

She pushes **Stuart** *aside and thrusts her hand between* **Laura**'*s legs.*

Angie I'll show you how the little bitch likes it.

Laura *starts to breathe heavily. She clings on to* **Angie**.

Angie That's it, you little slut. You like that?

Someone in the bed starts to masturbate.

This is how to do it.

Laura Oh yes, oh yes, that's it – oh finger me, finger me.

Angie (*to* **Stuart**) Do something useful with yourself and spank my fucking arse.

Stuart *starts to spank* **Angie**'*s arse.*

Angie That's it – spank my big fucking arse!

Mother *appears.*

Mother   Does this dress look terrible on me?

Laura   Oh God, that's so good – oh finger me!

Mother   I've got a bum like a baby elephant.

Stuart (*to* **Mother**)   Go away!

Angie   Spank my big fucking arse!

Mother   It wobbles like a big bloody jelly.

Stuart (*and the bed-wanker simultaneously*)   Go away!

Laura   Oh that's it, that's it, just there –

Angie   Spank me harder, you fucking bastard!

Mother   What do you want for your Christmas?

Laura   Oh God, that's good – rub my little cunt!

Mother   I've got a bum like a baby elephant's.

Mother *slaps her bottom. The rhythm falls into time with* **Stuart**'s *spanking of* **Angie**.

Angie   Spank my big elephant bum!

Laura   What do you want for your Christmas?

Mother   What do you want for your Christmas?

Angie   What do you want for your Christmas, then?

Furious, **Stuart** *gives up. Simultaneously, the girls go limp like dolls and* **Stuart**'s *'double' swings up, out of the bed, to sit on its edge.*

Stuart (*to* **Mother**)   Will you stop going on about your arse?! I don't want to think about your arse! It makes me want to vomit! I don't go on to you about my fucking balls, do I?! How would you like that?!

Pause. He sits on the end of the bed, mirrored in posture by his double.

Pause.

I'm sorry.

Mother   It's all right.

Pause.

Stuart   You know that aftershave stuff you bought me?

Mother   The stuff you said was cheap shite?

Stuart   I know, I know, but listen: I've still got it. And you know, if there was a fire, I wouldn't save my CDs first or my iPod or anything; the first thing I'd save would be that aftershave.

Mother   Don't be silly. If there's a fire you just get on with saving yourself.

Stuart   Well, obviously, yes, but – I'm trying to tell you something. I'm trying to tell you what it means to me.

Pause.

It's funny that, isn't it? Of all the really nice things you gave me – it's the cheap shite that means the most.

Pause.

Will *you* tell her to call me?

Pause. The sound of an ice-cream van. **Laura** *leaves.* **Angie** *bends over the toilet and vomits.* **Stuart** *kneels beside her, rubbing her back.* **Mullet** *bursts in.*

Mullet   Ice cream, ice cream, we all scream for ice scream!

Stuart   Too old for ice cream.

Mullet   What then?

Stuart   Don't know. Sorbet?

Mullet   Fucking sorbet! You're such an old wank! I'll bet you're even starting to like ready-salted!

Stuart   I am, actually.

Mullet   Come on – let's get some ice cream! A 99. Or a push-up.

Stuart   They probably don't have any ice cream. It's probably just smack.

Mullet   Get some of that then.

Stuart   I'll become an addict.

Mullet   So?

Stuart   So then we'll have to live in rubble. You wouldn't like that, would you?

Mullet   You're so boring and fat and emotionally stunted! Go and see if the post's here.

Stuart *looks at his watch.*

Stuart   Fucking should be.

Mullet   Go on then!

Stuart   It'll just be bills.

Mullet   It might not be. It might be a birthday card.

Stuart   It's not my birthday.

Mullet   So?

Pause. They exit, in a kind of synchronicity.

A light breeze blows sand across the stage. The light bulbs sway.

Stuart *enters, opening a bill.*

He stops, and reads it.

Stuart   What the fuck . . . ?

Pause.

I fucking paid that!

He throws it in the bin and puts the kettle on again. Pause.

What a bunch of cunts.

As he waits for the kettle to boil, he repeats the phrase, singing it to himself.

What a bunch of cunts, what a bunch of cunts . . .
What a bunch of cunts, what a bunch of cunts . . .

Music begins. He sings along, the orchestration becoming more elaborate.

Behind him, female dancers appear.

He becomes involved in a song-and-dance number. The lyrics consist only of the words 'What a bunch of cunts' and sometimes 'What a bunch of fucking cunts' for variety's sake.

Male dancers join in – they are blacked-up, like Al Jolson.

[Note: those of us who grew up in Britain in the seventies were treated, on Saturday nights, to a spectacularly incorrect show called The Black and White Minstrel Show, *which featured white singers blacked up. The point of this and the following small section might be lost in more enlightened times and locations, and can easily be substituted or omitted. But it should not be omitted on the grounds of offensiveness alone.]*

The song reaches a finale, then ends. Only then does **Stuart** *see the blacked-up male dancers.*

Stuart   What the fuck is this?

Minstrel 1   What?

Stuart   The blacking-up?

Minstrel 1   What about it?

Stuart   What *about* it?

Minstrel 2   We're the Black and White Minstrels.

Stuart   I know who you are. It's a bit fucking racist, isn't it?

Minstrel 3   It was your idea.

Stuart   It wasn't *my* idea.

Minstrel 1   Whose idea was it then?

Minstrel 2   It wasn't fucking mine, that's for sure – I feel a right twat.

Minstrel 3   Me too.

Stuart   It was whoever thought up *The Black and White Minstrels*.

Minstrel 1   Yeah, but you liked it.

Stuart   I didn't like it – it was just on.

Pause.

Right, well, just – fuck off, the lot of you.

Minstrel 2   Don't fucking worry.

Minstrel 1   It *was* your idea.

They leave. **Stuart** *pulls his trousers down and sits on the toilet.*

Stuart   It was just on.

Pause.

Yes, it was a big surprise to me. I'd always thought that you split up with someone because you'd stopped loving them, or realised you never did. But actually none of my relationships – my serious relationships – have ended that way. I've always loved them. There's been some other issue: a different outlook, a different dream; sometimes just practicalities. Nothing you wouldn't love someone for. Just things you can't live with peacefully. But I've felt the loss of every one of them, like a little death. It gets quite tiring after a while, the accumulation of losses.

He wipes his backside and looks at the toilet paper.

The accumulated losses. The accumulated losses of life.

Pause.

My next record? My next record is that one that's got the bit that goes 'I think I love you' that Angie used to play. If you're listening, Angie, please call. You said you'd fucking call.

[*Note: this is a reference to the radio programme* Desert Island Discs, *in which famous people choose their favourite records. In the original production, this scene ended with a repetitive sample of that one line 'I think I love you', taken from the song 'Take the Box' by Amy Winehouse, but this can be substituted. The point being that we often fixate on one line from a song. The sample then segued into a musical composition which served as the bridge between acts.*]

Music.

Above **Stuart***, a shower unit comes on and he is sprayed with water as he sits there. He turns his face up to it, letting it clean him.*

Lights fade.

Act Two: Afternoon

[**Stuart** *washes his clothes. He is insulted by a telesales call.*]

Stuart, *now dressed, enters with a basket full of dirty washing.*

Stuart (*singing*)
 What a bunch of cunts, what a bunch of cunts . . .

He opens the door of the washing machine and starts bundling the clothes in; but, from inside the machine, he hears his **Mother**'s *voice:*

Mother (*muffled*) Have you checked the pockets?

Stuart What?

Mother (*muffled*) Have you looked in the pockets?

He removes some of the washing.

Stuart What are you saying?

Mother I said, have you checked the pockets of your trousers?

Stuart Yes . . .

Mother Are you sure?

Stuart There's nothing in the pockets.

Mother Because you know what happened to those tickets.

Stuart *sighs.*

Mother Why don't you check? Better safe than sorry.

Stuart (*exasperated*) Right, I'll check the fucking trousers.

Mother There's no need for language.

Stuart (*fondly*) There's no need for language.

He drags out a pair of trousers and checks the pockets. He finds something.

Mother   What's that? Is that your bus pass?

Stuart   No.

Mother   So much for checking the pockets. Honestly, I think you'd –

Stuart *bundles the washing back in.*

Mother (*muffled*)   – forget your own head if you didn't –

Stuart   Yes, thank you, Mother.

He shuts the door. He empties powder into the tray, not sure how much to add. He sings a jingle from a washing-powder commercial:

'Washing machines live longer with Calgon.'

He crouches down to look at the settings.

What the fuck is a pre-wash? I never do a pre-wash. Maybe I should do a pre-wash?

Pause. He opens the door of the washing machine.

Mum – should I do a pre-wash?

A long pause. There is no answer. Of course not. He closes the door and turns the machine on. It trickles into life.

He looks in the basket. There's a sock in there.

Shit!

He tries to open the door but it's too late.

Exasperated, he takes the sock . . .

Right – you're going in the fucking bin!

. . . and throws it in the pedal bin.

He returns to the machine, watches it turn. The sound of the clothes sloshing.

Bored, he puts the basket on his head and clutches the slats as if they're the bars of a prison cell.

You've got to get me out of here!

This amuses him for a moment.

The sound of the machine gets louder and louder and more hypnotic. It reaches a crescendo and then stops.

The phone rings.

Stuart Hello?!

Salesman Is that Mr McWary?

Stuart Mr McQuarrie.

Salesman Oh, I beg your pardon – Mr McQuarrie: and can I just confirm with you that this is your home number?

Stuart Yes, obviously.

Salesman And is this a BT line, Mr McQuarrie?

Stuart Yes.

Salesman And if I was to tell you that you I could save you up to a hundred pounds a year on your phone bill, would that be of interest to you?

Stuart Em – not really, no.

Salesman I see. And what if I was to tell you that you could also enjoy over twenty extra channels of television at no extra cost – would that be of interest to you?

Stuart No, it wouldn't, but thanks – (for asking).

Salesman And you would also be able to enjoy free broadband at speeds of up to 8 MB depending on your area.

Stuart I'm sorry, but I'm really not interested. And I'm actually not that keen on being – (phoned at home).

Salesman Because all that can be yours with Teleport's Essentials package at an introductory price of just £13.99 a month for the first three months.

Stuart Right, well, you don't seem to be listening to me, but I'm really not interested, I'm sorry.

Pause.

Salesman You're not interested?

Stuart Sorry, no.

A pause, and then the **Salesman** *hangs up.*

Stuart Hello?

Nothing.

Fucking cheeky bastard!

Mullet *appears from under the bedding.*

Mullet You are one totally pathetic fucking loser!

Stuart What?

Mullet That guy just made an absolute cunt of you.

Stuart I know he did!

Mullet He made a fucking tit of you in your own house.

Stuart I know!

Mullet And you just let it happen.

Stuart Well, what was I supposed to do? I said I wasn't interested – I was trying to be polite.

Mullet Exactly. He basically said, 'I'm going to fuck you up the arse,' and you said, 'Yes, sir,' and spread your fat arse-cheeks.

Stuart Cheeky fucking bastard!

Mullet So what are you going to do about it?

The phone rings.

Stuart Hello?

Salesman Hello, is that Mr McWary?

Mullet *urges him on.*

Stuart   If by Mr McWary you mean Mr McQuarrie, then yes.

Mullet *is disgusted with him.*

Salesman   Oh, I beg your pardon – Mr McQuarrie: and can I just confirm with you that this is your – (home number)?

Mullet   Is that it?

Stuart   Eh?

Mullet   'If by Mr McWary you mean Mr McQuarrie' – is that all you're worried about? That he got your name wrong?

Stuart   I was just starting.

Mullet   You still said yes though, didn't you?

Stuart   What am I supposed to say?

Mullet   Tell the cunt to fuck off!

The phone rings.

Stuart   Hello?

Salesman   Hello, is that Mr McWary?

Stuart   No, it fucking isn't!

Stuart *looks at* **Mullet**.

Salesman   Oh – I'm sorry –

Mullet   Tell him to fuck off!

Stuart   Fuck off!

Pause. They seem pleased with themselves.

Salesman   Hello?

Stuart   He's still there!

Mullet   Give it to the cunt!

Stuart   Give him what?

Mullet   It's a Saturday afternoon, for fuck's sake!

Stuart   It's a Saturday afternoon, for fuck's sake!

Mullet *nods.*

Stuart   Would you like me phoning you on a Saturday afternoon?

Pause.

No, I didn't think so; and I don't want any more shit TV channels so fuck off and don't call me again!

The phone hangs up.

That told him.

Mullet   Yeah, but he still hung up on *you*. He's still got the power. He's phoned you up at your house, on your day off, and he's made you feel angry and bad.

Stuart   What can I do about it?

Mullet   Make *him* regret calling *you*. Spoil *his* fucking day!

Pause.

Stuart   All right.

The phone rings.

Hello?

Salesman   Hello, is that Mr McWary?

Stuart   No, it's Mr McQuarrie.

Mullet *is annoyed with him. but* **Stuart** *indicates to wait.*

Salesman   Oh, I beg your pardon – Mr McQuarrie. And could you just confirm that this is your home number?

Stuart   Yes it is. But listen – are you calling from Teleport?

Pause.

Salesman   Yes, I am.

Stuart   Oh good, I was hoping you'd call.

Pause.

Salesman   Were you?

Stuart   Yes, and listen, I'm very interested in your product but would you mind calling back in about ten minutes? It's just that I'm wanking at the moment.

Salesman   I'm sorry?

Stuart   I said I'm wanking at the moment – but I should have come in about five minutes so if you could call back then, that'd be perfect.

Mullet *is delighted.*

Salesman   Oh – right . . .

Stuart   I mean, unless you'd like to stay on the line and talk me through it, you know – say something like, 'Ooh yes, ooh yes, wank it,' over and over again. Would that interest you at all, you little fucking maggot?

Pause.

I'm asking you a question, you subhuman piece of shit – would that interest you?

Salesman   No, sir – it wouldn't.

Stuart   Right – well, then, *you* can fuck off!

The phone goes dead. They are triumphant. They run around whooping in triumph.

Mullet   That was fucking great!

Stuart   He'll think twice about doing that again.

Mullet   God, you were quite vicious there. 'Subhuman piece of shit'?

Stuart   Well, I'll take abuse up to a certain point –

Mullet   Yeah, but there's a line.

Stuart   But there's a line, and if you cross it – doesn't matter who you are –

Mother   Stuart!

They both jump out of their skins.

Mother   Stuart McQuarrie! What do you think you're playing at?!

Stuart   What?

Mother   Don't 'what' me! I heard the filth you were saying! What was the meaning of it?

Stuart   I didn't start it.

Mother   Who did then?

Stuart   The guy on the phone – he called me up, out of the blue –

Mother   I know what he did. I don't remember him saying any filth to you.

Stuart   No, well, he didn't; but when I said I wasn't interested, he just hung up on me. Which was pretty bloody rude.

She slaps him round the head.

Mother   There's no need for language!

Stuart   You shouldn't hit people on the head, it gives them brain damage.

Mother   I'll brain damage you.

Pause.

So he hung up on you. Which was rude . . .

Stuart   So I decided to be rude back.

Mother   Oh, the Big Man, is it? The Head Cheese.

Mullet *smirks.*

Mother   Making someone feel small over the phone.

Stuart   He hung up on me.

Mother   Did he? Are you sure that's what happened? Let's ask him, shall we?

Stuart   Ask him?

Mother   Yes – because he's here. Simon?!

She looks offstage.

Come and give him a hand.

Stuart *and* **Mullet** *look at* **Simon** *– who we cannot yet see – and then at each other.*

Mother   Come on then.

She nods them in an offstage direction. **Stuart** *makes* **Mullet** *acompany him. They exit.*

Muffled sounds of effort offstage.

They return with **Simon**. *He's in a wheelchair, attached to an IV drip.* **Mother** *helps bring him onstage. One of* **Simon**'s *arms is tiny and malformed.*

Mother   Simon, this – I'm ashamed to say – is my son. Stuart – this is the man you called subhuman.

Simon   Hello.

He extends his small hand. **Stuart** *and* **Mullet** *shake it.*

Stuart   Hello.

Mullet   Hi.

Simultaneously:

Simon   Why don't you –

Mother   Listen, I just –

Simon   Sorry –

Mother   No, you go ahead.

Simon   I just wanted to say that it's really all right. I completely understand – we get enough adverts thrown at us without people calling you up at home and trying to sell things. Believe me, I feel embarrassed every time I call someone. It's just that, obviously, given my condition, you know – playing for England was never an option.

Stuart   Oh, I don't know . . .

Mother   Stuart!

Stuart   Oh well, look – I'm sorry that you're disabled and all that and obviously I feel a bit bad. But it doesn't change the fact that as soon as I said I wasn't interested, you just hung up on me; and that's just rude, whatever . . . condition you're in.

Mother   Oh, and you're such a big know-it-all, aren't you? The Big I-Am. Well, tell him, Simon.

Simon   Oh really, it's all right. He wasn't to know.

Pause.

Stuart   Wasn't to know what?

Mother   It just so happens, Mr Smarty-Pants, that Simon didn't hang up on you; he actually had a seizure.

Pause.

Simon   I felt it coming on during the conversation. I'd have said goodbye but my jaw sort of locks, so I can't speak.

Pause.

Mother   Thank you, Simon.

Pause.

I hope you're proud of yourself, Stuart McQuarrie. Maybe you'll not be so quick to judge in future.

She wheels him offstage.

Stuart *and* **Mullet** *are left there, in their shame.*

The sound of the washing machine turning.

Mullet *sits by it and puts the basket on his head, as* **Stuart** *had earlier.*

Stuart *makes his way back to the couch.*

Pause.

The **Cat** *ambles slowly in.*

Stuart   Ah, here he is. Where have you been all night? Chasing all the girl cats I bet.

Cat   Fuck you.

The **Cat** *walks straight to the bowl of cat food and smells it.*

Cat   Muck.

And with this, he turns and walks slowly out again.

Stuart *tries to stroke him as he passes, but the* **Cat** *shrugs him off.*

Angie *enters. She's trying on clothes for an evening out.*

Angie   What's wrong with Galloway?

Stuart   He's spoiled.

Angie   Well, if he's spoiled it's because you spoiled him.

Stuart   I don't spoil him. They must have been feeding him salmon or something.

Angie   At a rescue centre? I doubt it. Anyway, don't change the subject.

Stuart   What was the subject?

Angie   You being a homophobe.

Pause.

Pleading the Fifth, I see.

Stuart   I don't care if you think I'm a homophobe. I know I'm not.

Angie   But being gay revolts you?

Stuart   I didn't say being *gay* revolts me.

Angie   What did you say then?

Stuart   I don't care if people are gay. I'm actually in favour of it.

Angie   Why, because it narrows the competition?

Stuart   Exactly. And they're all the best-looking guys as well. Everybody wins.

Angie   You said it revolts you.

Stuart   No, I said that if you're a heterosexual man – regardless of how enlightened you are – you find the thought of, you know –

Angie   What?

Stuart   The thought of coming into direct contact with another man's . . .

Angie   Cock.

Stuart   Yes –

Angie   You can't even say it.

Stuart   Can't even say what?

Angie   Another man's cock.

Stuart   Another man's cock.

Angie   There, you see? Still heterosexual.

She kisses him.

Stuart   You are so fucking annoying, d'you know that?

Angie   And you're a homophobe.

Pause.

And a racist.

Stuart   How am I a fucking racist now?!

Angie   Cos every time you tell me what Mr Rajah's said you put on that stupid accent.

Stuart   That's not being racist.

Angie   It is so . . . 'All reduced – Mr Rajah's all reduced!'

Stuart   That's how he talks!

Angie   You don't have to do the wee shake of the head.

Stuart   So *The Simpsons* is racist, is it?

Angie   Yes.

Pause.

Stuart   I'm not a fucking racist. There's not a racist bone in my body. In fact I go out of my way to not be racist.

Angie   How?

Stuart   Well – if an Asian shopkeeper –

Angie   'An Asian shopkeeper – '

Stuart   Yes – if an Asian shopkeeper gives me change, I always make a point of just making slight contact with his hand.

Angie   What's that supposed to prove?

Stuart   Well, you know – just to make sure he knows I don't think I'll get the Paki touch or something. And – if I get on a bus, and there's an Asian person sitting there –

Angie   Don't tell me – you sit beside them.

Stuart   Yes! Even if there are other seats!

Angie   You are such a fucking wanker, Stuart McQuarrie.

Stuart   Ah, but who's more of a wanker? The wanker, or the wanker that loves the wanker?

Angie *pushes him away.*

Angie   I don't love you.

Pause.

You love me.

Stuart   Yes. I do.

He embraces her. Pause.

Angie   D'you want to shag?

Pause. He looks at his watch.

Stuart   Yeah, all right.

She pulls him down behind the couch. We hear their voices, as they struggle off with their clothes.

Stuart   Can you bum your girlfriend?

Angie   Can I bum my girlfriend?

Stuart   Can *one* bum one's girlfriend? I mean – you hear about men bumming each other but you never hear someone say, 'I bummed my girlfriend.'

Angie   I'll fucking bum you.

Stuart   You'll bum me?

Angie   Will you shut the fuck up?!

We hear the sound of them starting to make love.

Father *enters and stops as he sees them.*

Father   What's going on here?!

Suddenly, from behind the couch, up spring **Stuart** *and* **Laura**, *looking flustered.*

Mullet *suddenly springs into life.*

Mullet   Stewpot, look! Porno!

He waves a tatty old porno mag that he's found.

Stuart   Not now!

Laura *runs out, distressed, clutching her blouse to her chest.*

Stuart *half follows her.*

Stuart   Laura!

Mullet *finds more pornography in the sand.*

Mullet   There's more, look! It's like treasure!

Angie *appears from behind the couch.*

Angie   You dirty bastard!

She storms out.

Stuart   Angie – it's not mine!

Mullet   Look at this!

Stuart *runs to* **Mullet**.

Stuart   I can't just now.

Mullet   But look at the fanny on that!

Stuart   Christ.

Mother (*enters*)   Stuart!

Stuart   I've got to go

Mullet   Later, then.

Stuart   Yeah, later.

Mother   Stuart, get over here now!

Stuart *runs back and sits on the couch, shamefaced.*

Father   Well, I think we have to tell them.

Mother   Oh, shut your silly mouth. We don't have to tell anyone anything.

Father   If it was the other way round, we'd want to know.

Mother   Have you met Laura's parents?

Father   No, but – (that's not the point).

Mother   Then shut your silly mouth, you old jessie.

Father   Don't call me a jessie, Margaret. Not in front of Stuart.

Mother (*mimics*)   'Don't call me a jessie, don't call me a jessie.'

Father   Right, well, you sort it out then; because I give up, I just bloody give up!

He walks out.

Mother   'I just bloody give up.'

Stuart *and his* **Mother** *share a conspiratorial laugh.*

Pause.

Mother   So – what are we going to do with the two of you?

Pause. **Stuart** *shrugs.*

Mother   He may be an old jessie, but you know what they say, even a stopped clock's right twice a day. When we've got Laura under our roof, we've got a duty of care. We've got a responsibility, to make sure she doesn't get up to anything that her parents wouldn't want her getting up to. You know what Jesus said: 'Suffer the little children.'

Stuart *looks confused.*

Mother   What do you think of her?

She pokes at him.

Stuart. Stuart.

Stuart   Who?!

Mother   Don't act the daft laddie. What do you think of Laura?

Pause.

Do you love her?

Pause. He shrugs uncomfortably.

Just a shrug.

Stuart Aw, Mum!

Mother Don't 'Aw, Mum' me, it's important. You put your swizzle-stick inside a girl and babies are what's next.

Stuart *groans and puts a cushion over his head.*

Mother Now don't be such a baby. It's a thing for a girl that age to have a child. She's just a little thing too. She's not got a big fat bum and hips like me. A baby'd rip her from front to back.

Stuart *groans. She prises the cushion away from him.*

Mother Listen to me, Stuart. You know what Jesus said: 'Respect your mother.'

Stuart He never said that!

Mother You weren't there, you don't know. Now listen to me: do you get all excited when you think of her? And I don't mean your swizzle-stick –

Stuart Stop saying that!

Mother I mean, down your back, a little shiver. And do you want to say her name over and over? Do you find excuses to say it? Laura Laura Laura!

She teases him.

And do you hug the pillow and pretend it's her?

He throws the cushion aside.

Stuart No!

Mother Ah, you see – a picture tells a hundred tales.

Pause.

And is it like all the other girls just disappear? Like they don't exist? Like she's the only girl in the world?

(*Sings.*)
    'If you were the only girl in the world,
    And I was the only boy . . . '

She smiles. Pause.

Well, you listen to me –

He covers his ears. She wrenches the cushion away, so seriously it startles him.

I'm being serious, Stuart, this is important!

Pause.

Don't you pay any mind to what anyone says. There's nothing worse you can do in this world than marry for the sake of appearance. If you feel all those things about a girl, then maybe she's the one. But if you don't, or if you think you might not feel them ten years down the line, then you let her go, no matter how she cries; and do it sooner, not later. Let her be free to find someone who does feel that. You be alone rather than that; rather than fight like cat and dog all your life; rather than die a bit at a time. That's what a real man does for a woman. That's what he does for himself.

Pause.

Don't you settle for less than love, than true love, do you hear me? Don't you settle for less!

Pause.

Laura *enters.*

Mother   Here she is.

Laura *sits on the couch with* **Stuart**.

Mother   You feeling better?

Laura *nods.*

Laura   I like your mirror.

Mother   Which?

Laura   The big one in the hall.

Mother   That was my mother's. Yes.

Pause.

My mother gave that to me.

Classical music plays, and **Stuart** *lies down to listen to it. With one hand, he half conducts.*

Mother, *bare-footed and parasol in hand, walks across the sand.*

[Note: in the original production, this next scene played out as if on a beach, but the location, in itself, is unimportant and you may wish to change it depending on your stage design.]

Mother *walks around a rock pool. She stares up at the sun.*

Suddenly she becomes unsteady on her feet, totters slightly, and then collapses, face down.

Bystander 1, *who has been talking on his mobile phone, runs to her. He crouches down beside her, unsure what to do.*

Bystander 2 *rushes in, having seen the collapse.*

Bystander 1 *calls for an ambulance.*

Seeing a coastguard, **Bystander 2** *rushes offstage towards him.*

Father *enters, in holiday clothes, carrying a bag of shopping. When he sees his wife collapsed, he drops his shopping and runs to her, but it is too late.*

He cradles her in his arms.

Bystander 2 *returns. Lights fade on this tableau. The music ends. The washing machine churns to a halt.*

Act Three: Night

[**Stuart** *has something to eat. He watches television. He goes to bed.*]

Stuart *looks at his watch.*

He gets up and goes to the fridge, opens it.

He takes out a ready meal.

Laura *enters.*

Laura   Oh Stuart!

Stuart   What?

Laura   What's that?

Stuart   It's a prawn curry thing.

Laura *is disapproving.*

Stuart   What?

Laura   I'll bet it's full of E-numbers.

Stuart   What's wrong with E-numbers?

Laura   They're bad for you.

Stuart   Everything's bad for you.

Stuart *pierces the film, puts the meal in the microwave and starts it cooking.*

Laura   You shouldn't use microwaves either. They make you infertile.

Stuart   Good. Won't have to bother with johnnies.

Laura   Don't say good. What if we want to have children?

Stuart   Laura, for fuck's sake – will you get off my back? If you want to go out with a leaf-eating, non-smoking, rice-eating wank then do it. But stop trying to turn me into one.

Pause.

Laura   I'm just saying it because I don't want you to die.

Stuart   Awww.

Laura   Who'll look after all the animals if you die?

Stuart   Oh I don't *know* . . .

Laura   Oh, oh – I've thought of another one! Koala bears! We've got to have some koala bears!

Stuart   Aren't they vicious?

Laura   Koala bears? They're lovely!

Stuart   I stand corrected.

Laura   But we'll have to grow eucalyptus trees because that's all they eat.

Stuart   Yeah, well – we're growing bamboo for the pandas anyway.

Laura   I think we'll have to build another biosphere, just for plants.

Stuart   This started out as a small farmhouse in France and now it's like Blofeld's fucking secret complex. Who's going to pay for all this?

Laura   I am!

Stuart   You are? Because it's going to cost about a billion pounds.

Laura   Yeah, well, it's a dream house. You can't put a price on a dream house!

She exits.

Stuart   You can't put a price on a dream house . . .

The microwave pings.

Stuart *takes out the meal. He peels back the film, stirs it, then places it back inside.*

He sits on the couch. Only the light from the TV on his face, which is fixed in an inane grin. A high-pitched noise sounds.

The doorbell rings. Lights up again. **Stuart** *looks puzzled.*

The doorbell rings again. He gets up to answer it, leaving the stage.

The light bulbs sway. A breeze shifts the sand. Pause.

Paul *enters, carrying a bag.* **Stuart** *is displeased.*

Paul   I know, I know – you said you were doing nothing.

Stuart   Yeah, and I sort of meant it.

Paul   Yeah, well, there was nothing going on at the Duck. Fucking girlfriends, I'm telling you – they're ruining the world. D'you want to stick these in the fridge?

He hands him some cans of beer. **Stuart** *groans.*

Paul   We don't have to drink them all. We'll just have a beer and see how it goes; if you still 'vant to be alone', I'll piss off – Scout's honour.

Stuart *puts them in the fridge.*

Paul *sits on the couch. He unwraps some food.*

Paul   I got you some chips.

Stuart   I just put something in the microwave.

Paul   What?

Stuart   A prawn curry.

Paul   That'll go with chips. What's this? *Millionaire?*

He opens a can of beer and hands one to **Stuart***, then opens one for himself. They fill their glasses.*

Paul   Look at this cunt. He's used a lifeline already and he's not even up to five hundred.

Stuart*, resigned to his fate, sits on the couch beside him.*

Paul   D – Jon Pertwee.

Again only the TV light plays on their faces. They stare at the television, with those same inane grins. The same whining sound. It suddenly ends and they return to normality.

Paul   That was shite. It's about time they put that to bed. What's on the other side?

Stuart   Let's just see the headlines.

Again – the light, the grins, the sound. Lights up.

Paul   The Israelis are a deeply misunderstood people.

Stuart   Fuck . . .

Paul   What?

Stuart   I had a dream . . . something to do with Israel . . .

Paul   What's this?

*Once more – the lights, the sound. but only **Stuart** is grinning. **Paul** immediately falls asleep. Lights up. **Paul** wakes.*

Paul   Who did it?

Stuart   The guy with the haircut.

Paul   His mate?

Stuart   Yeah.

Paul   Told you. Shall we partake of another 'tinnie'?

Stuart   Yeah, go on.

Paul   On you go then.

Stuart   Me?

Paul   You're the host.

Stuart   Didn't get much choice in the matter, did I?

Pause. He sighs.

These are nice chips.

*He gets up to go to the fridge. **Paul** watches him intently.*

Stuart   Fuck . . .

Pause.

Paul   What is it?

Pause.

Stuart   I feel really funny.

Pause.

Fuck . . .

He drops to his knees. The chips spill out of his hand across the floor.

Paul, I'm not joking – something's really wrong . . .

He rolls on to his back. **Paul** *gets up to look at him.*

Stuart   Call – an ambulance –

Paul   Can you move?

Stuart   No –

Paul   Try and move your hand.

Pause. Nothing.

Stuart   Oh Jesus – what's happening to me?

Pause. **Paul** *looks around. He takes a cushion from the couch.*

He squats down beside **Stuart***.*

Stuart   Paul –

Paul   Have you got anything to say?

Stuart *can barely even make a sound.*

Paul   Stuart – look at me; have you got anything to say –
you *cunt.*

Pause. With great effort:

Stuart   Tell Angie – that I love her. Tell her – I don't
know – why I left her – like I did.

Pause. **Paul** *nods.*

He places the cushion over **Stuart**'s *face.*

We hear his muffled shouts for a while, then they fade.

After a while, **Paul** *removes the cushion.*

Breathing heavily, **Paul** *stares down at* **Stuart**'s *corpse.*

The doorbell rings, startling him.

For a moment he doesn't know what to do.

The doorbell rings again.

Paul   There in a minute!

With great effort, he drags **Stuart**'s *body out of sight.*

Mullet *appears, peering over the back of the couch, watching this.*

The doorbell rings again.

Paul *enters, out of breath.*

Paul   Just a moment!

And then he sees **Mullet**. *Their eyes meet.* **Paul** *puts his finger to his mouth –* '*Shhhhh.*'

Paul *straightens himself up and goes to answer the door.*

The light bulbs sway.

Voices offstage.

Paul   Angie, hi.

Angie   Hi, Paul. Is Stuart here?

They enter.

Paul   Eh – he's not, actually.

Angie   Where is he?

Paul   I don't know. Is he not with you?

Angie   No, why? Did he say he was seeing me?

Paul   I think so . . .

Angie   No. I was meant to give him a call but I wasn't seeing him. Not as far as I know.

Paul   Oh right. I thought that was what he said.

She looks around the flat. **Paul***, nervous, positions himself in front of where he dragged* **Stuart***'s body.*

Angie   What are you doing here?

Paul   Do you want a beer or something?

Angie   No, I'm all right.

Pause.

What are you doing here?

Paul   We were down the Duck's Arse, you know – earlier. Had a couple of pints and then we were coming back here, but he had to do something – I thought he said he was seeing you, or calling you or something. So he said for me to wait here. I thought that was him.

She nods, obviously suspicious.

Angie   When was this?

Paul   Eight or so. I mean, I tried phoning him but . . .

Their talk fades, to be replaced by music. This is what we would hear them saying (or as much as you need for the moment).

Paul   . . . it always seems to be busy. I don't know, I just assumed maybe he was on the phone to you. To be honest I assumed you were maybe having a bit of a barney. Sorry, but you know how it is. Best not to interfere with these things. So, you know – I just made myself comfortable here, had a few beers, watched the TV, that sort of thing. But I am getting a wee bit worried. It's been a couple of hours now and if he wasn't seeing you, then I don't know who he could have been seeing. It isn't really like him whichever way you look at it.

Angie   No it's not.

Paul   I don't know – what do you think we should do? Maybe we should go out looking for him. I'm sure there's some explanation for it. Maybe he met someone. We could always try the Duck, maybe he's gone back there. I did sort of foist myself on him. Maybe he had some other plans that he didn't want to tell me about.

But instead . . .

A spotlight – signifying **Angie***'s point of view – moves across the floor, highlighting: the two glasses of beer, the two cans, the spilled chips and then the tracks left in the sand by* **Stuart***'s dragged body. The spotlight follows the tracks off into the wings.*

Mullet *still watches, silently, from behind the couch.*

The sound returns.

Paul   No, I'm sure there's an explanation for it.

Pause.

Angie (*scared*)   I'll try phoning him.

Paul   I've tried him a few times. There's no answer.

Pause.

Angie   Can't hurt to try again.

Pause.

Paul   Tell you what – let's try down the Duck. We can give him a call on the way.

He puts his jacket on. Pause.

Angie   All right.

They exit. **Angie** *casts a look backwards as she leaves.*

Pause. The sand shifts again.

A mobile phone rings: the ringtone is reminiscent of the ice-cream van heard earlier.

Mullet *slowly appears from behind the couch. He sits down cross-legged and starts eating the chips from the floor.*

Music.

From everywhere come the mourners, all moving slowly.

Laura *looks like a grieving supermodel, her movements strangely jerky as she walks to position.*

Stuart's **Father** *enters slowly, in a black suit.*

Stuart's **Mother**, *all in white, descends from the ceiling to come to a stop only feet above the ground.*

The **Cat**, *Galloway, enters, dragging a dead bird.*

They take their positions around the room, forming a bizarre tableau.

The music ends.

Mother   I remember one winter, it had just snowed – this was back when it snowed in winter – I looked out of the window of our house, down into the square, and I saw him in his little school uniform –

Father   He could never keep his shirt-tails in, could he?

Mother   No, that's right. Or his laces done up. But anyway, I looked down and – before he came into the stair – I saw him deliberately rolling in the snow, you know; getting it all over himself. So I'd make a fuss of him when he came in. Give him a nice bowl of home-made soup. I think that was the only thing I cooked that he actually liked.

Pause.

Laura   Yeah, cos I remember when it was snowing; and I think we'd had a bit of an argument. No, I think we'd actually split up; yeah, that's right. And we both spent about a week in misery but not knowing if the other one was bothered. And then one morning I came out of my mum's house to go to school and all this snow had fallen and it was all untouched; except outside my door, and on all the cars, and everywhere, someone had written 'I love you Laura'. Everywhere you could see.

Mother   Stuart?

Laura   He must've got up really early and come over to my house and done it all before I got up.

Mother   He did love you, Laura. I know you had your ups and downs; but he really did. And you, Angie. But I think you've always got a soft spot for the first.

Angie *shrugs, absorbing the veiled insult.*

Father   Well, that must've been the only time he ever got up early. D'you remember – he got into terrible trouble for being late at school?

Mother   Oh dear, yes. What a palaver that was. They had us in, didn't they?

Father   They were going to expel him!

Mother   That's right, they were.

Father   They were going to expel him if he was late just once more. So he came up with this foolproof system – he put a bucket of cold water by his bed. The theory being, when his alarm clock went off, rather than just turning it off and going back to sleep as usual, he would immediately plunge his whole head into this bucket of water. Well – come the morning – off goes the alarm, Stuart bolts awake, rolls over – takes one look at the water, says, 'Not a chance,' and just goes back to sleep again!

Laughter.

Angie   If he had to leave before me in the morning, he'd always put one of my teddy bears in bed beside me, with its little arm over me.

Affectionate nodding. Pause.

Mother   Galloway – you must have a few stories about Stuart?

Pause. Galloway considers it.

Cat   He was a prick.

Pause. **Father** *raises his glass.*

Father   To Stuart.

They raise their glasses.

All   To Stuart.

Music.

Stuart *appears now. They all turn to see him.*

They begin to clap. They applaud him as he walks down to them, his arms open, almost messianic.

He kisses **Angie**.

He shakes his **Father***'s hand and tries, awkwardly, to hug him.*

He hugs his **Mother** *tight.*

He attempts to stroke Galloway, but the **Cat** *swipes him with his claws.*

He high-fives **Mullet**.

Finally, he embraces **Laura**.

Laura *and* **Angie** *remove his clothes until he is as he was at the beginning of the play.*

His **Father** *and* **Mother** *prepare his bed.*

The **Cat** *picks up the dead bird and leaves.*

Stuart *is led up to the bed. His* **Father** *tucks him under the covers. His* **Mother** *kisses his forehead. They exit.*

Mullet *takes one last look at his friend, peaceful in bed now, then leaves.*

The bed slowly lifts up to a vertical position. Over this:

Stuart (*on tape*)
    And now I lay me down to sleep
    I pray the Lord my soul to keep
    And if I die before I wake
    I pray my soul the Lord to take.

Stuart *sleeps, as if we are looking down on him.*

The phone rings. He wakes and answers it. **Angie** *is voice only.*

Stuart   Hello?

Angie   Stuart? It's Angie. Did I wake you?

Stuart   Eh – no, no.

Angie   Are you in bed?

Stuart   Yeah, but I'm awake. I thought you were going to call me.

Angie   I am calling you.

Stuart   I thought you were going to call me earlier.

Pause.

Angie   You wanted to speak to me.

Stuart   Yes, of course –

Pause.

Angie   I don't care about my things. Throw them away if you want.

Pause.

Stuart   That's not what I wanted to say . . .

Angie   What then?

Stuart   Is it a bad time?

Angie   A bad time?

Stuart   You seem in a hurry.

Angie   It's late.

Stuart   Whose fault is that?

Angie   Don't start or I'll hang up.

Stuart   Don't hang up.

Angie   Then say what you've got to say.

Pause.

Stuart   Jesus, Angie – does it have to be like this?

Angie   Like what?

Stuart   Look – I know you won't believe me, Angie. But I love you. I really do.

Pause.

Angie   Stuart . . .

Stuart   And I know, so why did I finish it? But you've got to believe me when I say – I don't know. I truly don't know. There was no reason for it; I'm not seeing anyone else, I wasn't unhappy. I didn't do it because of what's happening now. I did it because – of what would happen in the future.

Pause.

Angie   Why are you telling me this?

Stuart   Because I don't want to live without you.

Pause.

Angie   What does that mean?

Stuart   It means what it means. It means that I love you. That's a precious thing. Do you know how precious that is?

Pause.

I know you're hurt. But let's not throw everything away.

Angie   You're really confusing me.

Pause.

What are you saying? Are you saying you regret it – what?

Long pause.

Stuart   No. I'm not saying I regret it. I think it was the right thing to do, for both of our sakes. But I didn't do it because I don't love you.

Pause.

Why don't we meet up?

Angie   No.

Stuart   Why not?

Angie   You know why not.

Pause.

It's over, Stuart. It has to be.

Pause.

Stuart   We can't even be friends?

Angie   I don't know. Not now.

Stuart   But some day.

Angie   I don't know. Maybe – who knows? But for now – stop calling me. Please. Please, Stuart.

Pause.

I have to go now.

Stuart   Not like this.

Angie   What do you mean?

Stuart   I mean let's not make it a big goodbye. I can't handle it, not just now.

Pause.

Just talk to me for a while. Talk to me like we'll be seeing each other tomorrow.

Pause.

Angie   What do you want me to say?

Stuart   I don't know. Anything.

Pause.

Angie   How's Galloway?

Stuart   He's fine. Surly, as usual.

Pause.

Angie   What did you do today?

Stuart   Today?

Pause.

Fuck all.

The lights by now have faded to black.

Optional Epilogue

[*In the original production, the following happened. Obviously, it was an expensive sequence and the play will work without it. If it can be done, it should be, but it may be omitted if there is no reasonable way to achieve it.*]

A box is flown in.

When the lights come up, it is revealed as a kitchen. The furniture – the washing machine, the cooker, the fridge, etc – is exactly the same as that which was dotted around the set, but is now in its proper place. It looks very real.

A door opens and **Stuart** *enters. He then proceeds to make himself, in real time and with little fuss, a cup of tea. This done, he sits at the kitchen table.*

Angie *enters, wearing a dressing gown. She takes the washing out of the washing machine (a stray red sock has caused the whites to come out pink). Irritated, she leaves.*

Stuart *sits there.*

The lights come up. The audience gradually realise they are expected to leave. **Stuart** *continues drinking his tea.*

Eventually, the theatre empties.